The Idea of Europe

European Studies

AN INTERDISCIPLINARY SERIES IN EUROPEAN CULTURE,
HISTORY AND POLITICS

Series Editor

Menno Spiering (*University of Amsterdam*)

Board Members

Robert Harmsen (*Université du Luxembourg*)
Joep Leerssen (*University of Amsterdam*)
Thomas M. Wilson (*Binghamton University, State University of New York*)

VOLUME 37

The titles published in this series are listed at *brill.com/es*

The Idea of Europe

The Clash of Projections

Edited by

Vladimir Biti, Joep Leerssen, and Vivian Liska

BRILL

LEIDEN | BOSTON

Library of Congress Cataloging-in-Publication Data

Names: Biti, Vladimir, 1952- editor. | Leerssen, Joseph Th. (Joseph Theodoor), 1955- editor. | Liska, Vivian, 1956- editor.
Title: The idea of Europe : the clash of projections / edited by Vladimir Biti, Joep Leerssen and Vivian Liska.
Description: Leiden ; Boston : Brill, [2021] | Series: European studies, 1568-1858 ; vol. 37 | Includes index.
Identifiers: LCCN 2020058157 (print) | LCCN 2020058158 (ebook) | ISBN 9789004449220 (hardback) | ISBN 9789004449442 (ebook)
Subjects: LCSH: Nationalism–European Union countries. | Group identity–European Union countries.
Classification: LCC CB203 .I335 2021 (print) | LCC CB203 (ebook) | DDC 940–dc23
LC record available at https://lccn.loc.gov/2020058157
LC ebook record available at https://lccn.loc.gov/2020058158

Typeface for the Latin, Greek, and Cyrillic scripts: "Brill". See and download: brill.com/brill-typeface.

ISSN 1568-1858
ISBN 978-90-04-44922-0 (hardback)
ISBN 978-90-04-44944-2 (e-book)

Copyright 2021 by Koninklijke Brill NV, Leiden, The Netherlands.
Koninklijke Brill NV incorporates the imprints Brill, Brill Hes & De Graaf, Brill Nijhoff, Brill Rodopi, Brill Sense, Hotei Publishing, mentis Verlag, Verlag Ferdinand Schöningh and Wilhelm Fink Verlag.
All rights reserved. No part of this publication may be reproduced, translated, stored in a retrieval system, or transmitted in any form or by any means, electronic, mechanical, photocopying, recording or otherwise, without prior written permission from the publisher. Requests for re-use and/or translations must be addressed to Koninklijke Brill NV via brill.com or copyright.com.

This book is printed on acid-free paper and produced in a sustainable manner.

Contents

Notes on Contributors VII

Introduction 1
   Vladimir Biti, Joep Leerssen, and Vivian Liska

PART 1
Rethinking the Idea of Europe

1   Jan Patočka on Europe in the Aftermath of Europe 17
      Rodolphe Gasché

2   Post-imperial Europe: The Return of the Indistinct 36
      Vladimir Biti

3   Can the European Heritage Be Redeemed? Confessions of an Europeanist 53
      Gerard Delanty

4   Europe and a Geopolitics of Hope 66
      Luiza Bialasiewicz

PART 2
Crisscrossing Projections

5   Eurotypes after Eurocentrism: Mixed Feelings in an Uncomfortable World 85
      Joep Leerssen

6   Rock, Mirror, Mirage: Europe, Elsewhere 99
      Lucia Boldrini

7   You Say *Liberté, Égalité, Fraternité?* Japanese Critical Perceptions of the Idea of Europe: A Preliminary Reflection for the Regeneration of Universal Humanism 121
      Shigemi Inaga

8 East Looks West and West Looks East: Images of Russia 136
   Aage Hansen-Löve

PART 3
The Heterotopias of Europe

9 On the Margins of (the Idea of) Europe: A Tale of Two Galicias as Constructive Comparativism 151
   César Domínguez and Nikol Dziub

10 United Europe and Disunited Yugoslavia 170
   Damir Arsenijević

11 'A Marvellous Leeway': Walter Benjamin's Idea of Europe 186
   Vivian Liska

Index 201

Notes on Contributors

Damir Arsenijević
is Professor of Literary and Cultural studies at the Department of English, University of Tuzla, and a psychoanalyst in training. Among his books are *Gender, Literature, and Cultural Memory in the Post-Yugoslav Space* (co-author, 2009), *Forgotten Future: The Politics of Poetry in Bosnia and Herzegovina* (2010), and *Unbribable Bosnia: The Fight for the Commons* (2015). His forthcoming book is *Love after Genocide*.

Luiza Bialasiewicz
is Professor of European Governance at the University of Amsterdam. Among her books are *Spazio e Politica: Riflessioni di geografia critica* (w. C. Minca, 2004), *Europe in the World: EU Geopolitics and the Making of European Space* (ed., 2011) and *Spaces of Tolerance: Changing Geographies and Philosophies of Religion in Today's Europe* (co-ed. w. V. Gentile, 2019).

Vladimir Biti
Emeritus Chair Professor of Slavic and Comparative Literature at the University of Vienna, is currently Distinguished Chair Visiting Professor at Zhejiang University. Author of *Literatur- und Kulturtheorie: Ein Handbuch gegenwärtiger Begriffe*, Rowohlt, 2001, *Tracing Global Democracy: Literature, Theory, and the Politics of Trauma*, De Gruyter, 2016 (second, paperback edition 2017), and *Attached to Dispossession: Sacrificial Narratives in Post-imperial Europe*, Brill, 2018, among others. Editor of the volumes *Reexamining the National-Philological Legacy: Quest for a New Paradigm*, Rodopi, 2014 and *Claiming the Dispossession: The Politics of Hi/Storytelling in Post-imperial Europe*, Brill, 2017, among others. Co-editor of *arcadia: International Journal of Literary Culture* and Chair of the Academy of Europe's Literary and Theatrical Section.

Lucia Boldrini
is Professor of English and Comparative Literature at Goldsmiths College, University of London. Among her books are *Autobiographies of Others: Historical Subjects and Literary Fiction* (2012) and *Experiments in Life-Writing: Intersections of Auto/Biography and Fiction* (ed. with Julia Novak, 2017).

Gerard Delanty
is Professor of Sociology and Social & Political Thought at the University of Sussex, Brighton, UK. He worked as fellow and visiting professor at York University,

Toronto; Doshisha University, Kyota; Deakin University, Melbourne; Hamburg University; the Federal University of Brasilia; and the University of Barcelona. His most recent publication is *Critical Theory and Social Transformation* (Routledge, 2020). Other publications include: *The Cosmopolitan Imagination* (Cambridge University Press, 2009), *Formations of European Modernity*, 2nd edition (Palgrave, 2019), *Community* 3rd Edition (Routledge 2018), *The European Heritage: A Critical Re-Interpretation* (Routledge 2018). He has edited many volumes, including the *Routledge International Handbook of Cosmopolitan Studies*, 2nd edition 2019) and, with Stephen P. Turner, the *Routledge Handbook of Contemporary Social and Political Theory* (2011), He is also the Chief Editor of the *European Journal of Social Theory*.

César Domínguez
is associate professor of Comparative Literature of the University of Santiago de Compostela. Among his books are *Literatura europea comparada* (ed., 2013), *Cosmopolitanism and the Postnational: Literature and the New Europe* (ed. with Theo D'haen, 2015), *Introducing Comparative Literature: New Methods and Applications* (w. Dario Villanueva & Haun Saussy, 2015); he is co-editor of the *Comparative History of Literatures in the Iberian Peninsula* (2007–16)

Nikol Dziub
is a faculty member of the Université de Haute-Alsace. Among her books are *L'Ashiq et le troubadour* (co-ed., 2017), «Son arme était la harpe»: *Pouvoirs de la femme et du barde chez Nizami et dans Le Livre de Dede Korkut* (2018), *Voyages en Andalousie au XIXe siècle* (2018), *Traduction et interculturalité. Entre identité et altérité* (co-ed., 2019), *Comparative Literature in Europe: Challenges and Perspectives* (co-ed., 2019).

Rodolphe Gasché
is Eugenio Donato Professor of Comparative Literature and SUNY Distinguished Professor of Comparative Literature at SUNY (Buffalo). Among his books are *The Honor of Thinking: Critique, Theory, Philosophy* (2006), *Europe, Or The Infinite Task* (2008), *The Stelliferous Fold: Toward a Virtual Law of Literature's Self-Formation* (2011), *Geophilosophy* (2014), *Storytelling and the Destruction of the Inalienable in the Age of the Holocaust* (2018).

Aage Hansen-Löve
is Professor Emeritus of Russian Literature at Ludwig-Maximilian-Universität München. Currently, he is teaching at the Institute of Comparative Studies at the University of Vienna. Since 1999, he is member of the Austrian Academy of Sciences. He is also founder and editor of the journal *Wiener Slawistischer*

Almanach (since 1978; 160 vols.). Author of *Der russische Formalismus* (Vienna 1978, Moscow 2001), *Der russische Symbolismus* (3 vols., Vienna 1989, 2003, Moscow 2014), *Über das Vorgestern ins Übermorgen* (Paderborn 2016) and *Schwangere Musen – Rebellische Helden: Antigenerisches Schreiben. Von Sterne zu Dostoevskij, von Flaubert zu Nabokov* (Paderborn 2019), among others.

Shigemi Inaga
is Professor at the International Research Center for Japanese Studies, Kyoto, and between 2016 and 2018 served as its Deputy Director-General and also served as Dean of the Post-Graduate University for Advanced Studies, Hayama. Among his books are *L'Orient de la peinture : de l'Orientalisme au Japonisme* (1999), *Images on the Edge: A Historical Survey of East-Asian Trans-Cultural Modernities* (2014), *In Search of Haptic Plasticity* (2016), as well as *Modernity of Japanese Art History and its Exterior* (2018).

Joep Leerssen
is Professor of Modern European Literature at the University of Amsterdam. Among his books are *Imagology* (ed. W. Manfred Beller, 2007), *National Thought in Europe* (3rd ed. 2018), *Spiegelpaleis Europa* (3rd ed. 2015); *The Rhine* (ed. W. Manfred Beller 2018) and *Encyclopedia of Romantic Nationalism in Europe* (ed., 2018). He was awarded the All European Academies' Madame de Staël Prize 2020 for Cultural Values.

Vivian Liska
is Professor of German at the University of Antwerp, Belgium as well as Distinguished Visiting Professor at The Hebrew University of Jerusalem. She has published extensively on German Modernism and Literary Theory. Her most recent book is titled *German-Jewish Thought and its Afterlife. A Tenuous Legacy* (Indiana UP, 2017)

Introduction

Vladimir Biti, Joep Leerssen, and Vivian Liska

Recent developments within and beyond Europe have variously challenged the very idea of Europe, calling it into question and demanding reconsideration of its underlying assumptions. Since Aristotle's times, Europeans have typically associated themselves with dialogic openness and inclusiveness, as opposed to the despotic exclusiveness and violence that has marked other manners of rule (*Politics*, III, 1285a 6-7; VII, 1372b 24-339). The tradition of singling out peaceful, cosmopolitan European self-perception against a background of bellicose, non-European provincialism is well documented.

For example, Johann Gottfried Herder argued, in the second half of the eighteenth century, that the 'general spirit' of Europe amalgamates the 'tribal formation of many European nations' (*Ideen*, 705). Over the centuries, in this climatically privileged part of the world, ethnic narrow-mindedness had evolved and improved so that 'everything in Europe tends toward a gradual suspension of national characters' (706). As with plant life, according to Herder, the environmentally bound non-European races and peoples flourish and then wither (571), but it is within the more mobile and advanced European races that culture moves on (*rückt fort*, 628), taking on the seeds of withered peoples in order to continue nature's vital creation (*lebendige Schöpfung*, 573). This is why cosmopolitan Europeans are predestined to carry forth the torch of humanity towards future freedom. However, Herder's European idea of a dialogically oriented, generous and self-educating people rests upon endless geopolitical devaluations, marginalizations and exclusions. Even while establishing an ideal type of 'human nature', it excludes and dismisses those who fail to conform to it: Jews are a parasitic people 'hanging onto almost all European nations and drawing more or less profit from their juice' (702) and 'Gypsies' are 'good for nothing but harsh military discipline' (703). By contrast, Germans have 'protected the culture that remained after the storm of the epochs, developed the common spirit of Europe and slowly and conspicuously ripened to effectuate all the world regions on earth' (805).

Thus, the idea of progress, entangled as it had become since the Renaissance in colonialism—yet tending to avoid a clear realization of that entanglement—was necessarily accompanied by exclusions, oppression and also the atrocities of the past century. Bearing this in mind, our intention here is to re-examine this uncanny legacy in the post-Eurocentric contemporary world. To what extent can present-day power asymmetries be seen as the aftermath of plantations, factories, and colonies, the principal laboratories of European progress? Does the purportedly universalist idea of humanity constitutively rely upon a gap which divides humanity into separate interest groups? Does democratic freedom in the European political space come at the price of violence applied beyond its borders and the concomitant normative pressures intensified toward its frontiers? And, if so, what can today's world apprehend and hope for from contemporary Europe, burdened as it is by the various projections to which it is now subjected?

Further on, what is the contemporary status of European values now that they have lost their axiomatic self-evidence? For the fact is that Europe has, until today, permanently reinvented its *singularity* against the background of external and internal others' *particularities*. Even its acknowledgement of the colonial and genocidal aspects of its history has been co-opted into a discourse of self-doubt and guilt-acceptance as a sign of moral superiority or at least maturity. At the same time, an Enlightenment ethics of even-handed justice and critique of hegemonism ironically underpins today's critiques of European hegemonism and eurocentrism. From its very beginning, the European self needed non-European others for its enduring background, and for this very reason could never relinquish them. It could not assert its uniqueness without exempting itself from non-European stereotypes. This has recently been corroborated in some influential interpretations of Europe. According to Zygmunt Bauman, 'we do not know who we are' and 'even less do we know what we can yet become' (*Europe*, 12). Non-European cultures, he says, remain unaware of being distinct, as they are unrelated to other cultures; European culture, however, differs starkly, for it 'feeds on questioning the order of things – and on questioning the fashion of questioning it' (12). As Rodolphe Gasché explains, this ultimately renders European culture an 'infinite task' of consistent self-singularization against a background of other, putatively non-European, historical, geopolitical and cultural particularizations (*Europe*, 27, 343).

Going back to the conference held at the University of Vienna in September 2017 and enriched by some new contributions, this volume endeavors to examine how Europe has been conceptualized by both its engineers and its Others – located both within and beyond Europe. Their diverse projections of an image of Europe have achieved prominent and powerful, albeit sometimes undesired, expression in the course of recent developments. How have they contributed towards shaping and forging the idea of Europe as a historical legacy, a contemporary presence and a future agenda? The studies assembled here address this question by way of general philosophical and theoretical considerations, transregional analyses, and focused case studies. They are divided in three sections.

1   Rethinking the Idea of Europe

In his opening essay 'Jan Patočka on Europe in the aftermath of Europe', Rodolphe Gasché departs from Patočka's thesis on the end of Europe in the sense of its loss of economical and political supremacy in the world, an end that ought to be taken as a chance for its re-conceptualization. In the process of the Europeanization of other cultures, Europe was amalgamated with traditions that are foreign to its spiritual substance because of their archaic origins. This has alienated it from its origin in the Greek 'care of the soul' that, through its gaze at an idea beyond all ideas, aimed at rational clarity and intelligibility. However, this sublime motif was not only spoiled by importing irrationality from other cultures but also by 'a native irrationalism peculiar to Europe' itself, i.e. its own archaisms. What Patočka means by this irrationalism are in the first place motifs that are native to Christianity and, through their practical orientation toward the things in an entirely objectified world, aborted the rational principle of the care of the soul. Especially in its Protestant form, upon whose soil Greek rationality enjoyed its renewal in Europe, it introduced the subject as an imperialist entity from which the world in its entirety can be drawn. 'At the root of the catastrophe of Europe is this theologically motivated reduction of rationality to the objectified world and expansion of the soul to an absolute subject'. Patočka therefore tries to rethink Europe without falling back on these errors, i.e. by carefully distilling its rationality out of the mud of its irrationality. For him, demanding such a radical renewal of Europe means returning it to its genuine task. No other culture can take critical issue with their assimilated Europes to the extent that Europe itself can by freeing its rationality and universality from native irrationalisms and archaisms. At this point of his argumentation, Gasché leaves behind the reconstruction of Patočka's theses, stating that even the notion of the 'idea' restricts Europe's universal thrust by rendering Europe as something given rather than as an infinite task. As long as Europe remains an 'idea', it is not free from the traditional burden of Greek metaphysics, unless one 'revives to this notion the strangeness that in fourth-century Greece must have been peculiar to it'. In order to accomplish that, it is necessary to conceive of an idea 'beyond the idea', i.e. one that comes from the other rather than from itself, as is the case when Europe attaches itself to a fixed identity. This other does not imply some exotic otherness, but rather its own strangeness, its own untapped resources that can exhibit new features. The idea beyond the idea thus allows Europe to expose itself to the gift from the other, i.e. to open itself toward that which it is not yet.

Vladimir Biti's essay 'Post-imperial Europe: The Rise of the Indistinct' singles out and deals with post-imperial Europe's two interconnected faces. The first, subaltern one was revealed through the dissolution of the East-Central European empires during the aftermath of the First World War; the second, superior one came to the fore through the crumbling of the West European empires in the aftermath of the Second World War. In the first case, through the Treaty of Versailles, the Western nation-state powers introduced the principle of national self-determination into the post-imperial East-Central European region. However, this process of 'civilizing' East-Central Europe induced general disappointment in its newly established states since it only exacerbated the extent to which they lagged behind their Western models. As is testified to by their populations' huge enforced migrations, instead of benefiting from modern European mobility, they were victimized by it. To defend themselves from their new masters, they forged alliances with one another, jointly subverting the civilizing techniques that were applied to them. In this way, in lieu of consolidated nation states, religious, ideological, class and gender transborder communities arose as the unprocessed residues of undertaken national translations. These hybrid formations were the first manifestation in which Europe's indistinct 'past' reemerged with the effect of ruining its goal-oriented differentiation. The second form of the return of its indistinct past was the resurfacing of 'animality' within its humanity's progress. After the Second World War, decolonization spawned the homecoming of colonized peripheries into the colonial countries that had, for a longtime, kept them at a distance as the dumps of their systematic cultivation. This 'return of the repressed' blurred the distinction that they had achieved, initiating a sense of commonality with their formerly denigrated compatriots. Forced to confront its imperial past, Western Europe started to expiate it. Many prominent modern philosophers attempted to solve this predicament by reattaching Europe to its task of rescuing universal humankind, but the difficulty that they faced was that the very agency called upon to rescue it increasingly acquired indistinct traits. If Europe failed to accomplish ultimate distinction, either through its translation into nations, as undertaken by its East-Central subalterns after the First World War, or humanity, as undertaken by its Western superiors after the Second

World War, this happened because its superior and subaltern faces repeatedly contaminated each other. They could not rid themselves of their traumatizing proximity. As a result, whoever acts as its ultimate carrier, a Janus-like Europe steadily reopens the very division that it is at pains to overcome. Instead of figuring as a solution for the imperiled human common being, it remains an open problem that must always be coped with anew.

Gerard Delanty's essay 'Can the European Heritage be Redeemed? Confessions of a Europeanist' defends the European heritage that recently came under attack from all sides for almost completely losing its specificity. The historical event that has most seriously interrogated the European legacy is of course the Holocaust. However, following Levy and Sznaider, Delanty argues that, instead of causing the European heritage's destruction, it can become the basis of its new understanding. Next to its symbolic components, it would then also include the cognitive and normative ones, thus opening European culture toward the non-European ones. 'I argue that Europe cannot abandon questioning its dark side, but it cannot also entirely see this as the only way it can relate to the past.' Taking the Holocaust as the trigger for its revision, it opens its heritage towards marginalized, forgotten or traumatized counter-memories, initiating the search for alternatives to the received view of history in the identification of that which has been hidden. In addition, 'a more critical approach to the past would include giving greater acknowledgment of what has come to be seen as a non-European tradition as constitutive of Europe'. The intention is not so much to assimilate these neglected and excluded histories but to reshape the whole historical narrative by means of them, transforming it into a site of cultural reinterpretation and reevaluation. In lieu of simply affirming Europe and fostering its reputation, European heritage must be a laboratory for the re-signification, re-codification, and cross-fertilization of divergent memories that makes place for traumatic legacies and counter-memories. Delanty renders it as a cosmopolitan mosaic that enables dialogue, exchange, and resistances between its constituents. It can only detach itself from Eurocentrism by embracing alterity, accepting difference, and the plurality of its traditions. In this regard, the self-critical currents that have been constitutive of Europe's past acquire particular importance. 'The argument I am making is that a critical cosmopolitan critique of Europe is itself one of the legacies of the European heritage'. The essay concludes by singling out 'three currents that might redefine the idea of Europe for the present day: peace, social justice, hospitality'. Although the commitment to peace after the First World War 'did not stop the descent into the worst war in the history of human societies', it 'offered a legacy on which Europe could rebuild itself after 1945'. Equally essential are concerns for social justice and individual human rights, the latter being 'the enduring feature of contemporary Europe which offers an antidote to its divisions'.

Luiza Bialasiewicz's essay 'Europe and a Geopolitics of Hope' departs from the well-established image of Europe as the generator of hope or an aspirational *civitas futura* (Cacciari). There is a visible tendency, not only in the interpretations of Europe's leading thinkers but also in its Constitutional Convention, to transcend the territorial understanding of a European political community by reconceptualizing it as a set of basic conditions that any applicant country must meet. The engineers of the idea of Europe avoided its territorial definition in order not to exclude 'potential Europeans' from it. The latter are more efficiently attracted if Europe is defined as a flexible and extendable 'area of human hope', however counter-factual this definition turned out to be after 'Europe's borders have become more and more deadly' and after Europeans have faced unequal effects from 'common' European developments. The resistance of facts has not hindered the applicants in proliferating their hopes. To explain this phenomenon, Bialasiewicz presents Bauman's thesis that the European geopolitical reality always lagged behind the projected 'essence of Europe'. In fact, the very practice of Europeanism has moved people away from the 'absurd accidentality' (Borges) of their geopolitical location toward the fiction of an 'unfinished project' that never stops questioning itself. On top of that, Europe used to see itself as a global 'civilian power' entrusted to domesticate international relations by transferring its internal policies to them (Duchène). It is true, external perspectives have starkly opposed this self-aggrandizing self-representation of Europe by criticizing it as 'oddly unreflexive about its own imperialisms' and involved 'in the production of exploitative and oppressive relations'. Even among today's EU member states, there are divergent understandings of what Europe was and is, and they multiply on a daily basis. Such rifts force thinkers to define Europe's geopolitical identity and its world role in much clearer terms, as demonstrated in Habermas's, Balibar's, Todorov's and in particular Derrida's most recent reflections. In conclusion, the author states that the appeals to Europe by those who, despite the hard realities of geopolitics, continue to seek access to its space of rights, should not be disregarded. The hope for a better Europe continues to demonstrate a powerful mobilizing potential. 'Indeed, many of those fleeing the horrors of the real Europe often attempted to make 'better Europes' elsewhere. It is vitally important to recall these histories of the loss and re-making of Europe today',

2   Crisscrossing Projections

Joep Leerssen's essay 'Eurotypes after Eurocentrism: Mixed Feelings in an Uncomfortable World' opens with the basic premise of imagology, that the establishment of national identity uses Others as its differential background. This implies that a European identity would take on very different characteristics depending on what serves as its background (America, Asia, or Africa). It is because Europe has been contrasted with so many different 'Others' over the centuries that its 'archival memory' contains such contradictory characteristics, which never stop resurfacing. While all these Eurotypes are Eurocentric in one way or another, Eurocentrism has meanwhile lost its unargued, aprioristical status and needs to be revised. However, unlike political history, cultural history does not render its past obsolete but searches for alternatives to it. 'Culture is a historical accumulation of its past productions, layered sediments and memories, always in a potential transition between functional and archival memory, between latency and salience, suspension and activation'. This is why the multifarious images of Europe continuously interact and crisscross with each other. One of these Eurotypes, which the author tries to disentangle, characterizes Europe by Christian virtues, whereas its Other is cruel and licentious, and was firmly established over the course of the Renaissance. The next one is 'Europe as plain, its Other as refined', which coincides with the Enlightenment and a more critical attitude towards Christianity. Its later, Romantic revalorization entails an 'imageme' of the Orient as despotic yet refined, cruel yet enticing. The next Eurotype is '(Western) Europe as individualistic, its Other as despotic and collective', which was reinforced during the European colonial expansion. The next Eurotype is 'the West as bland, its Other as ancient and authentic' and has its origin in the seventeenth century, while 'Europe declining in an awakening world' takes America on the rise as its background. Over the course of the eighteenth century, the Romantic Eurotype emerges of '(Northern) Europe as reasonable and philosophical, its Other as passionate and unreliable', drawing on the propaganda of the Reformation. In the second half of the nineteenth century the counter-image of '(Northern) Europe as stolid, its Other as vivacious and emotionally intense' is on the rise. All of this is caught up in the second great crisis in the European Self-Image, that of a guilt-ridden Europe as epitomized by Joseph Conrad's *The Heart of Darkness* (1900). It was followed by the images of Europe rising above its tyrannical chauvinisms, a haven for political correctness, and in danger of being subverted by its Other. All of this amounts to a steady intersection of progressive and conservative, positive and negative valorizations of Europe.

Ultimately, Europe may realize that it is complex, and willing to live with that complexity.

Lucia Boldrini's essay 'Rock, Mirror, Mirage: Europe, Elsewhere' perfectly fits into the frame set by the volume's title 'The Idea of Europe: The Clash of Projections'. It is a mosaic of vignettes that deal with the Croatian, Moroccan, Palestinian, Nigerian, Jewish, German, Catalan, Italian, and Algerian perspectives on the idea of Europe by distilling them out of such different sources as essays, novels, pamphlets, manifestos, photos, poems, artistic maps, stories, interviews, reviews, treatises and scholarly works. Putting together these most varied perspectives and sources, Boldrini lets her own Italian-British-European 'fragmented thoughts' cautiously meander between them, thoughts that are in their turn, as she confesses, very much influenced by the still fresh traumatic experience of Brexit. Of course, none of these perspectives and sources is isolated, self-sufficient, and autonomous but rather is included into an ongoing open dialogue that incessantly shifts their boundaries. There is no such thing as a *real* Croat, Moroccan, Nigerian, Italian, Jew, or, last but not least, European. Who among us is 'real' and therefore entitled to stand for a proper 'we' remains to be decided 'elsewhere', in a time that is always-yet-to-come, which probably means 'never'. In fact, the very idea of the essay is to 'expose the shortsightedness of any idea of solid borders, of purity, of national rootedness as the mark of identity, when the smudging of those borders, the evolution of traditions through constant encounters, clashes, equivocations, exploitations, has not only already been happening for centuries but is intrinsic to the European expansion over other territories'. The final establishment of European (or, by consequence, any national) boundaries would necessarily imply the exclusion of the 'citizens of nowhere', deprived of protection and rights, respectively the disenfranchisement of large swathes of those 'who think differently, who like a different food or have different memories'. Such an establishment of British boundaries took place over the duration of the Brexit process, which is precisely why it must not happen with regard to Europe. On the contrary, Europe has to remain an 'everchanging but capacious 'we' that has emerged from, and that continues to be shaped by, our encounters, exchanges, conflicts, similarities and divergences; of the emotional bonds that these encounters, and sometimes clashes, engender; of our responsibility to engender them; of how we always, inevitably, cause the 'we' to shift because we cannot but walk into the frame'. Such a Europe ought to figure as a necessary 'elsewhere' for each and everyone of its national identities.

Shigemi Inaga's essay 'You Say – Liberté, Égalité, Fraternité? Japanese Critical Perceptions of the Idea of Europe: A Preliminary Reflection for the Regeneration of Universal Humanism' opens by stating the imbalance in the flow of information between Japan and Europe: 'European literature is fully accessible in Japanese translation but not vice versa'. In addition, 'most cultural theories are European or Western products and it is rare that non-European reflections on Europe have been seriously taken into account'. Instead of being considered as equal partners in the cultural exchange, non-European cultures were treated as the suppliers of raw data for European theories. It is not only that the European style educational system, 'in the name of human rights', has colonized the rest of the world, but the latter has also fallen victim of the English-American linguistic imperialism. The colonialism of European culture that tended to believe in the universal validity of its own criteria when judging other cultures, on the top of that, induced the wounded self-respect among many of them. Many Japanese felt humiliated by the European perception of them. However, also some eminent Europeans experienced an identity crisis in their encounters with Japanese culture. In the second part of his essay, the author introduces three case studies of Japanese intellectuals ranging through various generations from the second half of the nineteenth century to the first half of the twentieth century, who interrogated the three fundamental ideas of Europe that were elaborated in the French Revolution, namely *liberté*, égalité and *fraternité*. The first is Mori Ōgai (1862-1922), one of the first Japanese medical students to stay in Europe, now remembered as a prolific writer and translator of many European works of literature into Japanese. He faced Europeans with their betrayal of the proclaimed fraternity among the Red Cross constituents and was, interestingly enough, celebrated by some of them for that. The second is Takeyama Michio (1903–1984), an exceptionally talented intellectual from the privileged elite who was appointed associate professor at Tokyo High School when he embarked for Europe in 1927 to stay there until 1930. He was astonished to see that in almost every European country counterfeit money was used to cheat, in the first place, foreigners who were the easiest victims. This is how the Japanese professor, having 'learned how to pay cultural tax at the inter-cultural border crossing', experienced the ruination of the European idea of equality. The third is Kudō Tetsumi (1935–1990), the famous Japanese artist and performer. He experienced Europeans, instead of serving the idea of liberty as expected, as bound to the idea of 'human noblesse', which he found hypocritical. Through these interactions with strangers who crossed the idea of Europe's borderlines, its intrinsic possibility was revealed in terms of its universal crisis.

Aage Hansen-Löve's essay 'East Looks West and West Looks East: Images of Russia' departs from the thesis that prejudices are central facts of every culture and belong to the crucial factors guiding their internal and external self-reflection. Although they have little to do with facts, or precisely because of that, they are necessary for the self-maintenance of any culture. 'We look towards the alien, the foreign, the other so as not to discover our own culture in it, and we look towards our own culture so as not to have to see the different one'. This is precisely how the West has 'invented' Russia as 'something highly exclusive'. However, the author is not so interested in special features ascribed to Russia, but rather the strategies deployed, in Russia and the 'West', to define their own uniqueness and exceptionality. As for the West, Leibniz deprived Russia of history by making it into tabula rasa, i.e. an empty surface suitable for Western wishful projections. As for Russia, the Russian philosopher Peter Chaadaev invented a distinctive flipping technique for conceiving his own country, which begins with the paradoxical veneration of the negative and deficient (Russia as a totally isolated, pale copy that is untouched by the universal education of the human race, alien even to itself, barren and void) and ends with the triumph of lack and want. These denigrating projections were eagerly adopted by Russians themselves, who blended them together with homegrown images of their own selves. 'The main strategy of self-characterization here is not only a masochistic inferiority complex, but also the countertendency to revalorize the negative characteristics into positive ones'. It generates the paradoxes of the self-Orientalization of Russia, the Russian apocalypse now and forever ('an untamable wish to arrive at the end and at the same time to negate that end'), and the 'Russian idea' as the salvation for all, as we know them in the first place through the works of Dostoevsky. But there exist, at the same time, Western stereotypes of Russia that were generated after 1900: an entirely alien country, homeland of the irrational (Spengler), which can nevertheless or precisely therefore rescue Europe from its decay (Nietzsche, Friedell). The essay continues by singling out the Russian response to Freud's psychoanalysis that has 'left out none of the then-current cultural cliches about Russia' by promoting it in this way into the West's 'unconscious'. A further significant Western stereotype of Russia was its identification with literature and art, as epitomized in Friedell's work among others. Finally, in post-Soviet conceptual art (Kabakov, Groys), Russia is rendered as the West's 'alternative', which demands a 'higher degree of universality' than it itself does. From this point of view, Russia has nothing that is genuinely its own, but it has it more radically so than anyone else.

3 The Heterotopias of Europe

César Domínguez and Nikol Dziub's essay 'On the Margins of (the Idea of) Europe: A Tale of Two Galicias as Constructive Comparativism' is an attempt to apply Detienne's concept of constructive comparativism in literary and cultural studies by resorting to two prima facie incomparable objects, namely, Western European Galicia in the Iberian peninsula and Eastern European Galicia in the frontier region between Poland and Ukraine. The idea is to maintain these two distant regions' sameness and difference in tension and thus to examine the politics of comparison. The points of departure are Manuel Rivas's novel *En salvaxe compaña* (*In the Wilderness*; 1993) and Andrzej Stasiuk's collection of stories *Opowieści galicyiskie* (*Tales of Galicia*; 1995), and the question that is raised is whether we can, from the work of one writer, learn something new about the region of the other. As the authors point out, following Detienne (2008, 26), 'incomparability is a provocation that results in the disintegration of a familiar category'. Rivas's novel follows its main protagonist Rosa from her childhood through to her adult life as a wife and a mother, i.e. from the Spanish Civil War to the early 1990s, enmeshing her malleable memories into the series of historical events. As her rape can be compared to the sixteenth-century Spanish taming of the Kingdom of Galicia, Rosa's story may be read as Galicia's (hi)story. In Stasiuk's collection, which gives a platform to voices that are not usually heard, the Galician community lives in an 'in between' state and its factual narratives look like fantastic nightmares telling the story of a dismembered reality. 'History and memory are both obsolete here: history because the Galician world has come to an end, and because Galicia seems to be banned from the historical cause and effect chain; memory because the 'last' people or objects are not remnants, but ruins without any temporal background, and because photographs do not bear witness anymore to the past presence of an object'. Both works are impregnated by a 'post'-atmosphere, haunted by the ghosts of the past, meaning that both Galicias are inhabiting transitory, adolescent spaces. Their space and time are clearly 'out of joint'. For both Galicias, 'history is a nightmare' and 'memory can only be retold *against the wind* by returned or to-be-returned ghostly figures'. Both turn out to be *non-lieux*, with neither past nor future available. These European post-colonies are typical 'zones of indistinction' (Agamben) where life and death cohabitate and mix. Precisely as such, they prove to be 'an important testing ground for a different conceptualisation of Europe'.

Damir Arsenijević's essay 'United Europe and Disunited Yugoslavia' opens with the humorous sketch of the Bosnian group *Top lista nadrealista* (The Surrealists' Hit Parade), entitled *United Europe and Disunited Yugoslavia*, in which Europe protects itself from war-torn Yugoslavia with a huge concrete wall, topped with barbed wire. While the last surviving Yugoslav, who is permitted to cross the wall and invited to join a feast devours the food, the various Europeans start fighting amongst themselves about the origins of the war in Yugoslavia.

We then see a reporter standing on a ladder on the Yugoslav side of the wall, talking about a hundred-year war in Europe. When he climbs down the ladder, he pushes it to the ground, lest some 'fool' from war-torn Europe climbs over into Yugoslavia. This bitter video clip interrogates the cynical relationship of Europe towards its borderlands, and vice versa, which is this essay's center stage. The first reproduced photograph shows a deserted waiting room in the forgotten railway station in Tuzla, in which a refugee prays to Allah, maybe to let him pass the EU-border and reach the Promised Land. 'The man's expulsion from his home brings to the fore the expulsion of the Yugoslav socialist future by the so-called transition into capitalism, evidenced in the photograph by the makeshift railway station offices'. Thus, what we testify to is the space of double expulsion, which creates and disseminates insecurity as one of the bases of new governance. Another such basis is trauma, opened with another photograph, in which a woman from Srebrenica holds a framed picture of 'three figures: the woman herself, a young man in uniform, and a young girl', i.e. the couple and their daughter. The man is wearing the uniform of the Yugoslav People's Army, the same army which killed him and buried him in a clandestine mass grave, leaving his wife and daughter with a traumatic desire to bring together and recreate the destroyed family around the missing man. Refusing to renounce Yugoslav political subjectivity, the woman opposes the new regime's ethnicization of trauma, which powerfully revises history. The third basis for new governance is poverty, evoked through a photograph of the post-industrial remnants of a former chemical plant in Tuzla. After extracting material value from such factories, the mercenaries of capital, supported by local ethno-nationalist elites, abandoned the toxic waste. Only the unemployed former workers, impoverished through the process of the factory's privatization, dare to approach this waste, picking through the site for scrap metal to sell. This work exposes them to toxic waste, leading to high numbers of premature deaths among them. In the logic of governance through poverty, pollution is weaponised. To oppose the delineated techniques of governance, workers organized protests to maintain production and increase their solidarity.

Vivian Liska's essay "A Marvellous Leeway': Walter Benjamin's Idea of Europe' reconstructs two decades of Walter Benjamin's hesitation to leave the European sphere that simultaneously figured as a support and resource and as a threat and burden to his life. Although he seriously considered America and Palestine as solutions for his suddenly endangered existence in Europe, neither proved to be a viable option for him, as witnessed by his consistent postponement of the decision. Benjamin was quite aware of the risk involved in this postponement but was nevertheless reluctant to definitely turn his back on Europe. He ultimately never solves this conflict, but its insolubility, demonstrated in frequently varied formulations, is linked to one of the core aspects of his thought. Europe is to him neither a geographical nor a political or ideological realm, but an indispensable workshop as well as a mode of thinking and speaking and an attitude towards life. Liska enlists the following motives *for* an emigration from Europe: initial encounters with Zionism; the need to learn Hebrew in the context of his studies on the German *Trauerspiel*; the emigration of acquaintances and friends; failed love affairs and an increasing feeling of isolation; disappointment at the failure of his university career; financial difficulties; hopes of professional opportunities outside of Europe; anti-Semitic violence in European cities; the increasingly dark social and political situation, which culminated in Hitler's seizure of power. The reasons for staying are more complex. First, there is his rejection of territorial Zionism and the need to situate Jewishness in Europe. 'Even as an outcast his place is in Europe, even if there is no place for him there'. Then there are doubts about the political, religious, and cultural conditions in Palestine. Finally, there is work that still needs to be completed before any departure and his need to stay in Paris to finish the Arcades Project. As a result, the simultaneity of the 'necessity' of departure and the inability to execute it turns out to be an ongoing philosophical problem. The core of all his considerations is delay, constant hesitations, conditions, reservations, and hints at vague difficulties and impossibilities, so characteristic of Kafka's writing. 'As with Kafka, hesitancy, *Zögern*, becomes the path itself: it makes it possible to ward off a decision. Yet this hesitancy is not merely a passive inability to decide'. Quite on the contrary, it opens a space, which is free of the dictates of 'foreign circumstances' and requirements and in which something else other than the given is conceivable. Or, to put it differently, it creates a space beyond necessity and impossibility, where the possibility of salvation lights up. Benjamin calls this space *ein herrlicher Spielraum*, a 'marvellous leeway', locating it 'in the middle of events' and expecting it to shelter him from the upcoming catastrophe. His idea of Europe amounts to precisely this 'marvellous leeway'.

Works Cited

Aristotle. 2013. Politics (trl. Carnes Lord; 2nd ed.; Chicago: University of Chicago Press).
Bauman, Zygmunt. 2004 *Europe: An Unfinished Adventure* (Cambridge: Wiley).
Gasché, Rodolphe. 2009 *Europe or the Infinite Task: A Study of Philosophical Concept* (Stanford: Stanford University Press).

Herder, Johann Gottfried. 1989 *Ideen zur Philosophie einer Geschichte der Menschheit* (ed. Martin Bollacher; in *Werke in zehn Bänden,* ed. Martin Bollacher et al., 6; Frankfurt: Deutsche Klassiker Verlag).

PART 1

Rethinking the Idea of Europe

∴

CHAPTER 1

Jan Patočka on Europe in the Aftermath of Europe

Rodolphe Gasché

Europe has been defined in several ways: as a project, a task, a dream, a promise, an image, a figure, but above all, and philosophically speaking more important, as a concept.[1] The characterization of Europe as an idea is certainly also one of the ways in which we have come to think and speak about Europe. In fact, it has become more common to refer to Europe as an idea than a concept. But does this equally philosophical designation fit Europe more properly than, say, a concept of Europe? What are the stakes of calling it an idea rather than something else? Does this representation of Europe as an idea best convey what we think of when we reflect on Europe, or has this term also intrinsic limits, making it possibly too narrow a representation for what might be meant by 'Europe', what I believe we *should* mean when we talk about Europe today?

I take my starting point in the 'Annexes' published to Jan Patočka's 2007 *L'Europe après l'Europe* (in the translation from the Czech into French by Erika Abrams).[2] From the title of the book – *L'Europe après l'Europe* – it is clear that after Europe has come to an end, we are not simply done with Europe. In fact, the end of Europe in the sense of the loss of its economical and political supremacy in the world, presents Europe with an opportunity; with a chance, as the Czech philosopher puts it, to reconceive of itself. In order to gauge the context for such a chance, it is important to realize that, as Patočka points out at the beginning of *Plato and Europe,* the end of Europe by way of Europe's self-destruction 'has drawn the entire world into this, just as she had appropriated before the whole world in a material fashion' (Patočka, 2002: 9). By forcing the rest of the world to engage in those horrendous enterprises of self-destruction by 'projecting the division of Europe upon a division of the world', inheritors of Europe have emerged who 'will never allow Europe to be [again] what it once was' (Patočka, 1996: 92; 2002: 9). It is important to see that this result is in fact the result of Europe's success; more precisely, of its successful Europeanization of the world. In *L'Europe après l'Europe,* Patočka notes that

---

1 A previous version of this essay has appeared as Gasché 2018.
2 The additions I will be concerned with, 'Ce qu'est l'Europe – Sept fragments', and 'L'époque posteuropéenne et ses problèmes spirituels', date from 1988 and 1974, respectively. All page numbers in the text refer to Patočka, 2007.

the collectivities that are in the process of awakening, as well as those who affirm themselves for the first time as political giants are ... formally Europeanized in the sense that indisputably they adopt technology, production and the forms of European organization

even though 'they remain intimately foreign to the spiritual substance of Europe' (Patočka, 2007: 208). The new emerging humanities not only remain foreign to it, 'their relation to this substance is even strained if not antagonistic', in that the rational foundations of what has been taken over from Europe are amalgamated with traditions and motifs that are not only hostile to Europe, but whose origins are often very archaic, some of which are traceable to the Stone Age (2007: 208, 211). If this situation is a chance for Europe to reflect upon itself and to have a future after its end, it is precisely because of the formal universality that it itself has taken on throughout the world, or to put into more contemporary language, in the thus globalized world. Indeed, this state of affairs confronts Europe with the fact that, paradoxically, it itself has remained foreign to its own substance. Not only that: if Patočka can characterize the successful Europeanization of the world as 'a generalization of the shipwreck of Europe', it is because the unforeseeable alloy that European rationality has undergone through its globalization rests upon and perpetuates the very reasons that have caused, to begin with, the European catastrophe from within (211). For this reason, the dismal situation of a successfully Europeanized world that takes over from Europe harbours the possibility of another Europe – I would say, of the *other* Europe (if not the Europe of the other), if that expression (the *other* Europe) had not already been reserved for Eastern Europe (for example, by Patočka himself).

In order to understand Patočka's argument, let me first recall that in distinction from Edmund Husserl, who, in the wake of a long tradition, retraces the idea of Europe to that of philosophy – that is, to the Greek idea of a rational science and a universal truth that not only meets the demand of being able to account for itself, but that also imposes itself without distinction on everybody – Patočka, by contrast, locates the origin of Europe in the Greek, Platonic conception of the 'care of the soul' (*epimeleia tès psychès*). Among everything that Europe has inherited, this conception is what after Europe's shipwreck could still 'affect us in a way so that we could again find hope in a specific perspective, in a specific future, without giving in to illusory dreams and without undervaluing the toughness and gravity of our current situation' (Patočka, 2002: 12). For Patočka, this conception of the care of the soul is not an altogether different motif from the Husserlian notion of reason and rationality. On the contrary, the motif of tending to the soul consists only in a recasting and deepening of the foundations of European rationality in order to be able to overcome the crises of Europe. Indeed, in the notion of the care of the soul, whose aim, as Patočka does not cease to remind us, is to endow it with full transparency and clarity, all the defining features of rationality find their first philosophical and historical articulation.[3] It is a clarity that the soul achieves as a result of looking into what is, into the most perfect being – the *eide,* the forms, or looks of what is – and which, as the most perfect beings, are also those that are entirely knowable. Their being is of such a nature as to have the potential (*dunamis*) of being fully cognizable because it is of the order of the intelligible itself. Ultimately, the gaze into what is, is a gaze into the idea beyond all ideas: the idea of the Good (*agathon*) which must not be understood in a narrow moral sense, but which has 'ethical' implications in a way that concerns the intelligibility of all that is.[4] It is, therefore, crucial to understand that the notion of the care of the soul is not simply an approach that concerns the life of the individual, but is, from the start, intrinsically tied to the life in community – a point that, though present from the beginning in Patočka's reflections on the care of the soul, is perhaps more forcefully emphasized in his later writings.[5] Furthermore, in these later writings, the cared for soul is characterized as an 'open soul'. Patočka writes: 'The open soul is in its essence, a soul that has been put in contact; it is not a being that is closed upon itself ... it is possible to say that in a way its essence is to be outside itself, outside itself in the world whose horizon it actively opens up.[6]

So, for Patočka, it is not the idea of a rational science and its implicit universality, but the inherent rational nature of the care of the soul that is the embryonic form of Europe.[7] Yet, as he argues, especially in *Heretical Essays in*

---

3 The metaphors of light, radical clarity, and the sun are intimately interwoven with the notion of the care of the soul, and with that of reason. See Gasché 2007.
4 For how 'goodness is fundamental in any explanation', see Annas 1981: 244–7.
5 Marc Crépon remarks in his 'Postface' to *L'Europe après l'Europe* that besides being an ontological project in that the 'soul becomes aware of the place that it occupies in the whole of what is', 'it is a critical and political project because the care of the soul cannot be reduced to the care of *one's* own soul. It is always at the same time and in constitutive fashion, a care for the *soul* of the community.' And thus it is also 'a project of life' (Crépon, 2007: 293–4).
6 2007: 239. For an extensive discussion of this notion of an 'open soul', which Patočka most likely borrows from Henri Bergson, see Tava 2016, especially 252-.
7 Patočka 2007: 149. As Patočka emphasizes in *L'Europe après l'Europe,* it is already in Greece that the notion of the care of the soul divides into two different pursuits: one which consists in the philosophical exploration of the essence of the world in view of a universal science (Democritus, and the materialists), and another that inquires into the possibility of a transformation of human life made possible by this universal science, that is, the Socratic-Platonic one. It is the ancient materialist pursuit that, starting with the sixteenth century, begins to dominate in Europe. See, for example, Patočka 2007: 135, 287.

the Philosophy of History, this conception has undergone a number of transformations, of which only the last, its Christian appropriation, is at the foundation of Europe. For what interests us here, namely, the reasons that have led to the end of Europe and its concomitant generalization in a globalized world, the turn that the notion of the care of the soul undergoes in the sixteenth century is what must concern us first and foremost. In a most succinct form, this turn occurs when in the life of Western Europe, 'another motif comes to the fore, opposing the motif of the care of the soul' – though not simply from the outside, but by a motif that, as Patočka notes, is 'originally held in captivity' by the Christianized conception of the care of the soul – namely the motif to dominate, the will to rule (Patočka, 1996: 83, trans. mod). He writes that this new motif that, beginning with the sixteenth century comes

> to dominate one area after another, politics, economics, faith, and science, transforming them in a new style [is] not a care *for the soul*, the care to be, but rather the care to *have*, care for the external world and its conquest. (83)

Since this motif of '*having* over *being* excludes unity and universality', 'the expanding western Europe lacks any universal bond, any universal idea which could be embodied in a concrete and effective bonding institution and authority' (84). Let us remind ourselves at this point that Patočka's concern with the care of the soul is an attempt at deepening the foundations of European rationality. More generally, the essays and fragments collected in *L'Europe après l'Europe* stand under the sign of the 'idea of an ultimate foundation', or an 'idea of the well-founded' (Patočka, 2007: 79, 81). This theme of 'the well-founded', which deserves a careful analysis of its own, guides Patočka's attempt to deepen the foundations of European rationality. Husserl is credited with having begun this urgent task in *The Crisis of European Sciences and Transcendental Phenomenology* (1970), and Patočka sets out to follow the direction that Husserl outlined, even though he failed to solve the problem. Even though hereafter I will repeatedly evoke some of the main aspects of Patočka's novel approach to the task in question, it may be appropriate to try, in spite of the dense, and at times elliptic elaborations in *L'Europe après l'Europe* (2007: 229ff), to pinpoint as succinctly as possible what Husserl's failure consists of. It seems to me that when asking why, besides the inertia of the tradition, ancient mathematics and the metaphysics of the Ideas related to it maintained themselves for such a long time, Patočka's response – that the force of this metaphysics and the secular theology that it implies – is rooted 'in the deepest layers of human existence ... layers from which the drive emerges to call and exhort the souls to live a life in truth which constitutes what is most proper to them' (232). As we will see, for Patočka, Husserl's answer to the task of recasting the foundations of European rationality by way of an objectivation of subjectivity in the form of the transcendental ego falls short of accomplishing this. On the contrary, a deepening of the foundation of rationality can only be achieved through 'the Socratic-Platonic idea of a total reflection' (235), by which the first reflection originating in the deepest layers of human existence, and the second reflection that concerns our appropriation and domination of the content of the world, are dialectically overcome in the conception of an 'open soul'. [8]

At this juncture, it may be appropriate to recall that, according to Patočka, the idea of rationality that emerged as such only in Europe emerges simultaneously with the idea of its opposite, namely, 'the anonymous tradition of non-reason', or irrationalism, which is constantly displaced by reason (Patočka 1996: 83, trans. mod). This latter conception of irrationalism is one, he writes, 'that also could only emerge on the European soil, and thanks to the means that Europe provides' (Patočka 2007: 187). For this very reason the idea of irrationality is twofold. First, Patočka uses it to refer to the myths or traditions of other civilizations. Indeed, in view of Europe's culture of reason and rationality, the foreign traditions and archaic motifs that have become amalgamated with European rationality in the process of the Europeanization of the world are inevitably of the order of the irrational. But this motif of irrationality is of particular significance in *L'Europe après l'Europe* in that European civilization is shown here to harbor its own peculiar irrationalisms as well. It is important to note that these irrationalisms that include archaisms, certain traditions, and nativisms are not simply particularities or idiomaticities of singular cultures. They are defined negatively with respect to the rational, whereas particularities and idiomaticities concern the way the universal is articulated in a culturally different way in each case, given that all testimony bearing to the universal

---

8   In addition to these reasons for Husserl's failure to accomplish the task he has set for himself in the *Crisis* book, there is, I think, another, deeper reason for Patočka's criticism, which concerns the status of the formal and ideality. Tentatively, only the following: regarding the relation in ancient mathematics between mathematical idealities and the realm of the ideas, as opposed to modern mathematics' concern with universal formal structures that are the correlate of operations on the universe of reality, Patočka objects to Husserl for not having sufficiently seen that modern mathematics' concern with a universe of purely formal structures for gaining access to the universe of realities implies a forgetting of what *The Heretical Essays* had qualified as ancient mathematics' concern with the 'content, and the donation of the form', as opposed to modern mathematics' 'emphasis on product over content, on mastery rather than understanding'; in short, a forgetting of the intrinsic connection between the Platonic reign of the Ideas and the motif of the care of the soul (Patočka 1996: 86). See, in particular, Patočka 2007: 211.

can only take place through the particular, and in an inevitably particular form. Whereas the particular is an inescapable mode for articulating the universal, archaisms, nativisms, and irrationalities have a debilitating effect on it. Certain motifs that are specifically European, and that are not simply of the order of inevitable particularity, are mixed into Europe's self-defining concern with reason and universality – with the idea of Europe itself. In the same way, as is the case with all the other, non-European traditions, there is also 'a native irrationalism peculiar to Europe' (210). In his characterization of the assimilation by other cultures of the European heritage, Patočka qualifies the native content and form with which European rationality undergoes unexpected alloys, as archaisms (see, in particular, Patočka 2007: 211). Let me linger for a moment on this notion of 'archaisms', which, in distinction from the native irrationalism that both Europe and other traditions share, Patočka reserves for certain substrata that non-Western cultures mix into their appropriation of European rationality.

Greek philosophy, as it begins to take shape in the sixth century, is not the result of what has come to be known as the 'Greek miracle'. As Jean-Pierre Vernant remarks, 'there is no immaculate conception of Reason' (1965: 123). In the case of the Pre-Socratics, it has been shown that, on the contrary, it is the result of a methodic translation through a manifold of stratifications of what Clemence Ramnoux has called 'the archaic', a cultural stratum of representations with its own vocabulary, structures, and modes of concatenations, and that is reinterpreted by philosophy so as to give rise to an entirely new kind of style and structure of thought, that is, rational thought with its language freed of all such archaisms and reduced to abstractions and essentials (Ramnoux, 1970: 27–35).[9] The question raised by this accomplishment of Greek philosophy in which a recourse to archaisms takes place, but in order to completely recast them in view of a universal discourse free of archaisms, is whether non-Western cultures have been at all involved in a similar process; in other words, whether the archaic has undergone a similar 'laicization' in other cultures, in particular when they became Europeanized through the assimilation of certain aspects of European rationality which they permeated with native archaisms. Patočka does not seem optimistic in this respect, be that as it may. In any event, the native irrationalisms that are present in Europe's actual conception of reason and universality, and to which Patočka draws our attention, are not to be understood as of the order of archaisms to begin with. Rather than belonging to archaisms, to what Ramnoux calls 'le lointain' – the far-off, the distant, the remote – they are of the order of what is close, in fact, rather

---

9 For how this same principle applies to Plato's thought, see Joly 1974.

close, namely, the relatively recent phenomenon of Christianity, historically, in the context of which a rediscovery and renewal of the Platonic notion of the care of the soul find its latest articulation. What has caused Europe to self-destruct in a process that, through the Europeanization of the rest of the world has drawn the non-Western world into the same movement, derives from the pernicious amalgamation of the idea of rationality and universality with irrational motifs native to Christianity.

Undoubtedly, the idea of reason, and hence of universality, originates with Plato and is thus Greek in origin. But as Patočka argues, the original meaning of Plato's discovery of universality undergoes a significant change when it is taken up by Christian theology. For Plato, the signification of this discovery of reason and universality concerns, first and foremost, the soul as the place of knowledge, and consists in the conviction that the new consciousness to which it gives rise leads to a complete transformation of the human being – in a process which Patočka refers to as 'a reflective renewal of life' – with the effect of thoroughly reforming not merely the individual but the collective form of his existence; the political nature of his existence, in particular (Patočka, 2007: 236). Yet, when this attempt at 'a reflective renewal of life' is taken up by Christian theology and its conception of history, and Europe is thus born, the possibility of organizing European humanity in an unprecedented and unheard-of fashion on the basis of the spiritual principle of the care of the soul is quickly aborted by the tenets of theology itself. More specifically, this process in which the relinquishment of the political dimension of the motif in question takes place is historically grounded in Europe's expansion to the West, and the simultaneous essential transformation by the Reformation 'of the orientation of Christian praxis, turning from the sacred to the secular, acquir[ing] that political significance that will manifest itself in the organization of the North American continent by Protestant radicalism' (Patočka 1996: 84). As regard the specific forms that the irrationalisms native to Europe take and that become amalgamated with the ideas of reason and universality involved in the care of the soul, Christian style, I can limit myself here to evoking only the two most important ones.

First, at the moment God becomes the one who alone has true knowledge, what is proper to the human being, namely, the soul's ability to look into the essence of what is -'the being which agelessly, eternally is' and to which it thus becomes bonded – loses the weight that it enjoyed in Greek thought (Patočka, 1996: 108). As a consequence, the authentic nature of what is human, rather than being understood in terms of a knowledge of the Good through which human beings could, in a way, become immortal and equal to the Greek gods, is in Christianity held to reside in man's practical attitude, in the operative actions in which he is involved – labor, in short – at the service of God in this world, in the down here (Patočka 2007: 227).[10] Transposed to a world entirely disenchanted and de-divinized by Protestant theology, the Greek idea of reason and universality generates, as Patočka remarks, a new attitude 'that until then was unknown to the spirit, an attitude that one could qualify as purely objective (*sachlich*), consisting in understanding things from the things themselves and their thingly structures without mixing anything heterogeneous into them' (227–8). Needless to say, this new attitude made possible by Christianity's practical attitude regarding work and service to God in a thoroughly secular world changes the nature of knowledge in its entirety, which from now on becomes a knowledge of domination of a thoroughly objectified world. The 'unique accomplishment' (236) of Christianity's appropriation of the Platonic motifs of reason and universality, which had been developed in the context of a concern with the soul and in view of a reorganization of community on universal grounds, thus amounts to an abortion of its initial goal (236). Oriented exclusively toward the things in the world in an objectivist, physicalist way, to the exclusion of the human beings within the world, the new attitude that emerges with Christianity 'necessarily skirts the content of the world' and thus also 'finds itself incapable of constructing a mundane science' (236). Indeed, as Patočka emphasizes, mathematics, now aiming at 'universalist tasks of a new style', as opposed to the role it enjoyed in Greek thought, plays a significant role in the new attitude toward the world that reigns in the sciences. Freed from the metaphysical realism of the ideal objectivities, mathematics as a purely formal discipline and as 'the model for the new reflection that aims at the world, and the down here', no longer seeks to map out the realm of the Ideas. Aiming at the universe of realities, it understands its formal structures primarily as the correlate of practical operations in and on the world (231). Such a mode of reflection, however, as Patočka submits, is unable to respond to the structures and real needs of European society in that it entirely abstracts from the opportunity that the renewal in Europe – or as Europe – of the idea of the care of the soul offers for 'reforming as a whole the tenor and collective form of [European humanity's] existence, particularly, of political life' (236).

The second motif that severely curtails the renewal of the principle of rationality and universality in Christian Europe concerns its very conception of the soul, or subject. Accord-ingtoPatočka, the correlate of the European sciences'

---

10   Patočka is referring here to the origin of the conception of labor as a devotion to God in the culture and life of the medieval cloisters, and which finds its culmination in what Max Weber qualifies as 'Protestant ethics'. By this reference it is also made clear that the seed of Protestantism is already planted in medieval Catholicism.

concern with an entirely objectified, or physicalist world, is a conception of the subject as an imperialist entity from which the world in its entirety can be drawn: a subject that is absolute and which, when speaking of European consciousness, he characterizes as 'a consciousness that one could say to be closed upon itself by way of its infinity' (216). He concludes: 'The *proton pseudos* of Europe is thus wed to its closure upon itself for having been rendered absolute' (216).

'Rooted in the deepest layers of our human existence', 'the impulsion to call upon the souls, and exhort them to a life in truth is what is most proper to these layers' (232). Yet, even though 'the secular empire of theology' has its source in these deepest layers of human existence (as is demonstrated by its ability to urge the discipline upon human beings to excel in worldly activity in a disenchanted and de-divinized world, and so to find a way to themselves by virtue of this trial), the disenchantment and de-divinization in question and the exclusive theoretical and practical concern with the world stifled the community of self and other to which the reflection on the soul's impulsion to a life in truth should have led. As a result of the secular empire of theology, the thrust of rationality is thus thoroughly reduced to the sphere of objectivity of a here below suspended from a beyond. At the hands of the sciences' mundane, or rather secular orientation, 'the Platonic-Socratic idea of a total reflection' that concerned the world *and* the human being is replaced by 'a partial reflection only, which, pretending to be total, in fact, condemned total reflection to oblivion' (235). At the root of the catastrophe of Europe is this theologically motivated reduction of rationality to the objectified world and expansion of the soul to an absolute subject. Further implications of the limitation of rationality and universality to the objective world of things, and the conception of the subject as absolute, will be spelled out hereafter. At this point let me only emphasize that the two motifs show Europe to be tied in the same way as all other traditions to a native irrationalism of its own, an irrationalism profoundly linked to Christianity in its Protestant form on whose soil the Greek idea of reason and universality enjoyed its renewal in Europe.[11]

This irrationalism, or hyperbolism of Europe's nativeness which emerged in the shape of a new rationality in Europe some 400 years ago, is what caused the end of Europe from within. But for Patočka, as we have seen, the end

---

11   It is also here that Patočka's reference to a heretical Christianity should be mentioned to overcome the continued indebtedness of historical Christianity and its conception of the care of soul to its Platonic solution through knowledge of what is. Only a heretical Christianity could truly accomplish the Christian conception of the care of the soul by way of a radical break with Platonism, and *a fortiori,* the thoroughly new beginning of Europe that it promised to be. See Gasché 2009: 241–7, 261–2.

of Europe has, perhaps, a positive signification. Indeed, for him, 'the post-European epoch stands under the sign of chance', on condition that in rethinking Europe, one avoids falling back on past errors (Patočka, 2007: 53). However, for this to take place, Europe will have to face the enormous task of 'deepening the foundations of rationality in relation to that at which one had arrived in Europe during the historical period dominated by it' (212–13). In *L'Europe après l'Europe* we read:

> It must suffice here to call to attention some of the fundamental conditions without which one cannot hope to succeed. One cannot generalize Europe as has been done hitherto contenting oneself with transplanting and taking up again results, but only by reflecting on the presuppositions that are responsible for the limits of rationality hitherto. (213)

Indeed, what is required is 'the urgent task of deepening the foundation of European rationality which alone could make a true debate with all the living traditions of the concrete world possible' (213). The deepening of Europe's foundation in an effort to yield a foundation that is 'well-founded', rather than an exercise of bending upon itself, is thus also predicated on an opening to other traditions within the concrete world. As we have seen, the post-European world is one in which the whole world has been Europeanized. A well-founded foundation would thus be one that would have inquired into the limits that native traditions, be they European or non-European, have imposed on the idea of reason and rationality itself. But only through a radical inquiry, first and foremost, into its own nativisms can Europe hope to develop a well-founded foundation, and thus reach out to others.

Let us remind ourselves again that for Patočka the idea of Europe is, in the same way as for Husserl, that of reason and universality. Let us also not lose sight of the fact that it has only been in Europe that this idea has arisen in explicit fashion, and that it is only in Europe that this idea has been involved in a, however failed, 'reflexive renewal of life' (236). In spite of the 'successful Europeanization' of the world, no other culture has taken the place of Europe's demanding of itself such a renewal. They have limited themselves to mixing their own historical patrimony into what they have taken over from Europe, namely, a certain conception of world-oriented rationalism, or become entrenched in nostalgic and at times violent fundamentalisms. If the non-Western world has become Europeanized as a whole, a reflection on the idea of Europe is certainly no longer the privilege of Europe alone. Yet if the non-Western world has become Europeanized without the spirit of Europe, it follows that it cannot draw on the resources of the European tradition to take critical issue with the form of rationality that they have assimilated. If Europe after Europe has, therefore, still a crucial role to play, it is because the idea of reason and universality which are, in Husserlian terms, its *telos*, or destiny, provide it with the task and the means to deepen its own understanding of what such a legacy demands of it. It alone would, therefore, seem to have the potential for bringing about a world capable of what Patočka calls a 'reflexive renewal of life' by freeing rationality and universality from native irrationalisms and archaisms. But if in order to do this, Europe must find ways of relating to other cultures in a way that is free of its past arrogance, the first step in this direction consists in coming to grips with its own native irrationalisms.

As Patočka avers, even though the conception of reason (and thus also of universality) that has dominated European thinking and its self-conception is 'insufficient, and has provoked crises', such as the crisis of 'Europe' itself, 'it remains that it will always be impossible to respond otherwise than through reason to the questions posed and the crises caused by reason' (190). This demand, although based on the very exigencies of reason, will immediately raise the objection, as Patočka himself acknowledges, that Europe's inquiry into its own limits and the means to overcome them amounts to nothing less than a perpetuation of the 'spiritual supremacy of Europe' (241). Yet, such self-inquiry in no way precludes an 'extra-European reflection, on the contrary, it sets it into movement and enriches it' (241). For Patočka, Europe's inquiry into the limits of reason, especially in the scientific and technical sense of reason, can avoid the suspicion that such a reflection only serves Europe's desire for supremacy by being accompanied by actions at other levels, such as those of economy and politics. But even though Patočka's inquiry into the nativism and irrationalities of European reason already goes some way toward accomplishing a reflection on 'the extra-European spiritual 'substances', the notion of universality implicit in reason demands, in my view, an even deeper exploration of the contingent native irrationalisms of Europe that prevent the reflection in question from becoming limited from within (241). It could perhaps be said that the task of scrutinizing the idea of reason and universality for the inevitable limits owed to its emergence in Europe is an infinite task bestowed on Europe by its very tradition.

In light of this pressing inquiry into the nativisms and irrationalities intertwined with the idea of Europe as the idea of reason and universality, I raise the question whether by thinking of Europe as the idea of reason and universality, the very notion of the 'idea' does not belong to a stratum – perhaps not of nativism and irrationality, but of a 'particularity', or idiomaticity – that even though it is indispensable to articulating reason and universality at all, nonetheless restricts its universal thrust. Undoubtedly, such a question seems far-fetched, even counter-intuitive, because the notion of the idea as a philosophical notion that refers to something purely intelligible – to an 'essence' (*ousia*) which per se denotes something universal, something *katholou*, free from everything sensible, hence from everything particular – is already intrinsically universal.[12] So how could the idea of Europe condition reason and the claim to universality that Europe, the idea of Europe, designates?

As a representation of an essence, a *noeton*, or mere object of thought, an idea grasps this essence in its very unification, uniqueness, and singularity. It establishes the essence that it represents as beyond all becoming, change, hence as self-subsistent. It thus refers to what strictly is – being itself – to what is eternal, atemporal, and ahistorical. If this is so, then the question can certainly be asked whether, when said of Europe, for example, this notion suggests that Europe, with its demands of reason and universality as trans-cultural demands in essence, are essentially European and belong to it as a privileged possession of something eternal. But at the same time a more important question arises, whether the notion of an idea of Europe resumes, or absorbs in advance what Europe could be all about, blocking in advance any possible development of reason and universality. Undoubtedly, to ask what Europe is, is to ask a question of identity, and the notion of the idea is an inevitable answer to this question, especially if Europe is not yet something that is, but a task: an infinite task at the limit. But if the nature of Europe is such that it still needs to be produced, or that it is something to come, then the notion of an idea of Europe which states in advance what it is, freezes it into a form that does not allow for further development.[13] Differently put, does the elevation of reason and universality to the status of an idea called Europe not permanently fix their nature, taking, as it were, the possibility of further reasoning about reason out of reason, thus preventing any attempt at deepening it in order to increase its universal range?

But there is more. To conceive of the rationalism and universality with which Europe identifies as an idea is not merely to suggest that content-wise it understands itself as originating in Greece, but also that it formally conceives of itself according to an exclusively Greek philosopheme, namely, the idea. Even though in the archeology of this notion from its archaic origins, and to some extent common understanding (in which it primarily refers to sensible looks,

---

12　The kind of question I am seeking to pose here is already prefigured in a sense by Patočka's recourse to a heretical Christianity to radically break with Platonism in historical Christianity in order to achieve a novel, truly Christian conception of the care of the soul that would make good on Christian Europe's initial promise.

13　This question is all the more important as Europe is not only an economical, but, above all, a political project.

or forms, such as the visible exterior form of an individual or a thing), to its philosophical status (in which it concerns invisible, that is, purely intelligible objects of thought), the Greekness of this Greek notion is not simply Greek any more in an idiomatic sense, the question arises, nonetheless, whether in order to secure the universal thrust of the idea of reason and universality associated with Europe, it might be necessary to uncouple this idea from the extraordinary charge that it carries as a remnant of Greek metaphysics.[14] Following Patočka, we have seen that certain native irrationalisms inherent to Christian Europe have obliterated the 'total reflection' that the Greek idea of the care of the soul comprehends. But must we not go one step further, and ask whether the conception of reason and universality is also limited from within by this intrinsically Greek concept of the idea, and hence by Greek metaphysics? Is it perhaps necessary to question the references to 'looks', forms, appearances, and shapes that inform this Greek concept, even there where their objects are solely intelligible, and to inquire into the implications that these significations have for understanding reason and universality itself? In order to secure the thrust of the demands that come with reason and universality as European ideas, might it therefore be necessary to liberate them of Europe's 'incorrigible Platonism', of which Derrida speaks in a section of the *Gift of Death* (1992: 28) that is largely devoted to Patočka?

In short, if Europe has come to an end, is it also, perhaps, because it has come to an end as an 'idea', and that if this end is a chance for a Europe after Europe, in a Europeanized world, the idea (of Europe) will have to make room for another 'representation'? Unless, of course, the notion of the idea still harbors an untapped potential of going beyond itself, beyond the idea itself; beyond the idea in a Greek sense. Considering the fact that in Greece itself the philosophical notion of the idea must have been received as something exceedingly strange, if not foreign, to go beyond the idea – apart from restoring and reviving to this notion the strangeness that in fourth-century Greece must have been peculiar to it – then involves an even greater strangeness and otherness: the double foreignness, as it were, of the idea beyond the idea.

If the idea of Europe is merely confined to the rational organization of its economy and its societies with their plural languages and cultures, as is mostly, although not exclusively, the case in the current union since it is no

---

14 See Gasché 2000. The point that Greek philosophical language is no longer idiomatic, hence, no longer a native language, has been forcefully argued by Martin Heidegger, for example. But can one hold as he does in *What Is Philosophy?* that Greek philosophical language is a language that transcends all idiomaticity without conceiving of such a liberation from the idiomatic as an infinite task? See Heidegger 1989.

less a project of a community of values, then the idea of Europe in an emphatic sense – as the project and promise of universal openness to, and responsibility for the other – has today, perhaps, more critical power than ever. Indeed, the European Union must not be conflated with Europe as an idea. One can also say, therefore, that Europe has certainly not lived up to its own idea in the traditional sense. But, the question that needs pondering, is whether conceiving of this idea of Europe as an 'idea' – as a representation in which Europe bends back upon itself in a loop of self-identification and gives itself to itself – is of the order of a last native irrationalism, perhaps, and thus a reservation that holds up its exposure and responsibility to the other. But if Europe, or rather its idea, is, as Husserl pointed out in the *Crisis* book, the idea of philosophy, then Europe cannot claim, as the sages did in early Greece or in other non-European cultures, that it possesses truth. It cannot on the basis of the fact that the idea of a universal and rational humanity has grown on European, and, in particular, Christian soil, claim and reserve rationality and universality as its own exclusive property, and in the same breath, pride itself on being the very incarnation of humanity itself (see Patočka 2007: 212, 235). As the idea of reason and universality, this idea demands of Europe the courage to critically put its own traditions and beliefs into question. Yet if this is the heritage that constitutes it, Europe must also proceed in renouncing any claim to a fixed identity, and, hence, of giving itself to itself. In other words, it must muster the courage to critically interrogate its status as an idea, through which it gives itself to itself, and by the same stroke arrests itself. Only thus will it be able to secure the universal appeal and thrust of its idea to begin with. This questioning would then also amount to a deepening of the concept of the idea, conceiving of a concept of the idea 'beyond the idea' in which the idea of Europe, rather than giving itself to itself in a movement of self-identification, would come to be an idea that comes from the other rather than from itself.[15] Indeed, in the globally Europeanized world, a novel idea of 'Europe' as the idea of reason and universality could, in principle at least, also come from the non-Western world.

The end of Europe and the beginning of a post-European world make it incumbent on Europe, which has understood itself so far from the idea of reason and universality, to revisit the concept of the idea with which it represented itself. Given its history in which it hegemonically ruled the world on the basis of its self-proclaimed superiority as the incarnation of humanity itself, its responsibility today consists in giving the idea of reason and universality a deeper foundation by going beyond the idea. If this is to be accomplished

---

15 I borrow the expression 'beyond the idea' from Jean-Luc Nancy, who in 'Finite History' (1993: 149) speaks of the need to rethink history 'beyond the idea' of history.

by uncoupling its idea not only from all native European irrationalisms, but also, and perhaps more fundamentally, from a Greek nativism, however subtle, concerning the idea itself, this cannot take place exclusively by Europe's opening itself to other native traditions, simply replacing its own traditions by other, exotic ones. The chance given to Europe as a result of the catastrophe of Europe in a post-European context is, to paraphrase what Patočka advanced about reason, to rethink, first of all, the idea of Europe as that of reason and universality, beyond the idea – not by abandoning this notion, but by way of the means that the very notion of idea possibly provides. This is the chance of conceiving an idea of reason and universality that rather than restricted to the idea of European humanity, would be one that, from the start, comes from the others as a task incumbent on humankind as a whole – without, if I may say so, the sole ballast of Greek and Christian metaphysics and theology. To put it differently: if the idea of Europe has come to an end, Europe needs another renaissance. One this time that is not based on the rediscovery of its own foreign origins in Greece, that is, not on the idea of rationality and universality in the form of a worldly science that it took in the West, but on the discovery of another kind of foreignness, the foreignness of the non-European others. Yet, and this is crucial, one that is *apart, and beyond* the latter's own archaic and native irrationalisms, in contrast to which the *idea* of an idea of Europe would still reveal itself as something merely native, thus not sufficiently meeting the philosophical demand of what Patočka calls 'the idea of what is well-founded' (Patočka 2007: 81).

A moment ago I held that in the aftermath of Europe, an idea of Europe that rather than being closed upon itself, but which from the outset is an idea of openness, must accomplish such a rethinking of Europe not by abandoning itself to some exotic otherness, but by exploring its own strangeness with respect to Europe itself. The first step in such a direction consists in the exploration of its own untapped resources. Instead of limiting oneself to rehearsing what the ideas of Europe have been so far – such as reason, freedom, democracy, etc. – and establishing the deficit of their realization, I thus propose that European reflection bend back upon itself, on its idea as an idea, not, however, with the intent of closing itself upon itself, but of capturing the potential for an openness to others within the idea as an idea. For the resources inherent to the notion of the idea to accomplish this, I turn to Martin Heidegger's (1987) elaborations in *Zur Bestimmung der Philosophie* on the relation between an idea and its object. With, unmistakably, Kant's elaboration on the regulative nature of ideas in the First Critique in mind, Heidegger points out that an idea is marked by a certain negativity, since unlike a concept, an idea 'does *not* give its object in complete adequation, in the completed, and full determinateness of its essential elements' (Heidegger 1987: 13–14, emphasis mine). 'Definite moments' of its object, but also singular characteristic ones must, of course, be given in its idea. Yet even though an idea illuminates its object only in an aphoristic, limited illumination, what is significant is that new characteristic moments of the idea's object -'new essential elements' (*Wesenselemente*) - can always become salient, and attach themselves onto (the term Heidegger uses is *Ansetzung*, that is, adding on, appending, or affixing) the already established features of the object, and modify them. The object, however, is allowed to keep its final indeterminateness. The idea, by contrast, as regards its own sense, leaves nothing open. It consists of 'an unambiguously delimited interconnection of the motivations regulated according to essential laws that concern the determinability of the never completely determined object of the idea, and that come into view as a unity of sense' (Heidegger 1987: 14). It follows from this that the object's final indeterminateness is not just any indeterminateness, as in the case of a fuzzy representation or guesswork, but a determined indeterminateness. The idea lets the object be undetermined, to remain autonomous, capable of exhibiting new essential features, and this possibility is what the idea gives to the object, whose indeterminateness, or incomplete determination, is, therefore, in Heidegger's terms, a determined one. This gift by the idea to the object is the idea's specific sense and accomplishment. Let us, therefore, look at this gift in greater detail. What it offers to the object is not a merely formal, empty, or arbitrary possibility, but a possibility that, as Heidegger avers, is 'determined, and always renewed according to essential laws', which are the object's own laws (14).[16] These laws must be laws that originate with the object itself because as heteronomous laws they would annihilate its autonomy, and especially the freedom of its openness to modifications by the outside, the foreign, or other. But if it is through its idea that the object receives this possibility of self-modification by way of the affixture of new and other features of itself, the implications are that the object has laws of its own only insofar as it is open to the outside, the foreign, or other. More precisely, the object receives laws of its own not by itself but as a gift from what is not itself. It is its idea that makes it possible to bequeath an autonomy on it as a gift received in its exposure to what it is not, and on the basis of this gift alone is it capable of self-modification. If the idea makes such self-modification of the object possible -and only if it is the object that modifies itself according to laws of its own that are a gift to it by what it is not, is there such a thing as a self-modification – this is not a transformation through which the object would close itself upon itself in self-sufficiency. On the contrary, it allows the

---

16 The idea lets the object have its own laws.

object to undergo modifications of itself by itself and by its outside, the foreign, or other.

To summarize: the relation between an idea as a determined unity of sense and its object is thus a relation in which the object is characterized by the structurally always open possibility of bringing to light new implications of its already established features, but also totally novel characteristics that are allowed to become attached to them, thus enriching and modifying them. This process is one according to essential laws of the object itself, but that, at the same time, it possesses only through its openness to otherness. It also follows from this that the idea allows its object to determine itself according to laws in a process that, in principle, never comes to a closure in full determination, and that structurally leave it open to further features, without ever freezing into a final identity. Such is the case, in particular, if the regulation or orientation that the objects' idea provides, allows for the *Ansetzung* of new features to the object that also come to it from its outside, the foreign, and the other, allowing for a modification of it by what is other than it, according to essential rules, of course – not only the rules of the unity of sense that constitutes the idea, but that are also 'proper' to the object in the complex way we have seen.

How do these reflections on the relation of an idea to its object bear on an idea beyond the idea called for where the idea of Europe is concerned? On an idea that given the Europeanized, or globalized world, is no longer one of Europe alone? By definition, an idea is an idea of reason: of universal intelligibility, in other words. It follows that an idea must allow its object to modify its determinations in such a way that it, by itself, meets this standard without which it would not even be what it is in all its distinctness. From what we have seen, an idea beyond the idea would be one in which its object is allowed to modify *itself by itself,* and at the same time *by what it is not,* through the *Ansetzung* to itself of new features that come both from itself and the other. However, such a self-modification is truly one only if it takes place freely, without irrationalisms; without retrenchment in nativisms, or archaisms. Rather than enabling Europe to give itself to itself by representing itself as an idea, the idea beyond the idea would thus allow Europe to expose itself to the gift by the other. Such an idea beyond the idea would also no longer be of the order of a re-presentation of Europe.

In a different context, I have shown that the idea of Europe cannot be an idea in the Kantian sense, that of the infinite approximation of a *telos*. But if the aim of rethinking the idea of Europe in post-Europe is to secure a 'well-founded' idea, an idea beyond the idea, then this structural potential of an openness to additions in its object, be that object Europe or humanity in its entirety – additions that, rather than arbitrary, are, to quote Heidegger (1987) one more time, 'regulated according to essential laws regarding the determinability of the object as a unity of sense' – must be given a *regulative* function in thinking or re-thinking the idea of Europe: regulative, not in the sense of an infinite approximation, but in the sense that this rule must be met in full at any moment (14).

Works Cited

Annas, J. 1981. *An Introduction to Plato's Republic* (Oxford: Clarendon).
Crépon, M. 2007. Histoire éthique et politique: La question de l'Europe. In: Jan Patočka, *L'Europe après l'Europe* (trl. E. Abrams; Paris: Verdier).
Derrida, Jacques. 1992. *The Gift of Death* (trl. D. Wills; Chicago: University of Chicago Press).
Gasché, Rodolphe. 2000. 'Feeling the Debt: On Europe', in: *Future Crossings: Literature between Philosophy and Cultural Studies*, ed. K. Ziarek & S. Deane (Evanston, IL: Northwestern University Press), 125–46.
Gasché, Rodolphe. 2007. 'In Light of Light: On Jan Patočka's Notion of Europe', in *The Politics of Deconstruction: Jacques Derrida and the Other of Philosophy*, ed. M. McQuillan (London: Pluto Press), 116–36.
Gasché, Rodolphe. 2009. *Europe, or the Infinite Task. A Study of a Philosophical Concept* (Stanford, CA: Stanford University Press).
Gasché, Rodolphe. 2018. 'Patočka on Europe in the Aftermath of Europe', *European Journal of Social Theory* 21.3: 391–406.
Heidegger, Martin. 1987. *Zur Bestimmung der Philosophie* (*Gesamtausgabe*, 56/57; Frankfurt /Main: Klostermann).
Heidegger, Martin. 1989. *What Is Philosophy?* (trl. W. Kluback & J. Wilde; Estover, Plymouth: Vision Press).
Husserl, Edmund. 1970. *The Crisis of European Sciences and Transcendental Phenomenology* (trl. D. Carr; Evanston, IL: Northwestern University Press).
Joly, H. 1974. *Le Renversement platonicien: Logos, Episteme, Polis* (Paris: Vrin).
Nancy, Jean-Luc. 1993. *The Birth to Presence* (trl. B. Holmes et al.; Stanford, CA: Stanford University Press).
Patočka, Jan. 1996. *Heretical Essays in the Philosophy of History* (trl. E. Kohak; Chicago: OpenCourt).
Patočka, Jan. 2002. *Plato and Europe* (trl. P. Lom; Stanford, CA: Stanford University Press).
Patočka, Jan. 2007. *L'Europe après l'Europe* (trl. E. Abrams; Paris: Verdier).

Ramnoux, C. 1970. 'L'Archaïsme en philosophie', in Id., *Etudes Presocratiques* (Paris: Klincksieck), 27–35.

Tava, F. 2016. 'The Brave Struggle: Jan Patočka on Europe's Past and Future', *Journal of the British Society for Phenomenology* 47.3: 242–59.

Vernant, J-P. 1965. 'La formation de la pensée positive dans la Grèce archaïque', in Id., *Mythe et pensée chez les Grecs* (Paris: Maspéro), 2.

CHAPTER 2

Post-imperial Europe: The Return of the Indistinct

Vladimir Biti

> How to escape the filth: not a new question.
> An old rat-question that will not let go,
> that leaves its nasty, suppurating wound.
> J. M. COETZEE, *Summertime*

∴

1 Post-Versailles Europe: The Compensatory Indistinct of Subalterns

The dissolution of East-Central European Empires in the aftermath of the First World War, followed by the founding of new nation states as well as the successor states to these empires, induced the region's traumatic post-imperial condition.[1] With the Treaty of Versailles, Western nation-state powers introduced the principle of national self-determination into the reconfigured East-Central European region, which endowed each nation with the political right to establish its own autonomous state. Such national modelling of the religiously, ethnically, culturally, and linguistically hybrid East-Central European states was not a unilateral imposition but a decision enthusiastically embraced by the carriers of their liberation movements who regarded the establishment of new states as a welcome opportunity for their own political affirmation. An ambiguous relationship emerged between the West-European 'mentors' and their East-Central European 'protégés' through this 'joint statism' (Guha 2002, 74) that inconspicuously merged the imperialist interests of Europe's centre with the nationalist interests of its periphery. The protégés highly coveted the respect of their mentors, yet were kept at a distance not only by their own sinister realities but also by their mentors' long entrenched prejudices against them. They were systematically treated as 'almost the same but not quite' subjects (Bhabha 1994, 122), destined to an interminable process of perfecting themselves and thus subject to a constant geopolitical and historical lag behind the model. As

---

[1] For an earlier version of this chapter, see Biti 2020.

Dipesh Chakrabarty aptly remarked, imperial centres allocated a pre-modern place 'elsewhere' and an outdated 'not yet' time to these 'barbarians', which relegated them to an enduring 'waiting room of history' (Chakrabarty 2000, 7). Although he primarily addresses Europe's relationship toward its *external* others, his description also perfectly fits Europe's attitude to its *internal* others. Since the age of Enlightenment, both 'axes' constituted Europe's 'joint venture' that, being from the outset exposed to a steady reconfiguration, acquired a statist shape with the Treaty of Versailles.

Although the delineated 'joint statism' that came into being in the aftermath of the First World War was expected to 'Europeanize' East-Central European states, it ultimately deepened their frustration. It firmly attached their peoples to the vague prospect of their independence, but by imprisoning them in an enduring dependence upon their mentors ultimately impeded the very aim of this attachment. Within a Europe that was determined to unify its constituencies, East-Central European states proliferated enemies and instigated new conflicts by spontaneously transferring on to their 'Oriental' European neighbours the stigma of inferiority that their West-European mentors had imputed upon them. Thus, instead of being abolished, Western 'Orientalism' experienced an unprecedented expansion (Bakić-Hayden). Far from being eliminated through the unification of all European nation states, 'Christian Europe's' discrimination of 'European Turkey' clandestinely became the basic principle for Europe's reproduction.

In the post-imperial East Central Europe of the 1920s and 1930s, disappointment was commonplace. The imperial *successor states* were involved in revengeful animosities with neighbouring states, such as Turkey towards Greece. Furthermore, they were torn by their majority population's hatred of domestic minorities, especially the Jews, but also the Armenians and Greeks in Turkey, or the Slavic minorities in Germany, Hungary, and Austria. In addition, they were bereft of tens of millions of their co-nationals who had remained in what were now foreign nation states, such as Austrians and Germans in Poland, Czechoslovakia, and Yugoslavia, Hungarians in Romania, Czechoslovakia, and Yugoslavia, and Russians in incipient non-Russian nation states. They were also exposed to huge influxes of these stranded external co-nationals, such as Turkey to the Russian and Balkan Muslims, Hungary to the Romanian, Czechoslovak, and Yugoslav Hungarians, or Weimar Germany to the Baltic, Polish, and Czechoslovakian Germans. Besides, the embitterment of the successor states arose from the territorial concessions that they were forced to make. The Ottoman Empire lost Russian, African and Balkan territories, Austria was obliged to 'return' the Sudetenland to Czechoslovakia and Upper Silesia to Poland, while Hungary was coerced into giving up its former territories to Czechoslovakia,

Romania, and Yugoslavia. They lost their former glory, like the Austro-Germans who were now 'transformed from a *Staatsvolk* of a Great Power into what they perceived as second-class citizens of third-class states' (Brubaker 1996, 124). This humiliation of their external compatriots rigidified the successor states' politics toward their borderlands and gave rise to various compensatory manoeuvres of national self-aggrandizement. Finally, the sensible intellectuals in some of them were plagued by war guilt, foremost those of Austria and Germany after they had confronted their compatriots' wartime hysteria against external and internal 'traitors'.

By contrast, the *newly established nation states*, plagued as they were by miserable social and economic conditions, poor infrastructures, unemployment, inflation, rigid and immobile social stratification, and corrupt and inefficient administrations in their countries (Berend 1998, 3–47), blamed this desolate state of affairs on long-term exploitations and humiliations inflicted upon them by former empires and foreign powers. The sense of backwardness was overwhelming and endemic, numerous obstacles to modernization fueled bitterness, hatred, and revolt. Being underprivileged in their new states, many of their constituencies, such as the Ukrainians, the Croats, the Slovaks, and especially the Jews perceived themselves as the Versailles Treaty's victims (Kożuchowski 2013, 8–9). The outbursts of frustration with the Treaty's outcome also induced revengeful animosities between the new countries, such as Poland and Czechoslovakia, Romania and Yugoslavia, and Italy and Yugoslavia. It ultimately paved the way for the establishment of populist dictators within them (for example Yugoslavia's King Alexander, Poland's Piłsudski, and Romania's Antonescu). Populism had been on a continual rise in East Central Europe since the turn of the century by systematically introducing in-distinction into the clear West-European distinction between socialist and communist ideologies on the one hand and nationalist, fascist, and anti-Semitic ones on the other. Taking advantage of the communicational, traffic and institutional networks, which had been established in East Central Europe in the last decades of the nineteenth century with the aim of implementing the mobility of modern West European democracies in the region, populists used it for the opposite purpose, i.e. to heal the population's feeling of uprootedness that resulted from such imposed mobility. Mobility, as the basic prerequisite of West European democracies, thus seems to have simultaneously acted as a West European ally and an East-Central European enemy.

If modernity has something to teach us, then it is that 'one man's imagined community is another man's political prison' (Appadurai 1998, 32). Not everybody benefited from mobility, the proudly flagged distinctive trait of modern European civilization. As soon as it entered the East-Central European space after the dissolution of empires, it replaced its West European liberating face with a coercive one, initiating huge and hitherto unimaginable migrations of populations. 'By 1890 close to 40 percent of all Austro-Hungarians had left their original place of Heimat and migrated to their current homes from another part of the monarchy' (Judson 2016, 334). Almost four million men and women moved overseas, but hundreds of thousands returned within a few years so that, as a result of all these immense dislocations, the populations of imperial cities such as Vienna, Budapest, Prague, and Zagreb enormously increased (Judson 2016, 335). The former empires' metropoles or core nations faced equally harsh consequences. 'The Fall of the Habsburgs automatically turned the 25 percent of the Viennese population born outside the frontiers of the new Austria into foreigners, unless they chose to opt for citizenship' (Hobsbawm 1996, 15). After the breakup of the Soviet Union, twenty-five million Russians who had been colonized in various territories across the Empire from the mid-sixteenth century until the mid-twentieth century (Brubaker 1996, 150) suddenly remained outside the Russian Federation (Brubaker 1996, 6–7). Three million Hungarians were left in Romania, Slovakia, Serbia, and Ukraine, two million Albanians in Serbia, Montenegro, and Macedonia, two million Serbs in Croatia and Bosnia and Herzegovina, and one million Turks in Bulgaria (Brubaker 1996, 56). It goes without saying that such a traumatic reconfiguration of post-imperial Europe's geopolitical circumstances deeply disquieted and disoriented the majority of its population, giving rise to an overwhelming sense of its disorientation and defencelessness.

However, to reiterate the central thesis of the two faces of the modern processes, such disabling dislocations of populations were coupled with some enabling effects. While post-imperial Europe's huge reconfiguration seriously endangered its population's material survival, it simultaneously immensely increased the mobility of its imagination (Appadurai 1998, 6). In the completely reshaped geopolitical space that now loomed large on the horizon, as Arjun Appadurai put it, '[e]ven the meanest and most hopeless of lives, the most brutal and dehumanizing of circumstances, the harshest of lived inequalities' became 'open to the play of the imagination' (Appadurai 1998, 54). This means that, however frustrating the enforced deterritorializations of the East-Central European populations were, they were nevertheless accompanied by some emancipating consequences.

To address their *frustrating aspect* first, late empires had already constructed their communicational, traffic, and mercantile networks to improve military control over their peripheral constituencies, to facilitate their economic exploitation, and to avert them from switching to other empires. Next to fostering the import of food and raw materials from these provinces (Barkey 1996, 106), late imperial traffic networks envisaged the subsequent export of the finished products in the opposite direction. Although modernization claimed to be equalizing all its participants, it thus deteriorated the economic imbalance between them still further (Berend 1998, 20–22). As in the case of the Austrian Emperor Joseph II's linguistic standardization that had taken place a century or so earlier, the following message underlay the integration of imperial provinces: Only those that succumb to it are regarded as progressive and modern. Those that remain loyal to their odd traditional habits confine themselves to their self-enclosed localities, excluding themselves from the universal process of civilization. They are stigmatized as backward. This is how modernization put the imperial provinces under pressure for accelerated adaption, which they, although poorly equipped, were forced to come to terms with.

Nonetheless, such subterraneous discrimination paved the way for the *emancipating aspect* of imperial modernization. It involuntarily provided the common background against which the provinces could learn their differences and homogenize themselves (Evans 2006; Cornwall 2006, 174–175). Through traumatic migrations that were induced by this modernization, they got the opportunity to make acquaintances with many other provinces that were hitherto barely known to them. Although the encounters with them were sometimes uncomfortable, discouraging and even terrifying, considering the geopolitical, religious, cultural, and linguistic differences that separated imperial provinces from each other, it enabled provincial communities to strengthen their resistance to the centres' discrimination by forging alliances with those who were equally subjected to it. Melting with them into transborder communities directed against their oppressor and perpetrator, they disregarded their huge differences.

Their resistance adopted the form which Homi Bhabha described as 'subversive mimicry' in his ground-breaking analysis of colonial circumstances (Bhabha 1994, 94–132). In terms of Bhabha's analysis, the colonized subject, in his or her reiterated attempts to erase the difference that separates him from the colonizer through the adoption of the latter's distinct achievements, reaffirms this difference by inadvertently distorting them (Bhabha 1994, 122). Although Bhabha applies his concept to the circumstances of European colonies, the population of European imperial provinces subverted modernization in the same way. They unwillingly or willingly turned its identifying techniques, which they were hard pressed to accept, upside down. This re-signification was a spontaneous act of affirmation of their anachronous habits. In this way, the late imperial age opened the door for the post-imperial rise of the indistinct. Let us recall what Nietzsche states in his famous analysis of *ressentiment* in *On the Genealogy of Morals*:

> While all noble morality grows from a triumphant affirmation of itself, slave morality from the outset says no to an 'outside,' to an 'other,' to a

'non-self'; and *this* no is its creative act. The reversal of the evaluating gaze – this necessary orientation outwards rather than inwards to the self – belongs characteristically to *ressentiment*. In order to exist at all, slave morality from the outset always needs an opposing, outer world; in physiological terms, it needs external stimuli in order to act – its action is fundamentally reaction. (Nietzsche 1996, 22)

To illustrate, the railways that were built to enable the centres' economic expansion gradually turned into the instruments of the periphery's resistance to it (Schenk 2013). Or, provincial elites who were educated in the imperially established provincial schools or in the imperial centres themselves engaged this very knowledge for their opposition to them (Barkey 1996, 110). If the idea of this education was to differentiate imperial *societies*, provincial elites engaged it to homogenize their *communities*. The modern invention of society thus inadvertently became 'the condition for the more exact profiling of the concept of community, inasmuch as it could now advance into a collective name for all that which cannot be subsumed in the concept of society' (Rosa et al. 2010, 37–38 (trl. mine)). However, it was not only the Habsburg Empire's political differentiation that systematically produced its unprocessed residues in the form of ethnic nationalisms that were 'forged in the context of Habsburg imperial institutions and in the possibilities these institutions foresaw' (Judson 2016, 452). The Ottoman Empire also raised vipers in its bosom since the wave of commercialization and monetization that contributed to its 'modernization and unification [...] eventually brought about various nation-based movements intent on separation from the empire' (Keyder 1996, 32).

The delineated operation of subversion by adoption, which was already germane of late imperial peripheries, re-emerged in the new nation states after the breakdown of the empires. However, if in the late imperial peripheries it was carried by the national elites as the subalterns of imperial centres, their carriers became *these same elites*' subalterns in the new nation states. As an outcome, across the post-imperial East Central Europe that had been expected to assimilate into West Europe by differentiating its nation states, transborder communities arose as the zones of 'national indifference' (Zahra 2010). Operating as the untranslatable residues of national translations, they developed a sort of intra-active transnationality against the officially imposed cosmopolitanism. Gradually, their proliferation subverted the nation-state platform of Europe's integration. According to Elisabeth Povinelli, such zones are reservoirs of suppressed possibilities that distribute their potentiality into the aggregate that they are (an unacknowledged) part of, setting in motion its disarticulation (Povinelli 2011, 3–4; 11–13). Enmeshing a multiplicity of small worlds into an interactive totality, such transborder communities created an alternative model of worldly mutualism. Their energy of longing for imagined homelands deactivated their sense of belonging to the given nation states. A series of contemporary political theorists such as Giorgio Agamben, Roberto Esposito, and Judith Butler interpret these internal 'pockets of resistance' to the imposed unification as the direct outcomes of the 'egalitarian discrimination' genuine to modernization's globalization. In their view, the collateral effects of the production of a homogeneous human world are the would-be humans, the spectral humans, and the non-humans who are prevented from becoming legible within the established space of humanity (Agamben 1998, 121; Esposito 2011, 209; Butler 2004, 92).

Indeed, the geopolitically reconfigured East-Central European space became a harsh political prison for many of its constituencies, which is why their sense of belonging to their newly formed nation states was replaced with a sense of longing for that which these states excluded from their constitutions and official memories. New state nationalisms befell and impoverished these constituencies, pinned them to the wall of dominating nations, stripped them of choice, silenced their alternatives, and nullified their complex identity by an imposed demonization of the 'other' (Brubaker 1996, 20–21). Since they longed for a different way to cohabit the political spaces that they were affiliated to, the door was wide open for forging alliances with the deprived from abroad who likewise felt 'stranded in the present' (Fritzsche 2004). However, while identifying with them across the newly drawn state borders along national, religious, class, gender, ideological, and/or cultural lines, they exposed the nation states to which they were affiliated to disintegration. By knitting together various frustrations into platforms that promised a remedy for them, they managed to mobilize the most heterogeneous victims for their agendas (Hanson 2010, xvi). In this way, amalgamate and explosive transborder communities came into being amidst the post-imperial states' politically established national communities. They turned out to be the most important agents of the rising indistinct in the geopolitically reconfigured East-Central European space after the dissolution of empires.

Before we turn to the response of West-European states to this unexpected 'perversion' of the nation state as the envisaged platform of European unification, it deserves reminding that these states' very establishment was discriminatory and violent.

> Ever since the fifteenth century (and in the case of England much earlier), Western Europe has embarked on a huge homogenization drive with various degrees of success (the Spanish reconquista, England's expulsion of the Jews in the twelfth century, the religious wars in France

and Germany), which, in conjunction with the strong dynastic states, had laid the foundations of the future nation-states. (Todorova 1997, 175)

As the French political philosopher Ernest Renan put it in his famous lecture 'What Is a Nation?', the essence of a nation is that its individual representatives erase atrocities committed by their compatriots from their memories. 'Every French citizen has forgotten St. Bartholomew's Day and the thirteenth-century massacres in the Midi' (Renan 2006, 46). In view of these violent purifications of West-European state bodies, which they were at enduring pains to expel from their official historical records, the East-Central European nation states' harsh exclusionary mechanisms represented for them a painful reminder of their own pasts. Their strong reservations toward such a demonization of others tended to prevent the traumatic return of this obliterated operation of self-establishment.

2   Postcolonial Europe: The Repenting Indistinct of Superiors

Already with the Enlightenment, West Europe launched the project of a gradual self-exemption from its violent past. One of its chief engineers, Immanuel Kant was at pains to emancipate man from his destructive habits. In the treatise 'Idea for a Universal History with a Cosmopolitan Purpose' (1784), he states that if history were delivered to man's naturally inborn base and selfish goals, it would amount to a 'senseless course' of devastation, upheavals and the complete exhaustion of human powers (Kant 2006, 42, 47). 'For each of them will always misuse his freedom if he does not have anyone above him to apply force to him as the laws should require it' (Kant 2006, 46). Kant's expectation, however, is that the united world society looming large on the horizon of his age will prevent citizens from living such an inappropriate, animally-blind life by subjecting them to the 'condition of compulsion' (*Zustand des Zwanges;* Kant 2006, 46 (trl. modified)) or the pressure of historical necessity. By his natural disposition constructed from 'warped wood', man needs mankind 'to break his self-will and force him to obey a universally valid will under which everyone can be free' (Kant 2006, 46). If he were not compelled to obey this supreme general agency, he would be destroyed by his essentially selfish and hostile nature, instead of developing the ability to reason that distinguishes him from animals. For Kant, the natural disposition is a wild compulsive force that must be domesticated through a patient self-overcoming of man under the custody of mankind. Modernity puts man under the pressure of such a persistent overcoming of his basically animal nature.

The difficulty that Kant's argument must face, however, is that man's self-willingness, compelled by mankind to discipline itself, *characterizes the very agency expected to discipline him*. The violence that had to be repressed thus returns. The agency called upon to supervise man's long journey to final freedom displays, in Kant's rendering, significantly coercive traits. While it encourages man to disobey his inherited identity, it commands him to obey his universal human duty. It thus repeatedly dooms him to an 'animal' bondage. Was not the same universal claim, that is now raised by 'reasonable' universal history, raised in the Renaissance by the Christian community that, subjecting people to God's transcendent law, produced ecumenical uniformity and equality out of diversity and differences (Badiou 2003, 109)? Is not Kant, in this manner, surreptitiously reintroducing into the Enlightenment the colonial difference between the 'humans' of proper faith and the 'animal' infidels that was established by the Renaissance *orbis universalis christianus* (Mignolo 2000, 725–726)? This is how his imperative for man and collectivities to relentlessly individualize themselves involuntarily reproduces man's violent disposition that it was expected to leave behind. Whoever adopts it necessarily subverts the idea of man as a being emancipated from his blind compulsions.

The project of European modernity as launched by the Enlightenment thus appears, from its very outset, to have been accompanied by a traumatic re-emergence of 'animality' within the envisaged 'humanity'. It involuntarily headed toward the 'indistinct' that it hardly strove to leave behind, which again forced it to renew and intensify its efforts at overcoming itself. On the eve of the dissolution of empires through the violent outbreak of their oppressed peripheries, Nietzsche became aware of the equivocal character of the Enlightenment project: 'My humanity amounts to a continuous self-overcoming [of its inhumanity]' (Nietzsche 1980, 276). Since inhumanity subversively resurfaces within its 'overcomer', its sublimation becomes an interminable task. He still believed that, through such persistent endeavor, the indistinct 'animal' hatred toward others transforms into a distinct 'human' love for them. In his *On the Genealogy of Morals* (1887), the contagious seed of 'a hatred the like of which has never been on earth' miraculously results in 'the deepest and most sublime of all kinds of love' (Nietzsche 1996, 20). In paragraphs 354 and 355 of his *Joyful Wisdom* (1882), Nietzsche presents his own persistently self-re-evaluating philosophical technique as the culmination of a long development that began with the 'denigrated and humiliated' mob; continued with the actor who had learned to command his instincts with other instincts; then the 'artist' like the buffoon, the fool, and the clown; thereupon, the proper artist; until the process was finally crowned with the 'genius' (Nietzsche 2010).

In his essay 'The Poet and this Time' (1906), Hugo von Hofmannsthal implicitly endorses Nietzsche's trust in redemption through self-dispossession, transferring it from the long-term axis of humankind onto the short-term axis of human life. Because the poet sees something that the blinded others overlook, he exposes himself to a common misunderstanding and contempt. However, despite such denigration, he must persevere with his sacrificial mission for these contemporaries' ultimate well-being. 'Living in the house of time, under the stairs, where everyone must pass him and no one respects him [...] an undetected beggar in the place of the dogs [...] without a job in this house, without service, without rights, without duty' (Hofmannsthal 1979, 66), only such a self-animalized poet can create a human world bereft of 'animal' hatred.

However, the post-imperial age shattered such late imperial trust in the 'animalized' human residues as the motors of new humanity. Taught by the devastating mass movements, for example, Robert Musil interprets these denigrated and humiliated agencies in a more equivocal manner. In 'A sort of introduction' to his *Man without Qualities*, his narrator states that next to nine identities attributed to 'every dweller on earth' by their internally diversified societies, there is a tenth attribute, which is 'difficult to describe', 'merely an empty, invisible space with reality standing in the middle of it like a little toy brick town, abandoned by the imagination' (Musil 2014, 34). But since this indistinct attribute *absorbs into its emptiness all the remaining identity attributes*, 'every dweller on earth' ultimately becomes a 'man without qualities', with his or her identity subjected to a persistent negation (Musil 2014, 220). A person who no longer feels at home in an extant community replaces it with a longing for such emptied communities. In such a way, a perilous 'organic' feeling grows at the heart of endangered belonging.

In his essay 'Beyond the Pleasure Principle', at the beginning of which he introduces the concept of 'oceanic feeling', Freud anticipates Musil's anxieties. In 'The Mass Psychology and the Analysis of the Ego', he argues that such blind mass binding to a leader eliminates the achievements of a long cultural development such as individual will, consciousness, self-control, logics, and a sense of reality (Freud 2001, 93). His thesis is that 'organic communities' are by no means an overcome phase of human history but rather a permanent disintegrating aftereffect of its development. Resulting from the dispossessed collectivities' and individuals' resurfacing desire for self-dissolution, they regularly re-emerge within the differentiated human society. This is how, for instance, the institutions of the army and the Church come into being (Freud 2001, 88–94). The proliferation of these supposedly surmounted modes of self-identification makes the present spectral and uncanny, saturated with the resonances of its terrifying past (Freud 1947, 'Das Unheimliche' 232; *Die Psychopathologie* 295).

As the confrontation between Nietzsche's and Hofmannsthal's enthusiasms on the one hand and Freud's and Musil's reservations on the other testifies, the re-emergence of the animal within the human is an equivocal phenomenon. Derrida, for example, once noticed how fascinating and fertilizing its disintegrating effects were for interwar European thinkers who felt stranded in their present: '[W]hy is [the uncanny] the best name, the best concept, for something which resists consistency, system, semantic identity? Why is it *the* experience, the most thinking experience in Freud and in Heidegger?' (Derrida 2003, 35) The uncanny also became the carrier of his own idea of Europe because Europe 'consists precisely of not closing itself off in its own identity and in advancing itself in an exemplary way towards what it is not' (Derrida 1992, *The Other Heading* 12). How is this denial of its devastating effects to be explained in the works of the late imperial and post-imperial West European thinkers?

In fact, from the outbreak of modernity onwards, Western philosophers relegated these perilous effects to the retrograde 'non-Europeans' or 'not-enough-Europeans'. It is for them, they say, that the 'proper Europeans' have to relentlessly expiate their distinction by reintroducing indistinction into it. Speaking of Slavs, for example, Herder already raises the question: 'Is it astonishing that, after centuries of subjugation and the deepest embitterment of this nation through its masters and robbers, their soft character has been degraded to the most cunning, terrible slavish inertia' (*Knechtsträgheit*) (Herder 1989, 698)? Their spiritual poverty engages mobility in the physical instead of the intellectual space as progressive peoples do. A century thereafter, in *The Crisis of European Humanity and Philosophy*, Husserl complains that the Roma 'incessantly rove around Europe [...] while we, if we understand each other correctly, will for example never become Indians (*die dauernd in Europa herumvagabundieren* [...] *während wir, wenn wir uns recht verstehen, uns zum Beispiel nie indianisieren werden*)' (Husserl 1954, 318–319 (trl. mine)). He attempted to solve the crisis of European humanity by reattaching Europe to its 'genuine' task of rescuing universal humankind by gradually suspending limitation caused by such benighted others.

But there are more recent 'engineers' of this *purely potential* indistinct constituent of Europe that attentively detaches itself from its restricted *physical* materialization. In the conclusion of his book *Europe, or the Infinite Task*, Rodolphe Gasché summarizes this long-lasting elaboration of European singularity as follows:

> From Husserl's discussion of a universal rational science having its roots in the life world, to Heidegger's linkage of an originary world to the history of a people, to Patočka's conception of a community of responsibility predicated on the absolute singularity of its members, to Derrida's claim that the concept or idea of universality as an infinite task emerges

in a finite space and time, we have seen that singularity can only identify itself by simultaneously appealing to universality. (Gasché 2009, 343)

Being open 'toward transcendence, toward the other, and what is other than Europe' (Gasché 2009, 27), an 'emancipating interiorizer of limited exteriorities" so to speak, Europe is for Gasché, thanks to such an extreme consideration of others, the most responsible representative of universal humankind (Gasché 2009, 31). It never stops questioning itself. Associating this consistently self-interrogating life with the spiritual rather than geographical Europeans, Gasché confronts every human being irrespective of his or her geographical location with this 'infinite task' of self-Europeanization (Gasché 2009, 27).

Although connecting on a different tradition, Julia Kristeva concurs with him by seeing Europe as the carrier of Montesquieu's *ésprit général*, a historically guided 'texture of many singularities' (Kristeva 1993, 32–33). In line with Gasché's argument, she states that unlike non-European civilizations inimical to contamination and overlaps with other traditions, Europe from the outset exemplified an exogamous society stipulating alliances outside the bloodline (Kristeva 1991, 45–46). The third prominent thinker, who interprets Europe's sacrificial self-de-identification as the prerequisite of its universal mission, is Zygmunt Bauman. He argues that unlike other cultures that are unaware of being distinct because they are unrelated to the others, European culture 'feeds on questioning the order of things – and on questioning the fashion of questioning it' (Bauman 2004, 12). This ultimately turns it into an infinite task of a consistent self-dispossession.

In order to defend Europe from a 'dispersal into a myriad of provinces, into a multiplicity of self-enclosed idioms or petty little nationalisms, each one jealous and untranslatable', Jacques Derrida also enthusiastically endorses the sacrifice of any given European identity for an 'infinite task' (Derrida 1992, *The Other Heading* 39). He expects Europe to exempt itself from any determinate identity into a pure potentiality of the 'New International', an eminently anti-organic community:

> It is an untimely link, without status, without title and without name, barely public even if it is not clandestine, without contract, 'out of joint', without coordination, without party, without country, without national community [...] without co-citizenship, without common belonging to a class. (Derrida 1994, 85)

Derrida formulates his idea of Europe as '[w]e know in common that we have nothing in common', underlining its relentless energy of self- and other-deactivation (Derrida 2001, 58). Instituting the 'global jurisdiction' (Derrida 1992, 'This Strange Institution' 72) of its all-pervading *nothing* as the 'most powerful powerless' (Attridge 2004, 131), his Europe ultimately uproots all identities grounded in a particular time, space, and culture. Because its dissemination exceeds, transgresses, and elusively surpasses the other, its non-community 'does not collect itself, it 'consists' in not collecting itself' (Derrida 1995, 354). In their 'plea for a common foreign policy, beginning at the core of Europe', Habermas and Derrida accordingly assume that, in proceeding thus, Europe substitutes a fully inclusive human community for an agglomeration of territorially entrenched entities (Habermas and Derrida 2003).

In a manner typical of weak messianism, Derrida thus deconstructs all small oppositions in favour of the big one between the Europe of free self-dispossessions and the non-Europe of the enforced ones. The first 'human' dispossessions take the upper hand over the second 'animal' ones. In line with the empowerment of the powerless as characteristic of Derrida's 'neither words nor notions' such as the *différance*, trace, undecidability, *tout autre*, or deconstruction, his Europe deprived of all identities operates as the 'law of laws' or the agency of justice. While it is itself safely withdrawn from any deactivation, it relentlessly deactivates all 'non-Europeans' (Derrida 1985, 121). Its vague and elusive character that lurks in the indistinct past behind the back of identifiable history promises an equally indistinct future to compensate for the long victimhood of its carriers. Paradoxically reintroducing the East-Central European populist retribution narratives— 'We have been naught, we shall be all'—Derrida's weak messianic Europe demonstrates the same *triumphant return of the indistinct*, which absorbs into its emptiness all 'petty' distinctions.

However, bereaving the idea of Europe of its geopolitical and historical particularity until it becomes such an indistinct entity, involuntarily uncovers the repentance of its creators for the crimes committed by Europe. For example, the myth of a multiethnic, multicultural and multilingual Central Europe equally sublimed its past atrocities. It acquired prominence after the almost complete extermination of the region's Jews, the deportation of its Germans, and a radical reduction of linguistic and ethnographic heterogeneity in its newly established nation states. Once the myth's traumatic background enters the daylight, it dismantles 'Central Europe' as a nostalgic, therapeutic, and falsifying back-projection established to heal its creators' wounds. Does not the same repentance underlie the recent indistinct idea of Europe?

Considering this suppression, it is significant to what degree Derrida's radically indistinct idea of Europe corresponds with Foucault's technique of ethical self-fashioning, which authorizes his indistinct 'soul' to engulf into its nothingness all his distinct identity attributes. For Foucault, the modern 'soul' is 'the effect' of the microphysical 'technology of power over the body' that consists of the systematic work of normative differentiation. As the most prominent counter-site of the modern self, it is the residue excluded from the modern society's rules of identity formation, which by the disconcerting resurgence of its unruly energy invokes further social regulation (Foucault 1984, 176–177). In Blanchot's interpretation, this in-different remainder of the social differentiation, which continuously sets a new horizon for the social operations, powerfully attracted Foucault (Blanchot 1993, 199). A 'man always on the move', he toyed 'with the thought that he might have been, had fate so decided [...] nothing or nobody in particular' (*un je ne sais quoi ou un je ne sais qui*; Blanchot 1987, 17). It was in the name of the unfathomable potential of this *je ne sais quoi* that he was ready to let his thought pass 'through what is called madness', to 'withdraw from itself, turn away from a mediating and patient labor [...] towards a searching that is distracted and astray [...] without result and without works' (Blanchot 1993, 199). One can hardly imagine a more radical dispossession of the West European self as undertaken in the name of its in-different remainder.

3   Conclusion

It is time to summarize the delineated developments in the post-imperial East Central Europe after the First World War and the post-colonial West Europe after the Second World War. Whether the distinction of Europe rests on its translation into nations or humanity, its carriers have to cope with the resurrection of their indistinct past. In the outcome, the idea of Europe displays two irreconcilable faces. Despite its fascinating appearance, the gap between them undermines its applicability as the remedy for the problem of human common-being. The idea of Europe is the 'thing' that we need to explain rather than to explain things *with*. It is never a self-evident toolkit but the site of an uncanny encounter. Instead of promising a harmonious reconciliation, it always implies an uneasy cohabitation with its untranslatable leftovers.

Works Cited

Agamben, Giorgio. 1998. *Homo Sacer: Sovereign Power and Bare Life* (trl. Daniel Heller-Roazen; Stanford: Stanford University Press).

Appadurai, Arjun. 1998. *Modernity at Large: Cultural Dimensions of Globalization* (Minneapolis: University of Minnesota Press).

Attridge, Derek. 2004. *The Singularity of Literature* (London: Routledge).
Badiou, Alain. 2003. *Saint Paul: The Foundation of Universalism* (trl. Ray Brassier; Stanford: Stanford University Press).
Bakić-Hayden, Milica. 1995. 'Nesting Orientalisms: The Case of Former Yugoslavia', *Slavic Review* 4.54: 917–931.
Barkey, Karen. 1996. 'Thinking about Consequences of Empire', in *After Empire: Multiethnic Societies and Nation-Building. The Soviet Union and the Russian, Ottoman, and Habsburg Empires*, eds. Karen Barkey and Mark von Hagen (Boulder, CO: Westview Press), 99–114.
Bauman, Zygmunt. 2004. *Europe: An Unfinished Adventure* (Cambridge: Wiley).
Berend, Ivan T. 1998. *Decades of Crisis: Central and Eastern Europe before World War II* (Berkeley and Los Angeles: University of California Press).
Bhabha, Homi. 1994. *The Location of Culture* (London: Routledge).
Biti, Vladimir. 2020. 'Post-imperial Europe: Integration through Disintegration', *European Review* 28.1: 62–75.
Blanchot, Maurice. 1987. 'Michel Foucault as I Imagine Him,' in *Foucault/Blanchot* (trl. J. Mehlman; New York: Zone).
Blanchot, Maurice. 1993. *The Infinite Conversation* (trl. S. Hanson; Minneapolis: University of Minnesota Press).
Brubaker, Rogers. 1996. *Nationalism Reframed: Nationalism and the national question in the New Europe* (Cambridge: Cambridge University Press).
Butler, Judith. 2004. *Precarious Life: The Powers of Mourning and Violence* (London: Verso).
Chakrabarty, Dipesh. 2000. *Provincializing Europe: Postcolonial Thought and Historical Difference* (Princeton, NJ: Princeton University Press).
Cornwall, Mark. 2006. 'The Habsburg Monarchy', in *What is a Nation? Europe 1879–1914*, eds. Tymothy Baycroft and Mark Hewitson (Oxford: Oxford University Press), 171–192.
Derrida, Jacques. 1985. 'Préjugés – devant la loi', in Jacques Derrida et al. *La faculté de juger* (Paris: PUF), 87–139.
Derrida, Jacques. 1992. 'The Force of Law: The "Mystical Foundation of Authority"', in *Deconstruction and the Possibility of Justice*, eds. David Carlson, Drucilla Cornell and Michael Rosenfeld (New York: Taylor and Francis), 3–67.
Derrida, Jacques. 1992. *The Other Heading* (trl. Pascale-Anne Brault and Michael B. Naas; Bloomington and Indianapolis: Indiana University Press).
Derrida, Jacques. 1992. 'This Strange Institution Called Literature', *Acts of Literature*, ed. Derek Attridge (London: Routledge) 33–75.
Derrida, Jacques. 1994. *Specters of Marx: The State of Debt, the Work of Morning & the New International* (trl. Peggy Kamuf; London: Routledge).

Derrida, Jacques. 1995. *Points: Interviews 1974–1994*, ed. Elisabeth Weber (Stanford: Stanford University Press).

Derrida, Jacques. 2001. *A Taste for the Secret*. Eds. G. Donis and D. Webb. (trl. G. Donis; Cambridge: Polity).

Derrida, Jacques. 2003. 'Following theory', in *Life.after.theory.*, eds. Michael Payne and John Schad (London: Continuum), 1–52.

Esposito, Roberto. 2011. 'The Person and Human Life', in *Theory after 'Theory'*, eds. Jane Elliott and Derek Attridge (London: Routledge), 205–220.

Evans, R.J.W. 2006. *Austria, Hungary, and the Habsburgs: Essays on Central Europe c. 1683–1867* (Oxford: Oxford University Press), 134–146.

Foucault, Michel. 1984. 'The Body of the Condemned', in *The Foucault Reader*, ed. Paul Rabinow (New York: Pantheon), 170–179.

Freud, Sigmund. 1947. 'Das Unheimliche', *Gesammelte Werke* (London: Imago), 12: 229–268.

Freud, Sigmund. 1947. *Zur Psychopathologie des Alltagslebens. Gesammelte Werke*, 4 (London: Imago).

Freud, Sigmund. 2001. 'Massenpsychologie und Ich-Analyse', *Gesammelte Werke in achtzehn Bänden* (Frankfurt: Fischer), 13: 73–165.

Fritzsche, Peter. 2004. *Stranded in the Present: Modern Time and the Melancholy of History*. (Cambridge, MA: Harvard University Press).

Gasché, Rodolphe. 2009. *Europe or the Infinite Task: A Study of a Philosophical Concept* (Stanford: Stanford University Press).

Guha, Ranajit. 2002. *History at the Limit of World-History* (New York: Columbia University Press).

Habermas, Jürgen and Jacques Derrida. 2003. 'February 15, or What Binds Europeans Together: A plea for a common foreign policy, beginning in the core of Europe', *Constellations* 10.3: 291–297.

Hanson, Stephen E. 2010. *Post-Imperial Democracies: Ideology and Party Formation in Third Republic France, Weimar Germany, and Post-Soviet Russia* (Cambridge: Cambridge University Press).

Herder, Johann Gottfried. 1989. *Ideen zur Philosophie der Geschichte der Menschheit*, ed. Martin Bollacher; *Werke in zehn Bänden*, ed. Martin Bollacher et al., 6 (Frankfurt: Deutscher Klassiker Verlag).

Hobsbawm, Eric J. 1996. 'The End of Empires', in *After Empire: Multiethnic Societies and Nation-Building: The Soviet Union and the Russian, Ottoman, and Habsburg Empires*, eds. Karen Barkey and Mark von Hagen (Boulder, CO: Westview Press), 12–16.

Hofmannsthal, Hugo von. 1979. 'Der Dichter und diese Zeit', *Reden und Aufsätze I (1891–1913). Gesammelte Werke in zehn Einzelbanden*, ed. Bernd Schoeller, 8 (Frankfurt: Suhrkamp), 54–82.

Husserl, Edmund. 1954. *Die Krisis des europäischen Menschentums und die Philosophie* (The Hague: Nijhoff).

Judson, Pieter. 2016. *The Habsburg Empire: A New History* (Cambridge, MA: Belknap/Harvard University Press).

Kant, Immanuel. 2006. *Political Writings,* ed. H.S. Reiss (trl. H. B. Nisbet; Cambridge: Cambridge University Press).

Keyder, Caglar. 1996. 'The Ottoman Empire', in *After Empire: Multiethnic Societies and Nation-Building: The Soviet Union and the Russian, Ottoman, and Habsburg Empires,* eds. Karen Barkey and Mark von Hagen (Boulder, CO: Westview Press), 30–44.

Kożuchowski, Adam. 2013. *The Afterlife of Austria-Hungary: The Image of the Habsburg Monarchy in Interwar Europe* (Pittsburgh: University of Pittsburgh Press).

Kristeva, Julia. 1991. *Strangers to Ourselves* (trl. Leon S. Roudiez; New York: Columbia University Press).

Kristeva, Julia. 1993. *Nations without Nationalism* (trl. Leon S. Roudiez; New York: Columbia University Press).

Luhmann, Niklas. 1989. 'Individuum, Individualität, Individualismus', *Gesellschaftsstruktur und Semantik: Studien zur Wissenssoziologie der modernen Gesellschaft* (Frankfurt am Main: Suhrkamp), 3: 149–258.

Mignolo, Walter. 2000. 'The Many Faces of Cosmo-Polis: Border Thinking and Critical Cosmopolitanism', *Public Culture* 3.12: 721–748.

Musil, Robert. 2014. *Der Mann ohne Eigenschaften* (Reinbek: Rowohlt).

Nietzsche, Friedrich. 2010. *The Joyful Wisdom* (trl. Thomas Common; Adelaide: Ebooks).

Nietzsche, Friedrich. 1980. *Ecce homo. Sämtliche Werke,* eds. G. Colli and M. Montinari, 6 (Berlin: De Gruyter).

Nietzsche, Friedrich. 1996. *On the Genealogy of Morals: A Polemic* (trl. Douglas Smith; Oxford: Oxford University Press).

Povinelli, Elisabeth. 2011. *Economies of Abandonment: Social Belonging and Endurance in Late Liberalism* (Durham, NC: Duke University Press).

Renan, Ernest. 2006. 'What Is a Nation?', in *Becoming National: A Reader,* ed. Geoff Eley and Ronald Grigor Suny (Oxford: Oxford University Press), 41–55.

Rosa, Hartmut et al. 2010. *Theorien der Gemeinschaft zur Einführung* (Hamburg: Junius).

Schenk, Frithjof Benjamin. 2013. 'Travel, Railroads, and Identity Formation in the Russian Empire', in *Shatterzone of Empires: Coexistence and Violence in the German, Habsburg, Russian and Ottoman Borderlands,* eds. Omer Bartov and Eric D. Weitz (Bloomington: Indiana University Press), 136–151.

Todorova, Maria. 1997. *Imagining the Balkans* (Oxford: Oxford University Press).

Zahra, Tara. 2010. 'Imagined Noncommunities: National Indifference as a Category of Analysis', *Slavic Review,* 69.1: 93–119.

CHAPTER 3

Can the European Heritage Be Redeemed? Confessions of an Europeanist

Gerard Delanty

There is not much left of the European heritage today, it would seem. It has been much debunked and attacked from all sides. My reflections might be dismissed as the delusions of a Eurocentrist, a futile attempt to clutch at straws since there is nothing left to be redeemed. But I think the European heritage can be redeemed and made relevant for the present without recourse to the traditional Eurocentric narratives that proclaim European uniqueness or exceptionality, narratives that are generally constructed on the basis of an origin, a dominant self and an external other.

Simply put: The origin has been constantly redefined; the self has been pluralised and the other has become opaque as a result of fuzziness between internal and external boundaries. Where does that leave the European heritage? Does it have any specificity? Can it be re-claimed? In other words, is it possible to be an Europeanist and even a Europhile but not be a Eurocentricist?

How we look back on European history and attempt to reckon with the past is an exercise that can only be done from a specific time and place. The time and place is Europe today.[1] The older positions – including many of their critiques – were all influenced by the context of their time. There is no transhistorical position. The argument I am putting forward in this chapter is an effort to advance beyond what I take to be two main positions that counteract against Eurocentrism and the 'dark side' of European history. Let me review these before setting out an alternative vision of how something can be salvaged from the past that is valuable for the present. I argue that a reorientation is needed around transnational perspectives on history and, from a more normative and critical perspective, cosmopolitanism.

There can be little doubt that any discussion on the European heritage has been influenced by the shadow of the Holocaust. It is difficult to escape the dark side of the past as the prism through which the European legacy must be viewed. This has irreversibly changed how we view the European heritage

---

1 The chapter was written in 2017. Much of the argument in the following pages draws on my *The European Heritage: A Critical Re-interpretation* (London, Routledge, 2018).

today in so far as normative standpoints are concerned. My position concedes that the possibility of a common understanding of history on a European scale has been more or less definitively refuted. As Hannah Arendt argued in *The Origins of Totalitarianism*, the historical experience of totalitarianism, and above all the holocaust, has shattered the possibility of common European heritage. If the European heritage begins with Athens, it ends with Auschwitz, as Christian Meier (2005) claims. Zygmunt Bauman's book, *Modernity and the Holocaust*, made a similar claim with the argument that modernity itself can be reinterpreted through the universal significance of the Holocaust (Bauman 1989). However, that memory itself has not remained constant. According to Daniel Levy and Natan Sznaider (2002 and 2006) as a result of a generational shift the Holocaust is no longer primarily a collective memory, but a historical memory that goes beyond the limits of a specific historical community. They call this variously a 'cosmopolitan memory' or a 'global memory.' The memory of the Holocaust provides the basic ingredients for a new and more cosmopolitan memory that is of global scope. In their view, the Holocaust can be memorialised and thus become the basis of a new understanding of the common heritage of humanity by people who no longer have any direct experience of it. In short, it has become re-contextualised for the present as it re-defines its relation to the past. This shift in the meaning of the holocaust is reflected in a European day of remembrance (27 January).

Such conceptions of the past are reflected in a broader notion of the past in terms of trauma. This has been most notably advanced by sociologists such as Jeff Alexander and Bernd Giesen (Alexander *et al.* 2004, Giesen 2005). In this approach, trauma is a category of experience that pertains to collective identities, and is not only manifest on the personal level. It structures a collective identity around narratives, whether real or imagined, of a victim and a perpetrator. Trauma can become normalised by repetition and enters into the dominant discourses in which a collectivity interpret themselves around notions such as guilt, revenge, atonement or responsibility. This perspective is an important one that is particularly pertinent to Europe, especially with respect to the problem of the dark side of history and the persistence of questions around suffering and guilt. It is relevant to the impact of the memory of war on the European heritage since 1918.

Public commemoration of war is centrally about symbolic acts of performativity, ever since Willy Brandt's famous genuflection at the memorial to the Warsaw Ghetto Uprising in 1970. However, cultural trauma analysis is not without its limits when it comes to address the wider domain of cultural heritage, as opposed to the symbolic dimension of culture and in particular the symbolic representations of collective identities and memories. Culture, including cultural heritage, extends beyond the level of symbolic representations to include normative as well as cognitive components and that this cannot be reduced to the symbolic level. The focus on cultural trauma has also been largely confined to the analysis of the shifting symbolic codes of national memories and thus does not capture the ways in which different collective and cultural memories interact. Nor does it tell us much about cultures learn from each other.

A relevant example of what I mean is the controversy in 2016 around demands for the removal of the statue of one of the symbols of British colonialism in Africa, Cecil Rhodes, at Oriel College, Oxford University. Here the question is how the memory of colonialism is handled, whether it is to be wilfully forgotten and rendered invisible through removal and renaming as symbolic acts or remembered in ways that challenge the physical presence of an older memory that has now been reinterpreted. The cultural politics of memory around symbols of colonialism is also an illustration of the impact of the global movement, 'Rhodes Must Fall,' that began at the University of Cape Town in 2015 and had world-wide impact on cultural heritage, since so much of heritage is under the shadow of colonialism.

I argue that Europe cannot abandon questioning its dark side, but it cannot also entirely see this as the only way it can relate to the past. The category of heritage also concerns the subversion of heritage by counter-memories that are not necessarily defined in terms of trauma, but in terms of demands for recognition of often marginalised or forgotten cultures and their heritage. In other words, there is something more than the shift from the monument to the memorial at stake in the question of how the past can be appropriated by the present. This unavoidably raises the question of future possibilities and claims to the validity of heritage. It is also where memory and history intersect.

A second general perspective is to view the past in terms of a plurality of different heritages, as opposed to one dominant one. This perspective is much influenced by the prominence of critical and postcolonial approaches to culture and to the past. In this case, a more critical approach to the European past would consist of the search for alternatives to the received view of history in the identification of that which has been hidden. I take this to be the most constructive outcome of post-colonial theory (in contrast to the orientalist critique that more or less negates the possibility of a counter-narrative and thus does not advance much beyond the pre-occupation with the dark side of history).

One expression of Eurocentrism is in the marginalisation of the non-European dimension, which is also constitutive of Europe and calls into question the notion of European uniqueness. Arab/Islamic thought, between the ninth and fourteenth centuries was very important in the making of the European heritage, but it is often reduced to its function of preserving and transmitting classical European thought. A more critical approach to the past would include giving greater acknowledge of what has come to be seen as a non-European traditions as constitutive of Europe. This can and must include writing in non-western sources of knowledge or giving them greater place. However, while correcting some Eurocentric thinking that cultivates the view that Europe is unique, such exercises do not necessarily offer an alternative view of Europe or of how the past should be evaluated other than the inclusion of that which has been marginalised. This in itself is not an insignificant endeavour, but it still leaves open the question whether there are other ways of approaching the European heritage beyond this task of the inclusion of what has been hidden.

Revealing hidden histories, however, may be more than a corrective exercise in the sense of adding in that which was missing, but otherwise not changing the narrative; it may in fact lead to fundamentally new insights if those histories reveal an alternative way of looking at the past. If this is the case – as in for example the way in which women's history reshaped the way we think about the past – it would require us to rethink the received views of the past in ways that go beyond mere pluralism. For instance, the relative neglect of colonialism in the formation of the modern history of Europe leads to a myopic view of Europe as something that can be understood without taking into account the formative impact of the rest of the world. A relevant example concerns the Anglo-centric memory of World War One in the UK which erased the presence of one million Indian troops and two million black soldiers. This forgotten history has only recently been reinserted into the British heritage.

So, there are two positions then: one that sees the European heritage as irredeemably mired by the dark side of history and one that aims to write in that which is missing. It seems to me that transnational approaches in history and cosmopolitan critical thought could open up further perspectives. I shall try to develop this now less as an alternative than a re-orientation of current ways of looking at the European heritage.

A brief clarification on what it means to speak of heritage to begin with will help at this juncture. The traditional view of heritage was two-fold: heritage as the universal patrimony of humanity or the patrimony of a specific people, generally a nation. The first is an inclusive understanding of heritage as the property of all peoples and the second an exclusive one. The two notions share a view of heritage as that which has been handed down by the past to the present and which defines the present. Both of these have been challenged by new understandings and practices of heritage. Universalistic notions of the patrimony of humanity have been in general challenged by collective identities seeking the recognition of their specific claims to heritage, claims that are often underpinned by cultural rights and the relatively new category of heritage rights. Such developments do not fit into the pattern of national traditions of heritage, since in many cases the groups in question are marginalised by the national culture, which has lost its integrative powers. The trend, then, is for universalistic and national traditions of heritage to be challenged by a new emphasis on marginalised and excluded memories seeking the acknowledgement of their heritage. This leads to new acts of remembering to counter-act the forgetting in the dominant national narratives. As I see it, this is more than a corrective exercise. The European heritage is a site of cultural re-interpretation and re-evaluation. However, as a cultural sphere of meaning, it is not only about the dominant cultures under-going change: minority cultures may also undergo changes in their self-understanding.

An illustrative recent example of cultural resignification is the Black Peter controversy in the Netherlands. Once a taken for granted feature of Dutch culture during the annual feast of St Nicholas on 5th December when people dress up in Renaissance costumes and paint their faces black, Black Peter has been recently denounced as racist and inseparable from the legacy of colonialism and racism. It is thus an example of a re-evaluation of the national cultural heritage as a result of new ideas and the influence of perspectives from outside the national culture. Such re-evaluations are not confined to everyday racism.

The Rijksmuseum in Amsterdam has been undertaking a reappraisal of the names and descriptions on many of its very large collection of paintings from the seventeenth century to the twentieth century and renaming those that might be considered to be offensive due to the use of racialized terms such as 'negro'. Many of these Dutch paintings from the colonial era featured peoples from colonial territories. Against arguments that such re-naming is censorship or the betrayal of history, the museum defends its policy with the claim that the terms were in most cases not given by the painters but were later designations and reflected the terms Dutch used for non-white people during the colonial era. These names have today lost their meaning and need to be changed.

A different example of renaming that in this case seeks to reclaim history from its instrumentalisation by the state, is the Budapest-based activist group, Eleven Emlékmű (Living Memorial), who created a living memorial to the victims of the Holocaust in 2014 on the occasion of the 70th anniversary of the mass deportation of Jews from Hungary. It was intended to be an alternative counter-memorial to the official government's controversial memorial in Liberty Square to the victims of WW2, which portrayed Hungary as a victim of the Nazis.

Another similar example is attempts in Belgium to foreground counter-memories in relation to the public statues of Leopold II. These actions can be seen as performative acts that make possible the counter-remembering of that which has been forgotten and challenges to the official monument. They are thus examples of what Young, in a classic essay, has called the 'counter-monument' (Young 1992).

In order for Europe to reinvent itself it will need to revisit its heritage, which cannot be a comfort zone or something that can be instrumentalized for the purpose of cultural diplomacy or for economic uses. National governments use cultural heritage to foster positive views of their nation. They very often take a nostalgic form suggesting that our heritage is that which we have lost but which can be recovered in the form of reminders based on place and objects. That sense of heritage as the fragments of the past lies behind Pierre Nora's famous work, *Realms of Memory*, published originally between 1984 and 1992, on the national heritage of France. He emphasised the survival of heritage in sites where it functions as a substitute for the absence of an integrative national memory. The EU, too, uses heritage in a similar way to promote positive views of Europe as exemplified in its classical architecture, the arts, festivals etc, except that in this case there is no memory as such that fragmented with modernity. Such projections in themselves are often unobjectional, but capture just one dimension of heritage, namely its affirmative side and which is normally expressed in tangible forms, as in architecture or the arts, as in the Europeana Foundation, the symbols on the Euro currency. However, this received view of heritage as the inheritance of relics of the past does not accord with the tremendous transformation in culture and in historical self-understanding.

Heritage has become a site in which previously excluded peoples can express their identity and make new rights based claims to the recognition of their heritage. The Holocaust memory has been one of the most important counter-memories. The very notion of the holocaust itself has result in a resignification of memory for other groups, for example it has been taken up by the Romas as a reminder to previously 'forgotten' the Roma Holocaust, also known as the *Porajmos*. A memorial was created in Berlin in 2012 to commemorate the 220,000 to 500,000 Sinti and Roman victims of Nazism. The holocaust memory has also made possible a recodification of memories of slavery, as Michael Rothberg has argued (Rothberg 2009). This does not mean that the shift to the victim can result in new and settled memories. The victim may be in the eyes of others a perpetrator. The Puritans who fled from oppression in Europe were refugees in the New World, but for those whom they encountered they were colonisers. This double movement has repeated itself many times in history.

The French who were victims of the German occupation collaborated in the persecution of the Jews. The Russians suffered from the Germans, but the peoples of central and eastern Europe were oppressed both by Stalin and by Hitler. The Irish nationalist movement complained about British rule in Ireland, but the Irish gladly participated in the colonial venture and contributed to white supremacism. Nonetheless, there has been a cross-fertilisation of memories.

I have referred to these developments as cosmopolitan heritage to capture the way in which heritage has ceased to be based on a single voice, such as that of the nation, but is polyvocal and sometimes the result of re-signification following recombination of different memories. The elements that make up many memories and claims to heritage are often the result of transnational movements in cultural production. While the unity of national narratives of heritage has been considerably pluralised as a result of new claims to recognition of marginalised or excluded people, this has not had a significant impact on the wider understandings of the European heritage. What is urgently needed is a vision of the European cultural heritage than will enable different groups to insert themselves and articulate their counter-memories. For this to happen, heritage will have to cease to be a comfort zone in which Europe only celebrates its achievements. It will need to move into and confront more directly the difficult and often traumatic legacies of history and the excluded and forgotten memories of many cultures, who also have claims to the European heritage.

The reality today is that European culture is no longer tied to a European people. There is no single European people, neither in a political or in an ethnic sense. The Europeans are those who live in Europe and those who have lived there in the past, including those populations expelled or exterminated. Europe is not underpinned by an objective reference, whether a state, a religion, a territory, an ethnicity. European culture is, like all of culture, de-referentialized; that is, it is not defined by immutable sources or an original culture that only undergoes pluralisation. Europe is a cradle of intermingling cultures, but also ones that are in tension with each other. It is this mosaic of differences that defines Europe.

Eurocentrism is not then an exhaustive category that includes within it all that can be said of the idea of Europe. A critical cosmopolitan view of the European heritage emphasises not only inclusivity but also the critique of particularity, including European particularity. It can be seen as a reversal of Orientalism. Where Orientalism posits only a relation of inequality between Europe and its 'Others', a cosmopolitan perspective, in contrast, would see the relation as admitting of the possibility of dialogue and exchange as well as resistances. The idea of Europe is today very much linked with the critique of

Europe. It is also associated with the shared experiences and interpretations of those experiences by Europeans as they re-evaluate themselves in light of those interpretations. The European heritage today might then be best seen as a site of resistances and of reflection. The dark shadow of the holocaust remains one of the core symbolic reference points for reflection on the European heritage. It has long cased to be a German specific memory, but has become a European one.

The two approaches I have looked at – cultural trauma and the search for hidden histories – have led to a general view of the European past as Eurocentric. We can agree that European heritage is contested and that pluralist approaches are needed in the sense of the recognition of that which has been hidden or marginalised. The European heritage can escape Eurocentrism, which is neither an all embracing entity nor its essential defining tenet. My argument is that when viewed through the lens of transnational history, Europe is unbounded and decentred within; it is not homogeneous but plural and many of its intellectual and cultural traditions embrace alterity, the positive acceptance of difference. The notion of Eurocentrism cannot be extended to embrace the entirety of the European heritage; nor can it be extended to encompass all forms of European self-understanding and knowledge. This is something that has been recognised by many major philosophers such as Karl Jaspers (1948), Jacques Derrida (1992), Hans-Georg Gadamer (1992) and Jan Patočka (2002). One of the challenges of scholarship on the European heritage is to identify the self-problematizing and critical currents that have been equally constitutive of Europe's past.

Whether Europe can escape Eurocentrism is very much a question of how the past is read and what weight is given to cosmopolitan currents in relation to those that fall under the rubric of Eurocentrism. Post-colonial critiques of Eurocentrism generally fail to address the diverse currents of the European heritage and the fact that nothing has ever been finally settled. The argument I am making is that a critical cosmopolitan critique of Europe is itself one of the legacies of the European heritage and gives to the present a possible direction for the future. This means that the European heritage contains within itself the resources to overcome itself. It is in this emphasis on an immanent critique of the European heritage that I depart from postcolonial theory. Viewing the European heritage in such terms, as unbounded and decentred, questions the unreflective use of the notion of Eurocentrism, which implies that Europe – or thinking about Europe – is somehow necessarily based on a centre and that it makes false claims to universality.

Moving forward, then, to a more positive account of what the European heritage might mean today, I think there are three currents that might redefine the idea of Europe for the present day: peace, social justice, hospitality.

Following the end of the First World War European intellectuals became increasingly aware of both common bonds that united the war torn European countries and the need to build upon their shared heritage (Harrington 2016, Rosenboim 2017). That commitment did not stop the descent into the worst war in the history of human societies, but offered a legacy on which Europe could rebuild itself after 1945. This heritage is still with us and has grown to encompass wide social strata. Until recently, the idea of Europe was the aspiration of elites, political and intellectual elites of both the right and the left. Initially it was more attractive to the right, but came to be accepted by the left.

Today the idea of Europe is part of the self-understanding of very large segments of the population, in particular of young people, who have been born as European citizens. Letting aside, for now, the extent of the Europeanisation of identities, the important point is that since 1945, but going back the interwar-period, a cognitive shift occurred that had far-reaching political and cultural significance. After 1945 the idea of Europe came to signify a profound opposition to war, as in the phrase *Nie Wieder*, 'never again war'. The generation who forged the project of European integration that culminated in the Treaty of Rome was animated by the belief in the need to create a lasting peace in a continent that had within living memory witnessed three wars. That sense of what Bo Strath (2016) has called a 'utopia of peace' has lost its force today, now that the goal has been achieved and the memory of the war no longer is a living or collective memory. However, I argue that the essential utopia of peace has survived and has entered the historical memory of Europeans in ways that are not always evident but exert a strong influence.

One of the defining features of European self-understanding is opposition to war. This has been recognised in the 2012 award of the Nobel Peace prize to the European Union. War within Europe has become a thing of the past. Significant progress has been made in resolving the last vestige of military conflict within the European area over Turkish occupation of Cyprus. Despite the discontents posed by Brexit, civil war in Northern Ireland is not likely to reoccur. External war is not to be discounted, as in the case of Iraq war in 2003, but here, too, there is little appetite for armed conflict. The world-wide tendency is towards an increase in civil strife within nations rather than between them.

This is all in stark contrast to the turbulent and often violent history of Europe. The past seventy years has been remarkably peaceful and can be seen as a part of a world-wide trend towards the relative decrease in violence. The exception is the war that followed the break-up of the former Yugoslavia in the early 1990s. It is of course the case that for several decades this peace existed within the context of a political order of dictatorships. The spread of democracy – since 1980 in the Iberian Peninsula and after 1990 in central and eastern Europe – has made it possible for Europe to re-appraise its history and forge a new self-understanding. This cannot be from the position of having reached the 'end of history' since this period has been marked by events that while largely peaceful have been nonetheless tumultuous. There may no longer be a major clash of political ideologies, but there is a cultural clash of identities and of socio-cultural milieus, as is evident from Brexit and the rise of the Alt-Right movement as well as the resurgence of radical right-wing populism more generally today. While a newly found unity has been attained in peace, new divisions have resulted from the very means that made this peace possible. Democracy does not overcome differences. It makes possible pluralisation and rights based claims. It also makes possible the reinterpretation of the past as the received accounts are discredited or contested. It has created the conditions in which the legacy of history can be examined from positions that previously were silenced. This situation when combined with the wider transformation of culture has opened up political community to new challenges.

It is thus my contention that since 1945 opposition to war has been a growing principle that has united Europeans and could be said to be the defining element in contemporary European self-understanding. It is a significant basis of European solidarity and can also be seen, following Walter Benjamin, as an expression of anamnestic solidarity with the victims of history. Anti-war solidarity made possible the largest protests in European history in 2003 when millions of people took to the streets on 15 and 16 February to protest against the Anglo-American led war in Iraq. The largest protests were in Rome with some three million people, 1.5 million in Madrid and one million sized protests in other cities, such as London and Barcelona. These protests, which were part of a global anti-war movement, reveal the shaping of a cosmopolitan ethic of solidarity and the centrality of the idea of human dignity and anti-war. The aversion to war in Europe since 1945 has been a strong force in shaping European consciousness and, with the dark legacy of the Holocaust, it has made possible a Europeanisation of memory in which older memories provide a pattern for new memories. It is in this sense, then, possible to say that despite the rise of radical right-wing nationalism there is something binding Europe together.

It can be argued that the concern with social justice is also one of the defining features of European modernity. A strong current in European history is resistance to a model of society based on the market. This can be variously related to anti-capitalist movements from socialism to social liberalism and social democracy. It is also what underpins the idea of a social model of capitalism that triumphed in western Europe in the post-1945 period. In the final analysis this is what distinguishes Europe from the rest of the world, that is the domestication of capitalism by political claims for social justice. In this sense, then, the language of social justice and solidarity entered into the political systems of modern Europe in at least two ways. One in the shaping of social policies, which is often what is meant by solidarity. The other is in a more general normative conception of society. Both of these senses are also reflected in the core documents of the EU, for examples solidarity is mentioned in the Treaty of Rome in 1957 and the Charter of Fundamental Rights in 2000. In the latter case it signifies social policies and in the former case a more general and elusive normative conception of society as both a goal and as an assumption. What is now needed is a fundamental shift in the very conception of Europe to more fully capture solidarity. This is more important than issues of mobility, markets or supranational governance.

There is a third legacy of recent history that in my view is a distinctively European one. One of the great achievements of the post-second world-war project of European integration is the principle of the legal recognition of the individual person as the bearer of rights and in particular human rights. As a result of the constitutionalization of the EU, a complex framework of rights has been consolidated. The EU is without doubt a major global champion of human rights. Human rights are deeply embedded in domestic laws as a result of EU law. Through the EU Charter of Fundamental Rights, the European Convention of Human Rights (ECHR) and the case law of the European Court of Human Rights in Strasbourg, human rights are not abstract rights but enshrined in the legal framework of all member states. Although the EU may not be greatly popular, it has had a positive and far-reaching impact on the lives of Europeans. It has made possible greater gender equality in employment and it has brought about the prohibition of discrimination on grounds such as religion, sexual orientation, disability and age. The upshot of this is that equality has been given an important basis in European law. It could therefore be suggested that in certain aspects of the legal framework of the EU, in particular those that pertain to the rights of the individual, there are wider normative aspects to European integration and which offer bonds of unity through solidarity.

To the extent to which it still holds normative force, the vision of a postnational Europe based on citizenship is not entirely devoid of substance. In several publications, Habermas (2001) defended the republican idea of Europe based on citizenship. The challenges to this normative model are now considerable and derive from systemic failure due to the nature of the single currency, which has led to new divisions within the member states. Despite these problems, it is arguably the case that the normative foundation of the EU is the individual, not the state. This is probably the most important legacy of the EU. It is an example of what I see as the enduring feature of contemporary Europe and which offers an antidote to its divisions.

The centrality of the individual has been one of the abiding features of the European legacy. It has been the integral to the liberal and the cosmopolitan tradition of thought. It is possible to see a clear link between the idea of Europe and the respect for the individual. In the cosmopolitical tradition of thought going back to Kant, it was expressed in the idea of hospitality. In *Perpetual Peace* in 1795 Kant established the principle of hospitality as the defining tenet of cosmopolitanism, which he contrasted to internationalism, which for Kant was based on treaties between states. Cosmopolitanism, in contrast, is based on the centrality of the individual and the need for the rights of the individual to be recognised even where the individual is a foreigner. It is this idea of cosmopolitan law, rather than the vision of global government, which Kant believed was desirable but not realistic, that has been the main legacy of modern cosmopolitanism. Its relevance to contemporary Europe cannot be underestimated.

To redeem the European heritage from the mire of history is a challenge for critical thought. I have argued from a cosmopolitan perspective that Europe is open to new definitions and that its identity is incomplete and that it can be built upon such currents as peace, social justice and hospitality. So, to answer my initial question, it is possible to be an Europeanist and Europhile without being a Eurocentricist.

Works Cited

Alexander, Jeffrey, et al. 2004. *Cultural Trauma and Collective Identity* (Berkeley: University of California Press).
Arendt, Hannah 2017 [1951]. *The Origins of Totalitarianism* (London: Penguin).
Bauman, Zygmunt. 1989. *Modernity and the Holocaust* (London: Polity).
Derrida, Jacques. 1992. *The Other Heading: Reflections on Today's Europe* (Bloomington, IN: Indiana University Press).
Gadamer, Hans-Georg. 1992. 'The Diversity of Europe: Inheritance and Future', in: D. Misgeld and G. Nicholson, eds, *Applied Hermeneutics* (New York: SUNY), 221–237.
Giesen, Bernd. 2005. *Triumph and Trauma* (New York: Paradigm).

Habermas, Jürgen. 2001. *The Postnational Constellation* (Cambridge: Polity).
Harrington, A. 2016. *German Cosmopolitan Social Thought and the Idea of the West* (Cambridge: Cambridge University Press).
Jaspers, Karl. 1948 *The European Spirit*. London: SCM Press.
Levy, Daniel & Nathan Sznaider. 2006. *Holocaust in a Global Age* (Philadelphia, PA: Temple University Press).
Levy, Daniel & Nathan Sznaider. 2002. 'Memory Unbound: The Holocaust and the Formation of Cosmopolitan Memory', *European Journal of Social Theory* 5.1: 87–106.
Meier, Christian. 2005. *From Athens to Auschwitz: The Uses of History* (Cambridge, MA: Harvard University Press).
Nora, Pierre, ed. 1996–98. *Realms of Memory: Rethinking the French Past* (3 vols.; New York: Columbia University Press).
Patočka, Jan. 2002. *Plato and Europe* (Stanford, CA: Stanford University Press).
Ricœur, Paul. 2004. *History, Memory and Forgetting* (Chicago, IL: University of Chicago Press).
Rosenboim, O. 2017. *The Emergence of Globalism: Visions of World Order in Britain and the United States, 1939–1950* (Princeton, NJ: Princeton University Press).
Rothberg, Michael 2009. *Multidirectional Memory: Remembering the Holocaust in the Age of Decolonization* (Stanford, CA: Stanford University Press).
Stråth, B. 2016. *Europe's Utopias of Peace* (London: Bloomsbury Academic Press).
Young, James 1992. 'The Counter-Monument: Memory Against Itself in Germany Today', *Critical Inquiry* 18.2: 267–96.

CHAPTER 4

Europe and a Geopolitics of Hope

Luiza Bialasiewicz

1   Hoping for Europe

Hopes and aspirations for Europe have always exceeded actually-existing Europe, both geographically, but also in the latter's capacity (and willingness) to fulfill them. As Maria Zambrano wrote in her 1942 *La agonía de Europa*, Europe is 'a projection towards a world always on the horizon, always unattainable. The landscape of Europe is pure horizon [...] its history is pure horizon' (Zambrano 2000). Over the past three decades (more or less since the demise of the Cold War order), a number of leading European thinkers have attempted to trace the 'geo-philosophy' of the European idea, focusing precisely on the idea(l) of Europe as an aspirational *civitas futura*, as Italian political philosopher (and two-term Mayor of Venice) Massimo Cacciari defined it in his seminal *Geofilosofia dell'Europa*.[1]

The characterization of Europe as hope or aspirational horizon has not only marked the work of cultural historians and philosophers of the European idea, however. The failed attempt at creating a 'Constitution' for Europe in 2004–2005 also appealed to just such an imaginary in order to frame the European project. The draft document of the Constitutional Convention opened its Preamble by appealing to Europe as a 'special area of human hope': a lofty pronouncement but one that drew upon a much longer series of political imaginaries of the European project as a distinct 'value space' – as Jurgen Habermas (1998, 2001) termed it – or a distinct 'structure of feeling' (as described by Jacques Derrida, 1991, 2010) – that did not and, indeed could not, have set territorial or temporal limits.

As I have argued elsewhere (Bialasiewicz, Elder & Painter 2005), the challenge facing the Constitutional Convention, was a unique one. It was not simply one of finding the right institutional shape, the right territorial 'fix' for today's Europe and, especially, for the Europe to come. It was not simply a question of finding the right borders for the 'special area of human hope'

---

1   Cacciari 1994. As Cacciari argued also subsequently, 'Europe has always been a term that designates what Europe will be, or would like to be, or should be. The figure of Europe has historically always been a task' (Cacciari 2006).

that was to be the new Europe. It was, rather, to (at least aspire) to transcend 'hard' territorial understandings of political community altogether. In fact, the reluctance of the Constitutional Convention to trace hard borders for the European project (or to trace these only in part) was remarked upon by many observers: the borders of the 'Europe' to be were, in fact, not defined anywhere in the draft text. The 'bounding' of the European project was defined, rather, in aspirational terms, stating that 'the Union shall be open to all European States which respect its values and are committed to promoting them together' (I-1.2). Rather than specifying the EU's limits territorially, then, the Convention defined a set of basic conditions, known as the Copenhagen Criteria, that any applicant country has to meet: stability of institutions guaranteeing democracy, the rule of law, human rights and respect for and protection of minorities; the existence of a functioning market economy as well as the capacity to cope with competitive pressure and market forces within the Union; the ability to take on the obligations of membership including adherence to the aims of political, economic and monetary union (SN 180/1/93).

Since any territorial definition would exclude 'potential' Europeans, the choice of using the Copenhagen Criteria allowed the Convention to define Europe's territorial limits 'aspirationally': open to all those who might become European in the future. Such an open (that is, non-territorial) approach to defining the borders of political community was not to be, however. The failure to adopt the Constitutional Convention's document (that fell hostage to two national referenda, in France and in the Netherlands) certainly reflected, among other things, the persistent discomfort of Member States to cede both institutional but also symbolic capital to the Union in key fields. Apart from the failure of the Constitutional attempt, however, faith in a revived European project as a 'special area of human hope' has also perished over the past decade on Europe's shores, as Europe's borders have become more and more deadly – and European border 'management' more and more inhumane. It has also perished in many Europeans' daily lives, as they have faced the profoundly geographically-unequal effects of the financial crisis.

And yet, Europe continues to inspire hope. To those willing to board smugglers' vessels across the Mediterranean or to entrust their fate to passeurs along the 'Balkan Route'; to protesters on the streets of Kiev, Skopje and Istanbul, Europe remains an aspiration. This dreamt-of 'Europe' is only partially accordant with the boundaries, territorial, as well as formal-institutional, of the current European Union. The 'Europe' hoped for is a set of legal rights and political and economic opportunities (Habermas' hoped-for European 'value space'), but also a set of ideas and aspirations for what 'Europe' could, in potential, be (Derrida's European 'structure of feeling').

2 Practiced 'Europeanism'

In thinking about Europe in aspirational terms, what are today being popularly defined as 'voyages of hope' of those fleeing to Europe, need to be understood as just the most recent episode in a much longer history and a much wider geography of longing 'for Europe': from those who tried to re-make Europe in new worlds, to Europeans expelled from Europe (by history, not geography), to those for whom Europe represents hope today (whether within or beyond the EU).[2] As the late Zygmunt Bauman has argued, to understand the essence of Europe, we should not consider the current-thing-called-Europe, but rather 'the practice of Europeanism'.[3] Indeed, what Bauman warns against, is the presumption of a total and complete correspondence of a specific geographical representation (i.e. what we conceive of as 'Europe' today) to all that is 'European'. As Bauman argues, 'the 'essence of Europe' tends to run ahead of the 'really existing Europe': it is the essence of 'being a European' to have an essence that always stays ahead of reality, and it is the essence of European realities to always lag behind the essence of Europe' (5). What is more, while the 'really existing Europe' – most visibly, the European Union, but more broadly 'that Europe of politicians, cartographers and all its appointed or self-appointed spokespeople' may be conceived as 'a geographical notion and a spatially confined entity, the 'essence of Europe' has never been either the first, or the second. You are not necessarily a European just because you happen to be born or to live in a city marked on the political map of Europe. But you may be European even if you've never been to any of those cities' (5).

He suggests, indeed, that it is in the conscious participation in what he terms 'the practice of Europeanism' (7), as an always evolving project of making and re-making something called 'Europe', that we can locate 'Europe' – wherever such practice (and its practitioners) may be located. To underline his point, Bauman cites Jorge Luis Borges, as 'one of the most eminent among the great Europeans in every except the geographical sense', who 'wrote of the 'perplexity' that cannot but arise whenever the 'absurd accidentality' of an identity tied down to a particular space and time is pondered, and so its closeness to a fiction rather than to anything we think of as 'reality' is inevitably revealed. This may well be a universal feature of all identities [...] but in the case of 'European identity' that feature, that 'absurd accidentality', is perhaps more blatant and perplexing than most' (5).

---

2   For a fuller discussion, see Bialasiewicz 2012.
3   Baumann 2004, 7. Further page references in the text.

The example of Borges may highlight, as Bauman suggests, the 'absurd accidentality' of European identity and its extensions across the world. But we need to also consider such extensions as part of a wider (again, both geographically and historically) project not just of making Europe and Europeans, but of also re-making the world 'as Europe'. Citing Polish philosopher and historian Krzysztof Pomian Bauman reminds us that Europe was

> the sole social entity that in addition to being a civilisation also called itself 'civilisation' and looked at itself as civilisation, that is as a product of choice, design and management – thereby recasting the totality of things, including itself, as an in-principle-unfinished object, an object of scrutiny, critique, and possibly remedial action. In its European rendition, 'civilisation' (or 'culture') [...] is a continuous process – forever imperfect yet obstinately struggling for perfection – of remaking the world. (7–8)

Bauman is not the first to have remarked on this aspect of 'European identity' or 'culture'. His argument draws heavily on Heidegger's distinction between the (taken-for-granted) realm of the zuhanden and that of the 'brightly lit stage of the vorhanden (that is, the realm of things that [...] need to be watched, handled [...] moulded, made different than they are)'. It is here that we can locate 'Europe's discovery of culture' – a culture that is self-aware, and that demands action: 'the world as zuhanden forbids standing still; it is a standing invitation, even a command, to act'. It is, Bauman suggests (9), precisely this 'discovery of culture as an activity performed by humans on the human world' that makes Europe unique: 'the discovery [awareness] that all things human are human-made' (emphasis in original); 'an incessant activity of [...] making of the world an object of critical inquiry and creative action' (11). But 'it was not just culture that happened to be Europe's discovery/invention. Europe also invented the need and the task of culturing culture. [Europe] made culture itself the object of culture ... the human mode of being-in-the-world itself was recast [...] as a problem to be tackled. Culture – the very process of the production of the human world – was [thus itself] made into an object of human theoretical and practical critique and of subsequent cultivation' (11).[4]

What does this mean? Bauman suggests that 'the outcome is that we, the Europeans, are perhaps the sole people who (as historical subjects and actors of culture) have no identity – fixed identity, or an identity deemed and believed to be fixed: 'we do not know who we are', and even less do we know what we

---

4 For further discussion of the 'self-awareness' of 'European culture', see the sections by Cacciari and De Vitiis in Alici & Totaro 2006, 21–34 and 189–204.

can yet become and what we can yet learn that we are. The urge to know and/ or to become what we are never subsides, and neither is the suspicion ever dispelled about what we may yet become following that urge. Europe's culture is one that knows no rest; it is a culture that feeds on questioning the order of things – and on questioning the fact of questioning it' (12). And such an aware, self-conscious and self-constituting identity is indeed very different from national-territorial 'cultures'/identities:

> another kind of culture, a silent culture, a culture un-aware of being a culture, a culture that keeps the knowledge of being a culture a secret, a culture working anonymously or under an assumed name, a culture stoutly denying its human origins and hiding behind the majestic edifice of a divine decree and heavenly tribunal, or signing an unconditional surrender to intractable and inscrutable 'laws of history' [...] (12)

The 'self-awareness', the self-doubting that characterizes European cultural identity, according to Bauman, has most recently been ascribed as a distinguishing marker also of Europe's geopolitical identity, as a number of prominent commentators have suggested over the past two decades. In the section that follows, I will briefly review some of their arguments, before moving on to a consideration of Europe's current geopolitical moment and persona.

3   A Doubting Actor?

Although political as well as scholarly reflection on Europe's possible geopolitical role is quite recent, the European integration project has had an external component seeking to promote a collective European role in the world since its very inception. The signing of the Treaty of Rome in 1957 established the European Development Fund (EDF) as a first common framework towards what were then mostly colonies and former colonies of European countries. The first explicit geopolitical visions for Europe started to emerge in the late 1960s and early 1970s, with the most prominent, in many ways, being François Duchêne's vision (1972, 1973) of Europe as a global 'civilian power'. Duchêne (much like Bauman) described 'Europe as a process' whose goal was to 'domesticate relations between states, including those of its own members and those with states outside its frontiers' (Duchêne 1973, 19–20). This 'domestication of international relations' referred to the transfer of 'the interior level of civilianized structures [of domestic policy conduct] to the international system' (Kirste & Maull 1996). Based on the goal of creating an interdependent area of peace and prosperity, Duchêne observed and advocated an international system of regulated interactions centred around institution-building, multilateralism and supranational integration, democracy, human rights and the restriction of the use of force in international politics.

Duchêne's ideas have since served as a key point of reference for a range of geopolitical visions of global 'EU'rope (cf. Bachmann & Sidaway 2009; Manners 2010). Many such visions calling upon an integrated Europe to play a leading role in world politics tend to forget, nevertheless, Europe's imperial history as the 'most civilized and best governed of all the world regions', as Bassin (1991) has argued and therefore with the innate right to 'teach' its model of political and economic organization to the rest of the world. Indeed, as Hooper and Kramsch have suggested, to those viewing the European project 'from the outside', 'EU'rope often appears

> oddly un-reflexive about its own imperialisms, past and present [...] The result is a geopolitical analysis which not only precludes recognition of the spatiotemporal complexities of empire, but masks Europe's current complicity in the production of exploitative and oppressive relations within as well as beyond its newly minted frontiers. (Hooper & Kramsch 2007, 527)

The lack of self-reflection remarked upon by Hooper and Kramsch has, indeed, been confirmed in various empirical studies of perceptions of the EU's 'actorness' abroad: in a wide-ranging research project on 'The External Image of the EU', Lucarelli and Fioramonti examined external perceptions of the EU, finding that the EU's role towards developing countries was, more often than not, criticized for 'double standards, protectionism and the vigorous pursuit of European economic interests' (Fioramonti & Poletti 2008; also, Lucarelli & Manners 2006).

This stands in stark contrast to the EU's self-representation as a 'helping hand' for the Global South (European Commission 2007). At the same time, Lucarelli and Fioramonti's research also revealed, however, positive perceptions of the EU with respect to its model of political-economic organization and its commitment to 'civilian' standards in international policy conduct, albeit its influence in this realm was generally regarded as limited.

Such apparent disjuncture between the appeal of the EU's 'geopolitical model' and concurrent resentment towards its 'geo-economic power' has been also noted by more recent studies of external perceptions of the EU's role (cf. Bachmann & Müller 2015). This is particularly visible in the EU's extended 'Neighbourhoods', South as well as East. I have written extensively elsewhere on the geopolitics of the European Neighbourhood Policy (Bialasiewicz 2009; Bialasiewicz, Giaccaria & Minca 2013), noting how the ENP from its outset has been framed around what Tassinari (2005) has termed 'the EU's political and ethical *mission civilisatrice*' (or, more recently, that which Dimitrovova and Kramsch refer to as the EU's 'universalization mission', deployed through the rule of norms and standards in its postcolonial spaces of action).[5] The EU's image as a normative and civil power and as a 'force for good' in international affairs, has also been (as was noted in the introduction) profoundly tarnished by its increasingly violent policies of border and migration 'management'. Romano Prodi's hopeful characterization of the nascent European Neighbourhood space in the far-off 2003 as a 'ring of friends' has now been re-christened as the 'ring of fire', as The Economist termed it in the summer of 2015. The EU's Neighbourhood is no longer envisioned in policy-speak as 'a space of opportunity' (whether for economic integration or, in more optimistic times, for the advancement of norms and values), but rather as a space of dangers to be contained, and whose possible 'spill-over' to EU shores and territory must be prevented at all costs.[6]

It would be difficult to conceive today of the EU's geopolitics in 'hopeful' or 'aspirational' terms. It is thus useful to cast our gaze back slightly over a decade, to the early 2000s, when a prominent number of leading European intellectuals imagined – hoped? – precisely such a role for the EU. It was indeed the 2003 invasion of Iraq and the ensuing 'war on terror' that served as a key Euro-organizing moment, certainly in the geopolitical arena. The Iraq war, on the one hand, unleashed a symbolic assault on the EU by U.S. neo-conservatives (but also European neo-populists), deriding the ambiguity and weakness of the European role in the international arena, depicting a cowering, doubtful (and highly feminized) Europe, lacking a clear sense of strategic purpose and geopolitical identity (Elden & Bialasiewicz 2006; Bialasiewicz & Minca 2005). But it was also the war that provided the occasion for some of the most original and wide-ranging initiatives aimed at re-imagining Europe's political role.

As a number of prominent commentators (from Etienne Balibar and Tzvetan Todorov to Jacques Derrida and Jürgen Habermas) argued on the eve of the invasion in early 2003, the war provided an important Euro-organising 'opening' for two key reasons. First, they suggested, what the mass protests against the war made evident (beyond the sheer strength of feeling) was the crystallization, for the first time, of a European public opinion: the emergence,

---

5 Dimitrovova & Kramsch 2017. See also Del Sarto 2016.
6 For a fuller discussion of some of the geopolitical visions justifying the securitization of the Neighbourhood, see Bialasiewicz & Maessen 2018.

in practice, of 'a common European public sphere' (to cite Habermas' assessment of the events). At the same time, the European reaction against the war was also seen as a strong stand against the US role in the Middle East and thus the emergence – here, too, for the first time - of an alternative vision and geopolitical role for Europe. That role was not uncontested, also among EU states, for the war quickly revealed fundamental breaks within the European whole. The most important was the divide that made itself apparent between a significant part of the public opinion in the countries of the EU15, and popular feelings within the 'New European' in Eastern and Central Europe (to use Donald Rumsfeld's infamous characterisation), where an important majority proclaimed themselves much closer to the American position than the 'Old European' one. Three Eastern and Central European states – the Czech Republic, Hungary and Poland – were among the signatories of the famous 'United We Stand Letter of Eight', pledging to support the American war effort.

The characterization of the divide by then-U.S. Secretary of Defence Rumsfeld as that between a 'New Europe' (largely corresponding to the Eastern and Central European states, together with Britain, Denmark, Italy, Portugal, and Spain), willing to share the American burden and rise to the challenge of the war and an 'Old Europe' (most markedly, France and Germany), cowardly, doubting and weak in its convictions, may have been overly simplistic, but it did capture a fundamental break in the European family, and a very different set of attitudes towards the War on Terror. It is a divide that has persisted in the years that followed, marking not only divergent geopolitical understandings (and behaviours) on the part of some of the new EU member states, but also highlighting divergent national understandings of what Europe was – and what it was for. The ideal vision of Europe as 'a special area of human hope' evoked by the Constitutional Convention – a space where certain rights and values were assured to one and all – clearly did not mean the same thing across the now 25-member strong EU.

We could say that, in this sense, broader geopolitical shifts simply allowed to come to the surface existing differences within the Union. At the same time, however, the 'geopolitical vertigo' opened up by the War on Terror made all Europeans crucially aware of the need to define Europe's geopolitical identity and its world role in much clearer terms. In their widely diffused intervention on the eve of the invasion of Iraq, Jurgen Habermas and Jacques Derrida argued that Europe could only define itself by defining and defending a European model

> that transcended the boundaries of Europe: a cosmopolitical order based on the recognition and protection of certain basic rights and the

principles of international law [...] being European should also mean rejecting certain practices, certain violations wherever they occur.[7]

Habermas's and Derrida's appeal hinted at a radically new conception of Europe's geopolitical identity, one that was 'future oriented [...] defined by setting off towards the new, rather than pointing towards a perfect past'. The (successful) transcendence of its national past had made Europe, the authors argued, a 'unique geopolitical subject, a unique polity of the future'.

Another important voice in the 2003 debates on re-thinking the European geopolitical subject was French political philosopher Etienne Balibar. In his book *L'Europe, L'Amerique, La Guerre* Balibar suggested that Europe must reject the essentialized geopolitical identities and civilisational divides inscribed by the War on Terror and reclaim, rather, its role as what he termed an 'evanescent mediator'. It was the role already ascribed to it by many outside of Europe, Balibar argued; those who saw in Europe the only possible alternative to American hegemony and the discourse of a putative 'clash of civilizations'. Indeed, he suggested that in constituting itself as a new political subject, Europe should reflect, first of all, upon the 'play of 'illusions and mirrors' within which it is imagined by others – and imagines itself within others' gaze' (Balibar 2003, 22). As a geopolitical actor, Europe could only be a 'mediator', Balibar noted, because there is no (and there cannot be) a singular European identity that can be delimited, distinguished in essential fashion from other identities. This is because there are no absolute borders between a historically and culturally-constituted European space and the spaces that surround it. Just as there are no absolute confines to those values, beliefs and traditions that make up a 'European inheritance': these, he argued, are present to various degrees, and in various 'reflections', throughout the world. The question for the European Union, then, should then be not one of tracing the contours of a European identity, but rather that of 'recognizing Europe wherever it occurs'.

Such an understanding of Europe has important consequences: it necessarily privileges, Balibar argued, practice over a singular identity; the deployment of 'European ideas' and 'European ways of doing', rather than any fixed 'European identity' (very much echoing Bauman's characterization cited above). Balibar's ideas found close resonance in the work of a number of other authors around the very same time. Tzvetan Todorov's notion of Europe as a '*puissance tranquille*', for example, similarly invoked the European geopolitical subject

---

7   Habermas/Derrida's original contribution appeared jointly in the German *Frankfurter Allgemeine Zeitung* and the French *Liberation* on 31 May 2003 and was subsequently translated and re-printed in a number of other major European newspapers.

as 'an evolving, becoming order, not prescribable, but existing in practice' (Todorov 2003, 42). The call to Europe to become a 'different' geopolitical model was, nonetheless, most clearly articulated in the work of Jacques Derrida (cf. Bialasiewicz 2012). In one of his final public addresses, in May 2004, Derrida made an impassioned plea for 'a Europe that can show that another politics is possible, that can imagine a political and ethical reflection that is heir to the Enlightenment tradition, but that can also be the portent of a new Enlightenment, able to challenge binary distinctions and high moral pronouncements'. In the address (entitled 'A Europe of Hope', subsequently re-printed in a number of European newspapers) Derrida summoned his audience to 'imagine a different Europe':

> I believe that it is without Eurocentric illusions or pretensions, without a trace of European nationalism, indeed without even an excess of confidence in Europe as it now is (or appears in the process of becoming), that we must fight for what this name represents today, with the memory of the Enlightenment, to be sure, but also with the full awareness – and full admission – of the totalitarian, genocidal and colonialist crimes of the past. We must fight for what is irreplaceable within Europe in the world to come so that it might become more than just a single market or single currency, more than a neo-nationalist conglomerate, more than a new military power. (Derrida 2004)

What was 'irreplaceable' within Europe, in Derrida's words, was precisely its ability to transform itself – and the world; here lay Europe's 'exemplarity'. Writing in *L'autre cap* (published in 1991 and translated into English as 'The Other Heading: Reflections on Today's Europe'), Derrida described how this 'exemplarity' brought with it also a host of ethico-political responsibilities: responsibilities to that 'which has been promised under the name Europe', but also the duty to open up this legacy to 'what never was, and never will be Europe' (Derrida 1991, 76–80).

The temporal dimension is of vital importance here. Elaborating his ideas further in 1993 in *Spectres of Marx: The State of the Debt, the Work of Mourning and the New International*, Derrida suggested that any 'politics of responsibility' must extend also to the past and future. Justice is due not just to today's living, he claimed, but also to the dead – the victims of war, violence, extermination, oppression, imperialism, totalitarianism – and to the not-yet-born. Derrida's reflections on responsibility and justice were articulated through the figure of the 'spectre'. In Derrida's understanding, spectres are both those he termed *revenants* (those who return), and *arrivants* (those still to come).

The present, he suggested, is unsettled as much by the return of the past as by the imminence of the future. Both temporal dimensions are integral part of what Derrida termed 'spectrality', encompassing at once that which is no longer and that which is not-yet-present: as he put it, 'the non-contemporaneity with itself of the living present' (Derrida 1994, xix). In Derrida's formulation, the present 'is never free of vestiges of the past and stirrings of the future but rather constantly filtered through the structures of memory and anticipation'.[8] According to Derrida, the belief in the impermeable solidity (and contemporaneity) of the present has always been key to totalitarian ideologies: every regime would like to eternalise its present in order to rule out the possibility of its future disintegration and to erase the barbarity from which it sprang. Such regimes, he argued, fear spectres.

In his attempt to sketch an alternative, 'exemplary', politics for Europe, Derrida (2004) thus invoked an ethico-political engagement with both past and future; with both 'memory and anticipation'. His call for 'what is irreplaceable in Europe in the world to come' thus appealed both to notions of Europe's unique 'inheritance' and its 'promise' (or hope). For Derrida, what can be inherited from any sort of 'European legacy' is only its promise: that which it defers, that which it postpones – and thus bequeaths to the future (Derrida 1994, 54). Indeed, the 'Europe to come' that Derrida calls upon is what he considers a 'paleonym': 'for what we remember – and for what we promise'. This, he argues, in no way weakens Europe's political/ethical potential: quite the contrary. It is only in its 'promise', in that which he terms 'the realm of im-possibility', that Europe's responsibility can be exercised (*ibid.*).

It is interesting that Derrida's call has been taken up by theorists in sketching out the actual spaces of Europe's political and geopolitical responsibility. In particular, juridical experts have emphasized the unique malleability of the European space of rights – and the political and geopolitical effects this carries. Scholars of international law such as Emmanuel Decaux have noted, for instance, that the 'exemplarity' (to borrow Derrida's term) of the EU space of rights comes from the fact that it allows (at least potentially) for claims to its law to come from and extend to also 'non-European' spaces and subjects Decaux 2004). Within the EU treaties, the safe-guarding of certain rights and values is opened up also to those not currently residing in the present territory of the Union; it is available (in potentia) to all those who call upon 'Europe's promise'; it extends also to the not-yet, im-possible Europeans (as various recent rulings of the European Court of Human Rights have highlighted).

---

8   See the discussion in Benjamin & Chang 2009 61; also, Silvano Petrosino, 'Scrivere 'Europa' con una mano sola: Derrida e l'anticipazione', in Alici & Totaro 2006, 206–17.

3 Europe's Future Promise

How do we place today's appeals to Europe in this context? How should we understand the seemingly im-possible hopes of those claiming physical or ideational access to Europe's space of rights? The calls of crowds massing in city streets for 'Europe to do something' that resonated in Kiev in 2014, in Istanbul in 2015, in Skopje in 2016, and most recently on the streets of two EU Member States, in Hungary and in Poland in the spring and summer of 2017 cannot be reduced to a naïve blue-flag waving optimism that simply fails to recognize the hard realities of geopolitics. So too the hopes of those willing to risk their lives to enter Europe seeking a better life. The glaring mis-match between what Europe should be and what it turns out to be does not appear to matter to those laying claims to its promise.

As countless observers have noted, historically Europe has always exceeded itself. It has done so most evidently in its imperial and colonial adventures and attempts to remake the world in its image (as a number of chapters in this volume highlight). But Europe has 'spilled over' itself in other ways as well, territorially as well as ideally. Across centuries, Europeans thrust out of Europe by wars or persecution were some of the most fervent believers in the European ideal. Indeed, many of those fleeing the horrors of the real Europe often attempted to make 'better Europes' elsewhere. It is vitally important to recall these histories of the loss and re-making of Europe today. Most directly and banally, because they are a reminder of the fact that many of us, Europeans, were also once migrants (even if only 'internal' exiles – as was the case of those torn from Europe by the Iron Curtain). But it is also important to recall these histories in order to understand how hope for Europe can serve as a powerful mobilizing force – and a powerful political and geopolitical ideal.

Today, the mobilizing potential of such hope-ful (geo)politics makes itself visible at less-than obvious instances and locations. One such instance were the rather muted celebrations marking the 60 years of the Treaty of Rome in March 2017: an event interpreted by most popular commentators as anything but a celebration of the achievements of the European Union, and rather a ridiculously-securitized and highly institutionalized performance piece, with EU leaders 'going through the motions' while Europe burns. And yet the fact that the event generated at least 5 different demonstrations and counter-demonstrations meant that for the thousands of European who travelled to Rome that week, the European project mattered: whether blamed as the root cause of all social, political and economic ills afflicting the continent (by the different Eurosceptic and 'sovereignist' movements that took to the streets in those days), or seen as entirely 'too little European' (by groups such as the Young Federalists that projected their desiderata for Europe in a light show on the walls of the Colosseum). For whatever little actually took place in the formal gatherings marking the occasion, shifting ones' gaze to their peripheries, to the streets and to the countless meetings taking place across the city, fundamental debates were taking place about what Europe was and what it should be – and especially what should be its purpose in today's world.

The curious turn of argument that emerged from the Rome discussions, however, was the suggestion, repeated by both institutional figures as well as activists, that it was precisely in this moment of internal crisis that an external 'mission' and common external action could provide the European project with the needed renewed purpose to also bolster legitimacy at home. For someone like myself following the emergence and evolution of the EU's geopolitical persona, this was particularly interesting because thus far internal discord regarding foreign policy priorities and directions was always seen as a block to coherent external action. Reversing the equation – that is, aiming to invoke a common external purpose to weave a harmony of 'internal' objectives – was thus a striking shift (cf. European Commission 2017).

One of the affirmations that most powerfully resonated from those days of debates was former Italian prime-minister Enrico Letta's call that 'we need to see the EU with the eyes of the world'. Letta has long been one of the Italian centre-left's most enthusiastic Europeanists, so his appeal was not particularly surprising. Yet in many ways it reflected a wider European 'structure of feeling' (to abuse Jacques Derrida's term) emerging over the past couple of years regarding 'Europe's promise'; a hope and wish articulated most forcefully, indeed, by those outside of European institutions, and outside of Europe.[9]

Two such external figures that had recently attempted to remind Europeans of their role and responsibilities to both to those within and beyond the EU's borders were former President Barack Obama and Pope Francis. Obama's Hannover 'Address to the People of Europe' in late April 2016 received significant media and political attention in its call for 'Europe not to doubt itself'. It would be easy to dismiss Obama's invocation in that moment as simply a geopolitical gesture in support of key EU allies. Nevertheless, it is important to note both the geographical and historical imaginations underpinning his call to 'the people of Europe not to forget who you are' in this moment of 'crisis':

> I am confident that the forces that bind Europe together are ultimately much stronger than those trying to pull you apart. But hope is not blind

---

9   The leading Italian political philosopher Roberto Esposito argues that it is only 'Europe's task in the global world' that can provide its necessary political 'energy' (Esposito 2016).

when it is rooted in the memory of all that you've already overcome – your parents, your grandparents. So I say to you, the people of Europe, don't forget who you are. [...] You are Europe – 'United in diversity'. Guided by the ideals that have lit the world, and stronger when you stand as one. [...] Because a united Europe – once the dream of a few – remains the hope of the many and a necessity for us all. (Obama 2016)

The second case was even more striking and came in May of 2016, on the occasion of the ceremonial award to Pope Francis of the Charlemagne Prize, a prize awarded 'for work done in the service of European unification'. Flanked by Jean-Claude Juncker, Martin Schultz and Donald Tusk and a number of EU heads of state, Pope Francis delivered an impassioned address calling for 'rebirth and renewal of the soul of Europe', and invoking the assembled leaders to remember Europe's founding purpose, 'a Europe that promotes and protects the rights of everyone, without neglecting its duties towards all'. In their speech at the award ceremony, Juncker and Schultz ironized that the EU must really seem in trouble if it has to look for guidance from the Pope in this moment of crisis of the 'European spirit'. The ironies of papal intervention aside, however, what was most striking about the Pope's speech was, as in Obama's address, the call for Europe to reclaim its purpose through a strengthened role in the world.

The EU Global Strategy (EUGS) published in the summer of 2016, has attempted to give formal shape, for the very first time, to the Union's geopolitical vision and persona. As described in its Foreword by High Representative Federica Mogherini:

> A fragile world calls for a more confident and responsible European Union, it calls for an outward- and forward-looking European foreign and security policy. This Global Strategy will guide us in our daily work towards a Union that truly meets in citizens' needs, hopes and aspirations; a Union that builds on the success of 70 years of peace; a Union with the strength to contribute to peace and security in our region and in the whole world. (European Commission 2016, 5)

As doubtful as many commentators have been of the EUGS's actual capacity to shape a single and coherent EU foreign policy (cf. Panke 2019), it is important regardless to recognize how such hope-ful geopolitical scripts can (and do) exert real geopolitical effects. The active role played by the EU in its Neighbourhoods, both as an economic but even more importantly as a 'stabilizing and securitizing force' may, in aspiration at least (as the EUGS purports) be 'guided by the values on which the EU is founded'. Nevertheless, such a framing of Europe's role risks 'simultaneously internalising and occluding prior visions of Europe and European world roles', as Bachman and Sidaway (2009, 105) argued some time ago. In imagining itself as an aspirational model for the world, today's Europe must respond to the hopes of those seeking it, but without (yet again) attempting to remake the world in its image.

Works Cited

Alici, Luigi & Francesco Totaro, eds. 2016. *Filosofi per l'Europa: Differenze in Dialogo* (Macerata: EUM).

Bachmann, Veit & Martin Müller, eds. 2015. *Perceptions of the EU in Eastern Europe and Sub-Saharan Africa: looking from the outside in* (Basingstoke: Palgrave).

Bachmann, Veit & James Sidaway. 2009. 'Zivilmacht Europa: A critical geopolitics of the European Union as a global power', *Transactions of the Institute of British Geographers* 34: 94–109.

Balibar, Etienne. 2003. *L'Europe, l'Amérique, la Guerre* (Paris: La Découverte).

Bassin, Mark. 1991. 'Russia between Europe and Asia: The ideological construction of geographical space', *Slavic Review* 50: 1–17.

Bauman, Zygmunt. 2004. *Europe, An Unfinished Adventure* (Cambridge: Polity Press).

Benjamin, Ross, & Heesok Chang. 2009. 'Jacques Derrida, The Last European', in Andrew Davidson and Himadeep Muppidi (eds.), *Europe and Its Boundaries: Words and Worlds, within and beyond* (Lanham, MD: Lexington Books).

Bialasiewicz, Luiza. 2009. 'The new political geographies of the European neighbourhood', *Political Geography* 28: 79–89.

Bialasiewicz, Luiza. 2012. 'Spectres of Europe: Europes past, present, and future'. In D. Stone (ed) *The Oxford Handbook of Post-War European History* (Oxford: Oxford University Press), 98–119.

Bialasiewicz, Luiza, Stuart Elden & Joe Painter. 2005. 'The Constitution of EU Territory', *Comparative European Politics* 3:333–363.

Bialasiewicz, Luiza, Paolo Giaccaria & Claudio Minca. 2013. 'Re-scaling 'EU'rope: EU Macro-regional Fantasies in the Mediterranean', *European Urban and Regional Studies* 20.1:59–76.

Bialasiewicz, Luiza & Enno Maessen, 'Scaling Rights: The Turkey "Deal" and the Divided Geographies of European Responsibility', *Patterns of Prejudice* 52.2/3:210–230.

Bialasiewicz, Luiza & Claudio Minca. 2005. 'Old Europe, New Europe: for a geopolitics of translation', *Area* 37.4: 365–372.

Cacciari, Massimo. 1994. *Geofilosofia dell'Europa* (Milan: Adelphi).

Cacciari, Massimo. 2006. 'Europa o filosofia', in Alici & Totaro, 21–33.

Decaux, Emmanuel. 2004. 'Valeurs démocratiques communes et divergences culturelles', *Questions internationales* 9: 32–5.
Del Sarto, Raffaella. 2016. 'Normative Empire Europe: The European Union, its borderlands and the 'Arab Spring'. *Journal of Common Market Studies* 54.):215–232.
Derrida, Jacques. 1991. *L'autre cap* (Paris: Minuit).
Derrida, Jacques. 1994. *Spectres of Marx: The State of the Debt, the Work of Mourning and the New International* (New York: Routledge).
Derrida, Jacques. 2004. 'Une Europe de l'espoir', *Le Monde Diplomatique* (3 November).
Derrida, Jacques, 2010 [1987]. *Heidegger et la question de l'esprit et autres essais* (Paris: Flammarion).
Dimitrovova, Bohdana & Olivier Kramsch. 2017. 'Decolonizing the spaces of European foreign policy: Views from the Maghreb', *Interventions* 19.6:797–817.
Duchêne, François. 1972. 'Europe's role in world peace', in *Europe Tomorrow: Sixteen Europeans Look Ahead*, ed. R. Mayne (London: Fontana/Collins), 32–47.
Duchêne, François. 1973. 'The European Community and the uncertainties of interdependence', in *A Nation Writ Large? Foreign Policy Problems Before the European Community*, ed. M. Kohnstamm & W. Hager (Basingstoke: Macmillan), 1–21.
Elden, Stuart & Luiza Bialasiewicz. 2006. 'The New Geopolitics of Division and the Problem of a Kantian Europe', *Review of International Studies* 32: 623–644.
Esposito, Roberto. 2016. *Da Fuori: Una filosofia per l'Europa* (Turin: Einaudi).
European Commission. 2007. *The EU in the World: The Foreign Policy of the European Union* (Luxembourg: Office for Official Publications of the European Communities).
European Commission. 2016. 'Shared Vision, Common Action: A Stronger Europe. A Global Strategy for the European Union's Foreign and Security Policy'. https://eeas.europa.eu/sites/eeas/files/eugs_review_web_0.pdf
European Commission. 2017. *Jean Monnet Seminar 'The Future of Europe: A Commitment for You(th)', Rome, 23–24 March 2017* (Brussels: European Commission, Directorate-General for Education, Youth, Sport and Culture).
Fioramonti, Lorenzo & Arlo Poletti. 2008. 'Facing the Giant: Southern Perspectives on the European Union', *Third World Quarterly* 29: 167–180.
Habermas, Jürgen. 1998. *Die Postnationale Konstellation* (Frankfurt /Main: Suhrkamp).
Habermas, Jürgen. 2001. 'Why Europe needs a constitution', *New Left Review* 11: 5–26.
Hooper, Barbara & Olivier Kramsch, 'Post-Colonising Europe: The Geopolitics of Globalisation, Empire and Borders: Here and There, Now and Then', *Tijdschrift voor Economische en Sociale Geografie* 98: 526–534.
Knut Kirste, Knut & Hanns Maull. 1996. 'Zivilmacht und Rollentheorie', *Zeitschrift fur Internationale Beziehungen* 3:283–312.
Lucarelli, Sonia & Lorenzo Fioramonti. 2009. *External Perceptions of the European Union as a Global Actor.* (Abingdon: Routledge).

Lucarelli, Sonia & Ian Manners, eds. 2006. *Values and Principles in European Union Foreign Policy* (Abingdon: Routledge)

Manners, Ian. 2010. 'Global Europa: Mythology of the European Union in world politics', *Journal of Common Market Studies* 48: 67–87.

Obama, Barack. 2016. 'Remarks by President Obama in Address to the People of Europe', https://obamawhitehouse.archives.gov/the-press-office/2016/04/25/

Panke, Julian. 2019. 'Liberal Empire, Geopolitics and EU Strategy: Norms and Interests in European Foreign Policy Making', *Geopolitics* 24.1:100–123.

Tassinari, Fabrizio. 2005. 'Security and Integration in the European Neighbourhood: The Case for Regionalism'. *CEPS Working Document* 226 (Brussels: Centre for European Policy Studies).

Zambrano, Maria. 2000 [1942]. *La agonia de Europa* (Madrid: Editorial Trotta).

PART 2

Crisscrossing Projections

∴

CHAPTER 5

Eurotypes after Eurocentrism: Mixed Feelings in an Uncomfortable World

Joep Leerssen

> Marbles of the dancing floor
> Break bitter furies of complexity,
> Those images that yet
> Fresh images beget,
> That dolphin-torn, that gong-tormented sea.
> W.B. YEATS, *Byzantium*, 1932

∴

> Don't be so gloomy. After all it's not that awful. Like the fella says, in Italy for 30 years under the Borgias they had warfare, terror, murder, and bloodshed, but they produced Michelangelo, Leonardo da Vinci, and the Renaissance. In Switzerland they had brotherly love – they had 500 years of democracy and peace, and what did that produce? The cuckoo clock. So long Holly.
> GRAHAM GREENE/ORSON WELLES, dialogue for *The Third Man*, 1949

∴

1   Eurotypes in Cultural Awareness and Archival Memory

Imagology,[1] the analysis of ethnotypes (ethnic stereotypes characterizing 'nations'), is based on the key insight that such characterizations are always articulated in a discourse of contrast, even if that contrast is elided or left implicit. To observe that the French are frivolous or that the English have a

---

1   On the theory and method of imagology, generally Dyserinck 2015 and Leerssen 2016. This article relies thorughout on the handbook Beller & Leerssen 2007 and on the materials, both theoretical and critical, collected on the website www.imagologica.eu.

stiff upper lip, means, implicitly or explicitly, to observe how such an attribute renders them different from the non-French or non-English. Nations are most characteristically themselves (so the assumption goes) in precisely those aspects in which they are most markedly different from other nations. For imagologists, this means that our analysis of ethnotypes will always involve an unpacking of the implied contradistinctions, and to establish what Others are used as a background against which the reputed 'character' or 'identity' (ethnotype) of a nation is silhouetted. Any notion of national identity invokes, overtly or silently, a discourse of differentiation, particularism or exceptionalism.

What does that mean if we want to tackle the vexed question of what constitutes a European 'identity', or even a characteristically 'European' position in the world? The topic has attracted inordinate amounts of commentary, hundreds of books and essays. Most of these begin with admissions of the impossibility of defining Europe; many of them then go on to address Europe as a aggregation of inner contrasts and diversities, usually labeled by nationality and themselves left unquestioned. Imagologists, however, would for a first reflex inquire into the implied contrast-frame: a 'European identity' as opposed to what, precisely? As opposed to America, or Asia, or Africa? The resulting European ethnotype (which I shall henceforth call 'Eurotype') would take on very different characteristics in each of these contrast-frames: Europe-as-opposed-to-America would be a continent of ironies, characterized by weary, disenchanted refinement, by a combination of high culture and great bloodshed, by a 'negative capability' of living in mixed feelings; all this (think *The Third Man*) as opposed to American vigour, simplistic moralism, brashness and energetic naiveté. Europe as opposed to Asia evokes connotations of historical development and a rationally-based civil society as opposed to the unchanging persistence of pre-civic traditionalism, a disregard for 'Western' rationalism and a propensity towards mystic trans-rationalism; or else 'Oriental Despotism' and collectivism (a continent of milling crowds). Europe as opposed to Africa evokes different ethnotypical frames again, this time more obviously colonialist: Europe as characterized by a self-disciplining social order and technical advancement vs. the brute or brutalizing forces of nature. And so 'Europe' can be framed, from case to case, as the continent of mixed feelings, civil society and social order; of Rembrandt and Captain Cook, Auschwitz and Chartres; scientific achievement and enervated decline; Augustine, Erasmus, Torquemada, Tolstoy, Mussolini and Derrida.[2]

---

[2] Summaries here and in the following pages of existing images of Europe and its Others rely on Beller & Leerssen 2007 and Leerssen 2015.

2 Selves and Others, Auto- and Hetero-images, as a Diachronic Accumulation

This remarkable array of contradictory characterizations is the result of the fact that Europe has over the course of the centuries been contrasted with so many different 'Others'. In the process, the discourse of silhouetting Europe has been so long-lived in its historical accumulation that it has left sediments and traces from different situations and different periods in Europe's archival memory, available for reactivation at any moment. I take the term 'archival memory' from Aleida Assmann's notion of *Speichergedächtnis* (as opposed to *Funktionsgedächtnis*, Assmann 1999). While active recall is current and present in society's *Funktionsgedächtnis*, the *Speichergedächtnis* contains older memories that are inert, without active or noticeable social presence, yet available for retrieval from the sedimented traces they have left in the documentary record. This conceptual distinction is highly apposite and useful for imagologists, who will often notice how certain commonplaces slowly oscillate between salience and latency, move in and out of active usage, re-emerge (after a period of social and cultural latency) from the *Speichergedächtnis* into which they may at some later point sink back. Old stereotypes, like outdated ideologies or world-views, never wholly disappear; they just go 'on standby', become inert, latent, and are suspended in an ontological limbo zone, in unread texts forgotten until further notice.[3]

The multiplicity of Europe's Others means that Eurotypes can be aligned, almost at will as the situation might require, in various ways. There is a Christendom/paganism axis, operative since the rise of Islam; a civilization-wilderness axis, operative since the colonial voyages of exploration, a North-South axis operative since the rise of climate theories, mercantilism and anti-absolutism. We are, then, at the receiving end of a layered sedimentation of successively accumulated paradigms in the self/other-characterization of Europe.

Most Eurotypes were, and remain, Eurocentric in one way or another. Throughout literary history, Europe has always had control over the means of its representation: the terms in which Europe was opposed to its Others were autonomously defined by Europeans. That luxury was not available to subaltern groups. However, in the present-day *crise de la conscience européenne*, Eurocentrism has lost its unargued, aprioristical status; and our understanding

---

3   Karl Popper's notion of a 'world-3' to describe an ontological status between the physical ontology of material objects (e.g. the Eifel Tower) and the ideational ontology of mental concepts (e.g. the value of π), is useful to conceptialize the ontology of archival memory (Popper 1978).

of Europe's current identity crisis may be improved by a closer investigation of that fact. Europe is being (re-)defined by those who dissociate from it.

At this historical juncture various characterizations and counter-characterizations of Europe are simultaneously present in discursive praxis; while each of these may have been originally formulated at different moments in history, all of them have left their traces and echoes into the present. Every Eurotype now negotiates, at one and the same moment, its shifting back-and-forth transitions between *Speichergedächtnis* and *Funktionsgedächtnis*.

Cultural history, it should be pointed out, does not proceed in the same way as political history or the history of technology. Those latter forms of history one might term 'serially successive': in the diachronic concatenation of causes and effects, events and occurrences, the new replaces the old. What's past is gone, its place taken by something more recent. A reign or government will come to its end and by succeeded by another reign, government or constitutional system; the phlogiston theory of combustion (i.e. how things burn up) has been replaced by that of oxidization; parchment has given way to paper, messenger couriers to mobile phones. What they leave is at best a cultural afterlife: memories, memorabilia.

Cultural history, by contrast, does not abolish the past by rendering it obsolete, but rather adds to it by finding alternatives. Music was innovated by Beethoven, Chopin, Wagner and Schönberg; but none of these abolished the work of precursors as the rule of Ayatollah Khomeini ousted that of Shah Reza Pahlavi in 1979, or rotary-dial telephones were replaced by touch-dial ones. Bach was still performed and listened to after Beethoven, Bach and Beethoven both after Wagner, all of the above are still present and active in musical culture nowadays. [4]

There is, to be sure, a limited bandwidth of what an individual or a society can keep 'on the air': canons are not infinitely elastic,[5] and as the new moves in, some of the old must give way. But the mastery of anatomy and perspective in

---

4   Of course there are variations and exceptions to the rule. Mechanically wound wristwatches maintained a niche market after the rise of battery-powered quartz ones; the sovereignty of Latvia was restored after 60 years of the country's incorporation into the USSR. But such vacillations do not take from the fact that the intermediate changes are of an abolute either/or nature, and shifting from one to the other means a choice against the past as well as a choice for the new. Latvia cannot be both types of country simultaneously, a wristwatch cannot run on a mechanical escape movement and a quartz movement at once. But while my music collection is divided between the incompatible carrier media of vinyl records, CDs and mp3 files, it unproblematically includes Palestrina alongside Miles Davis.
5   This is related to the principle, formulated by Ann Rigney (2005), of 'cultural scarcity', which, in her analysis, explains why the past in not remembered in all its detailed and contradictory variety, but in condensed narrativized form around *lieux de mémoire*.

Renaissance painting did not do away with Cimabue or Giotto. The worst that can befall outmoded culture is to be relegated to the archival part of cultural memory. Culture is a historical accumulation of its past productions, layered sediments and memories, always in a potential transition between functional and archival memory, between latency and salience, suspension and activation. Culture (and ethnotypes) moves through time like a pod of dolphins, now above, then below the waterline, constantly and varyingly weaving and bobbing between submergence and emergence. Seen historically, Europe resembles, to use the Yeatsian phrase, a 'dolphin-torn sea'.

So it is, I would argue, with the multifarious images of Europe, which all of them have their specific moment of origin and their long tails of persistence and aftereffect, each interacting and crisscrossing with the others.[6] In the following pages I offer an imagological attempt to disentangle, as far as possible, the resulting skein.

3 A Succession of Eurotypes: Dialectics, Valorization and Accumulation

[1a] *Europe as Christendom and characterized by Christian virtues, its Other as cruel and licentious.* A very old and long-standing stratum in the European auto-image opposes Europe, as the continent of Christendom, to the world of Islam. The image goes back to the eight-century Battle of Tours and was reinforced, first in the Crusades, then in the 1453 conquest of Constantinople and the 1492 conquest of Granada. By 1500, a religious opposition had become a geopolitical one, with the Pillars of Hercules and the Hellespont turning into Europe's 'natural frontiers'. The Spanish *reconquista* was not pursued beyond Gibraltar; Spanish expansionism instead turned westward, into the Atlantic. After the 1683 Siege of Vienna, Habsburg and (later) Romanov expansionism hardly looked beyond the lodestar of the Dardanelles and the Hagia Sophia. In this geopoliticized, Christian notion of Europe, Islam and the regions where it holds sway were characterized in terms of cruelty and sexual licence, combining harems, eunuchs and Janissaries, with slave-raids taking daughters and sons from their parents. Against this, Christendom is seen as familial, pious rather than fanatical. The abandonment of domestic slavery within

---

6 The stereotypes of Orientalism and Eurocentrism are too familiar to require extensive source-references in the following pages. Generally, see the relevant articles in Beller & Leerssen 2007, as well as the relevant bibliographical materials that can be interactively selected on https://imagologica.eu/bibliography.

late-medieval Europe (not, tellingly, in what would become Europe's colonies) reinforces this contrast.

[1b] *Europe as plain, its Other as refined.* Here as in many long-standing ethnotypes, a sudden, drastic revalorization can occur. As the geopolitical threat of the Ottoman Empire recedes after 1683, some tentative ameliorations of the image of the Islamic world become noticeable; these coincide with the Enlightenment and a more critical attitude towards Christianity (or rather, Catholicism). Montesquieu's *Lettres Persanes* (1721) and Mozart's *Entführung aus dem Serail* (1782) accompany the vogue for the Arabian Nights (following the first version by Galland, 1704–1721) and the first stirrings of Orientalist exoticism. Not that the switch was total: Voltaire's *Mahomet* (1741) still denounces Islam in time-hallowed fashion as fanatical and murderous; but Lessing's *Nathan der Weise* (1779) sees the three Abrahamic religions as a plural identity. In that constellation, Europe is sometimes seen as lacking in refinement, rough-hewn, short-sighted. The romantic contrast between the blunt warlord Richard Lionheart and the high-minded, courteous strategist Saladin (in Walter Scott's *The Talisman*, 1825) announces a revisionist, highly critical view of the Crusades. Following Washington Irving's Romantic *Tales of the Alhambra* (1832), Moorish Spain could be reframed as a tolerant, philosophy-friendly Golden Age – a sharp difference from the traditional image of Christian-enslaving Moorish tyrants; and also a sharp contrast when opposed to the harsh, Inquisition-dominated imagery characterizing absolutist, Catholic Spain. Later in the nineteenth century, philologists begin to speculate that the West-European transition, around 1100–1200, from warrior ethics to courteous chivalry, and the discovery of courtly love, may involve a certain 'cultural transfer' from Oriental sources, be it by way of the Crusader Kingdoms or Moorish Spain.

[1c] This later, Romantic revalorization does not abolish the earlier polarity but compounds it, overlays it. The result is an 'imageme' of the Orient as despotic yet refined, cruel yet enticing. The underlying European auto-image combines contradictory elements such as long-suffering families in enslaved parts of Europe, stalwart chivalric champions like El Cid or Jan Sobieski, the bloody-minded harshness of the Crusaders and the Inquisition.

[2a] *(Western) Europe as individualistic, its Other as despotic and collective.* A slightly later polarity situates Western Europe between the East and the New World. The period of emerges follows the Great Schism (1054) and the twelfth/thirteenth-century rise of the university as an institution of learning. The rise of scholastic philosophy and the later development towards the scientific revolutions is a development that takes place in Western (Catholic) Christendom and meshes with a West-European image as a space where learning is conducted as a progressive, transgenerational and institutionally consolidated enterprise;

this is opposed to an East where civic institutions are weak or non-existent, philosophy is wholly overshadowed and etiolated by theology and religious doctrine and tradition, and where Oriental Despotism has left individuals in a state of passive, docile servility. That image applies both to the Slavic world and to the Ottoman parts of Eastern Europe and the Levant.

In the sixteenth century, the learning of Western Europe is seen as its greatest asset in its colonial expansion. Map-making, navigation and the use of gunpowder furnish an explanatory frame for the domination of overseas territories, from the Americas to the coastlands of sub-Saharan Africa and the Indian ocean. In these theatres, Europe is habitually seen as a superior, technologically and intellectually advanced force vis-à-vis backward and sometimes 'savage' native populations. This Eurocentrism remains a powerful trope practically until the present; it plays through, not only in colonial supremacism but also in an Atlantic opposition which contrasts the age-won experience and wisdom of Europe with the inexperienced naivety of America.

[2b] *The West as bland, its Other as ancient and authentic.* That Eurocentrism is challenged by two powerful counter-images. In the course of the seventeenth century, accounts of Imperial China like those of Matteo Ricci represent that country as a philosophical, well-ordered state with a high standard of civilization, leading to what we may call, following Paul Hazard, the first 'Crisis in the European self-image'. The image of the 'Noble Savage' re-evaluates the simple and non-technological lifestyle of Pacific and American natives in terms of innate morality and unspoilt innocent honesty. Herder's ethnotyping of the Slavic nations, at roughly the same time, praises their meekness and gentle emotionality. These exoticist appreciations also remain powerful tropes until the present. Against them, Europe stands out as a continent caught up in a rigid and artificial over-refinement that risks losing sight of intuitive human morality. Rousseau's and Herder's ethnotypes obviously form part of an Counter-Enlightenment discourse; accordingly, Romanticism is marked by a strong tendency towards a positive, exoticist valorization of Europe's Others.

[2c] *Europe declining in an awakening world.* The stadial view of Europe (as opposed to America) as having an older civilization and possessing, as a result, a greater store of experience (as opposed to American naiveté and innocence) can tip over in an equally stadialist counter-image: Europe as decadent, beyond its prime, morally corrupt and depleted in its vital energies, as opposed to a younger, more energetic and more successful America (or, later on, other emerging industrial countries: Japan, Korea, China...)

[3a] *(Northern) Europe as reasonable and philosophical, its Other as passionate and unreliable.* In the course of the eighteenth century, a new, Romantic image emerges of a Nordic Europe, characterized (over against its Mediterranean

counterpart) by an aesthetics of the Sublime rather than the Beautiful, individualism rather than sociability, a middle class work ethos of work and virtue rather than an aristocratic ethos of status and honor. This North-South bifurcation draws on the propaganda of the Reformation and on old climatological notions of temperament. It revolves around a mercantile, entrepreneurial Europe of stock exchanges and business enterprises requiring civic reliability and a free market. The ethnotype runs all the way from Madame de Staël to Max Weber and beyond, and sees Europeans from Mediterranean climes (Catholic in religion, successors to a declined and fallen Roman Empire, usually speaking a Romance language) as unreliable charmers, superficially glib and elegant but essentially untrustworthy.

[3b] *(Northern) Europe as stolid, its Other as vivacious and emotionally intense.* A counter-image takes shape in the second half of the nineteenth century where Northern Europeans are represented as dull, plodding, pedantic, lacking in imagination and charm, the South as warm, sociable, gregarious, earthy. Narratives like Thomas Mann's *Tonio Kröger* (1901) or E.M. Foster's *Where Angels Fear to Tread* (1905) or *A Room with a View* (1908) play on this opposition, which is satirically subverted in films like *Bienvenu chez les Ch'tis* (2008).

[3c] In sum, an ambivalent North-South polarity is still strongly operative within European identity discourses. Notwithstanding romanticized views of Mediterranean Europe (as expressed in tourism publicity and advertisements for olive oil and Italian food products), an anti-Mediterranean ethnotype of laziness and venality has been activated during the monetary and economic crises in the Euro-zone.

[4a] All of this is caught up in the second great Crisis in the European Self-Image, that of *a guilt-ridden Europe*. The idea that European supremacy was in itself tyrannical in nature draws on the critique of Eurocentrism as signalled in [2b], on the idea of European decadence as signalled in [2c]; this discourse gains prominence as, in the late nineteenth century, reports of cruelties and abuse begin to reach Europe from its colonies (notably the Belgian Congo). A 'Heart of Darkness' discourse takes hold, in tandem with a 'Dr Jekyll and Mr Hyde' view of the human personality: under the veneer of European civility there lurks a frightful, atavistic inner savagery.[7] This Eurotype is massively amplified as a result of two World Wars and the genocides that stretch from Namibia to Auschwitz. (By contrast, Stalin's purges and the Gulag still tend to be externalized as a non-European form of 'Oriental Despotism', as does the Armenian genocide). Another factor in this amplification process was the rising tide of decolonization. European supremacism was denounced

---

7   Stevsenson's novella dates from 1886, Conrad's novel from 1899.

as tyrannical and identity-destroying by intellectuals like Frantz Fanon and Edward Said. That critique has been internalized by Europeans: many European academics and intellectuals are now in a 'postcolonial' paradigm, having accepted the validity of the Fanon-Said line of reasoning, and now eschew and criticize European triumphalism and Eurocentric chauvinism.

[4b] The recoil from totalitarianism and murderous mass oppression also gave rise to a counter-discourse about a *Europe rising above its tyrannical chauvinisms*, falling back on its tradition of liberal inquiry and remaking itself into a privileged forum for humane standards of civilization. This post-totalitarian Euro-idealism was internationalist in orientation. Rooted in the utopian pacifism of c. 1900 (Koskenniemi 2001), it re-emerged after the Great War in the thought of Coudenhove-Kalergi and of the Founding Fathers of the European unification: Denis de Rougemont, René Cassin, Robert Schumann, Jean Monnet (Judy 2007). Prior to 1974, dictatorial regimes (Franco's Spain, Salazar's Portugal, the Greece of the military regime, 1967–74) were refused membership ad hoc. In 1993, the conditions formalized in the Copenhagen Criteria adopted by the European Commission included the requirement of state institutions 'guaranteeing democracy, the rule of law, human rights and respect for and protection of minorities' (EU 1993). This Euro-idealism sometimes continues to evince certain continuations of older Eurocentrism: Nicholas Sarkozy's 2007 Dakar speech has become notorious for imputing that Europeans are better than Africans at getting over catastrophes (a recurrent Eurocentric trope) (Mbem 2008). On the whole, however, Euro-idealism is avowedly internationalist and cosmopolitan and tries to avoid the ethnocentric errors of the past.

[4c] *Europe as a haven for politically correct 'snowflakes' and bureaucratic over-regulation; its Other a savage, vindictive world of former colonies.* The critique of Eurocentrism has also become the object of an altogether different type of backlash. Drawing on the lingering traditions of European supremacism in an antagonistic relationship vis-à-vis the rest of the world (1a, 2a and 3a) a new European nationalism has risen in recent years denouncing the 'cultural Marxism' and 'political correctness' that, in the neo-nationalists' view, abolishes a sense of European identity and achievement, and plays into the hand of Jihadists, immigrants, disgruntled ex-colonials and other enemies of European peace and prosperity. This is framed as a 'clash of civilizations' with enemies threatening Europe from the outside and traitors threatening Europe from the inside. This discourse draws on post-fascist and racist publications such as *Europe-Action* (1963–67), one of the source traditions of the crucially important group around Alain de Benoist, GRECE (Chebel d'Apollonia 1998, Taguieff 1994). It informs what amounts to a further twist in this dialectically morphed Eurotype:

[4d] *Europe as a besieged fortress in danger of being subverted by its Other, an incoming population influx of alien provenance.* This outlook is manifested in xenophobic-populist fears of population displacement,[8] the nightmare scenario of a future 'Eurabia',[9] and dovetailing with [4c]-type denunciations of the culpable laxity of conniving eurocrats and 'cultural Marxists'.[10] This new Euro-centered chauvinism ranges from established party politics (the Hard Brexit faction of Britain's Conservative Party) by way of far-right parliamentary politicians (Le Pen, Farage, Baudet, Orbán), to extraparliamentary extreme-right activists (*Génération identitaire*, CasaPound) and neo-Nazis or neo-fascist extremists. The discourse evokes deep memories of earlier European-Islamic antagonism (indicated under [1a]) in the names of websites such as 'Gates of Vienna'.

These are, ordered roughly by the moment of their first emergence, are some of the discursive traditions that articulate a European ethnotype amidst the world's diversity. Their original texts are still available for the reading, still capable of exerting influence; their contending and continuing 'long tails' are still with us, forming the warp and the woof of the tangled web of European identity arguments.

4 The Present European Crisis and Beyond: An Emergent Eurotype?

In most of these textual traditions, we can see a dialectical pattern, from the [a] type to its [b] countertype and [c] the compounded inflection ([a] mixed with [b]). An initial characterization or valorization provokes, over time, a counter-valorization, the two then continuing to co-exist side by side as a legacy of 'mixed feelings'. This conforms to the imagological model of the 'imageme', where the characterological profile of a given nation may be sharply bipolar ('a nation of contrasts') as the result of earlier types and later counter-types coexisting in the textual heritage; thus with the 'sensual yet meditative'

---

8   The terminology is diffuse. It spans older Nazi concepts like *Umvolkung* (adopted by the New Right in the Netherlands as omvolking) and more recent variants like *Überfremdung* as well as the French idea of a *Grand Remplacement* (thus in the title of the book by Renaud Camus, 2012).

9   The title of an anti-Islamist book by Bat Ye'or (2005).

10 Calqued on the Nazi term *Kulturbolschewismus*, the term Cultural Marxism circulated among American conservatives, who claimed they had adopted and re-purposed it from the critical theory of the Frankfurt School. It gained notoriety when it was used in the 2011 manifesto of the exstreme-right Norwegian mass murderer Anders Breivik. It has since then been normalized and 'mainstreamed' by books such as Paul Cliteur's *Cultuurmarxisme* (2018), and is currently widespread as a denunciatory term for multiculturalism. Cf. Janin 2014.

Flemings, the French who are rigid Cartesian rationalists and gallant oh-là-là socialites, or the English combining a 'stiff upper lip' with a readiness for violent battle, James-Bond-style. So too it is with Europe: Chartres Cathedral, the Brussels EU offices, Dachau, Armani and *Trainspotting* are all in their very, very different ways equally 'Eurotypical'.

However, there is one remarkable break in the dialectics of the [a]-[b]-[c] pattern; and this break may help to explain the extraordinary aporia in which current Europe-debates find themselves. — In the first three tradition-strands, a Euro-celebratory register came first, provoking a Euro-critical counter-discourse in the second instance. In tradition [4] however, the dialectics have taken a different course: a Euro-negative image [4a] came first, its countertypes following as reactions.

Indeed, the most recent configuration of competing characterizations forms a four-cornered stand-off. The opposing valorizations of 'Europe' are a compound of contradictory oppositions, involving a postcolonial critique of Eurocentrism (progressive Euro-critical, [4a]), post-totalitarian Euro-idealism (progressive Euro-positive [4b]), unilateralist anti-European nationalism (conservative Euro-critical [4c]), and a new xenophobic European chauvinism (conservative Euro-positive, [4d]):

	Euro-negative	Euro-positive
progressive	4a: radical postcolonialism	4b: liberal internationalism
conservative	4c: populist Euro-skepticism	4d: populist Euro-chauvinism

The foregrounded effect of this configuration is a deep ambivalence in the current view of Europe among the new conservative nationalists. For them, Europe is either a 'we' with whom they identify (as the Judaeo-Christian 'Abendland' that has to be saved from immigration, Islamism and loss of identity) or as a 'they' that needs to be resisted (as the internationalist organization that threatens the sovereignty and identity of the European nation-states). Neo-nationalists accordingly position the nation against an oscillating Other with is located either in the World of Islam or in the office buildings of Brussels and Strasbourg.

For Europe, this means that its self-image now stands at the centre of a circular firing squad. 'Europe' is now subject to a swarm of mutually competing and irreconcilable Others, united only in their vehement anti-Europeanism. Something called 'Europe' is, albeit for sharply different reasons and in different manifestations, criticized by postcolonial academics, aggrieved citizens of former colonies, and Europe's native populists. A return to the simple discourses of a premodern world-view or an early-modern hegemony is no longer possible. And the most pressing need and most difficult challenge for Europe is now to articulate, against the bewilderment of being Othered by its former Others, a future-proof identity of its own, something it can stand for.

It cannot be the purpose of this article, or indeed of imagology as such, to offer 'market guidance' on how to successfully brand one's image in a world of limited and distributed sympathies. Even so, a few emerging force lines and perspectives can be tentatively outlined for those who see Europe as a subject they identify with, rather than as an object they dissociate themselves from.

It was a concomitant of Europe's hegemonic position that it could autonomously articulate its self-images, rather than having one imposed on oneself, to interiorize or to reject, by powerful Others. As a result, Europe in the course of its long autonomous history silhouetted its self-images against a host of successive Others, and this multiplicity of Others now comes back to haunt a post-imperial Europe, all of these offering a perspective from which to impugn Europe.

This long-accumulated reservoir of self-other distinctions is still a present reality. It seems that the images of oldest vintage are, at this political juncture, the most toxic ones politically. The old, pre-1900 tropes of anti-Islamism and white supremacy are now feeding populist nationalism and xenophobia. The auto-images of a Judaeo-Christian tradition or Enlightenment values, having fed the liberal internationalism of post-1918 and post-1945 Europe, are a little shopworn, challenged by postcolonialism, or else co-opted by the western-supremacist views of Euro-chauvinism.

[5] What seems to be re-emerging, however, is a Eurotype of *experience vs. simplistic naiveté*. The Other of an 'experienced, worldly-wise Europe' is now no longer the underdeveloped, inexperienced New or Third World (as it had been for Eurocentrism type [2a]), but rather neo-nationalist, populist strongman leaders such as Boris Johnson, Viktor Orbán, Recep Tayyip Erdoğan and above all Donald Trump, all of whom have voiced the various recent modes of anti-Europeanism ([4b, c d]). This Eurotype invokes disenchanted pragmatism, living with the mixed feelings of a chequered historical track record, where the guilt of great crimes and the glory of great achievements are two sides of the same coin, and where the overriding need to move forward in a world riddled by complexities is nonetheless imperative. This Eurotype may have emerged together with existentialism from the moral ruins of the Second World War, and involves a Keatsian notion of 'negative capability' – the power to live in uncertainty amidst unresolved complexities. I discern an early expression of this Eurotype in the film *The Third Man* (1949), scripted by Graham Greene, which, interestingly, had for it Others both the moral turpitude of

the multinational flotsam and jetsam of post-Nazi Vienna, and the simplistic, moralistic *naiveté* of the American anti-hero, Holly Martens. It was *The Third Man* which formulated the famous 'cuckoo clock paradox' which captured precisely this condition of mixed feelings and moral complication.

Throughout the period between 1945 until 1989, this Eurotype (mixing existentialism with Keatsian Romantic Irony) had the Manichean worldview of the Cold War for its Other. It found its most forceful expression in the art form that was the only one which could effortlessly and without sense of contradiction self-define as 'European': that of art-house cinema. The *nouvelle vague*, Fellini, Pasolini, Bergman, Saura, Fassbinder, Wenders, Makavejev, Kieslowski and Tarkovsky: all of these could, for all their mutual differences, be classed under the rubric of 'European cinema', defined by their opposition to the consumer entertainment offered by 'Hollywood'. Known in some US circles by the jocose moniker of 'full frontal nudity with subtitles', European art-house cinema scorned facile emotions, middle-class conventions and moralistic earnestness. Instead, it explored moral perplexities, aesthetic finesse and a certain ironic raffishness, which were, in the process, framed as European characteristics (Everett 2005, Sojcher 1996, Sorlin 1991). That Eurotype silhouetted itself against the hetero-image of American simplicity and naiveté – a long-standing trope, already deployed in Henry James.

This Eurotype obtained a new political edge after 1989, when 'Old Europe' showed reluctance to join George W. Bush's 'Coalition of the Willing' for a second Iraq War (Merkl 2005, Villepin 2003); it intensified when facing the unilateralist and uncouth America of Donald J. Trump (dismissive as he, and it, are of cultural refinement or moral doubts).[11]

Each auto-image requires a hetero-image; Europe, which may well be in the process of having a new type of Other thrust upon itself, may as a result reinvigorate a sense of self, *une certaine idée de l'Europe*. There is a possibility that in the face of the self-serving unilateralist chauvinism of new strongman regimes based on populist charisma, Europe may find a new auto-image in the realization that it, like life itself, is complex, and willing to live with that complexity.

Works Cited

Assmann, Aleida. 1999. *Erinnerungsräume: Formen und Wandlungen des kulturellen Gedächtnisses* (München: Beck).

---

11   Cf. Luiza Bialasiewicz's chapter in this book.

Beller, Manfred & Joep Leerssen, eds. 2007. *Imagology: The Cultural Construction and Literary Representation of National Characters. A Critical Survey* (Amsterdam/Leiden: Rodopi/Brill).

Chebel d'Appollonia, Ariane. 1998. *L'Extrême-droite en France. De Maurras à Le Pen* (Paris: Complexe).

Dyserinck, Hugo. 2015. *Ausgewählte Schriften zur Vergleichenden Literaturwissenschaft* (Berlin: Frank & Timme).

EU. 1993. 'Presidency Conclusions: Copenhagen European Council - 21–22 June 1993, art. 7a', online at www.europarl.europa.eu/enlargement/ec/pdf/cop_en.pdf (last accessed 19 July 2019).

Everett, Wendy Ellen, ed. 2005. *European Identity in Cinema* (2nd ed. Bristol: Intellect).

Jamin, Jérôme, 2014. 'Cultural Marxism and the Radical Right', in *The Post-War Anglo-American Far Right: A Special Relationship of Hate*, ed. A. Shekhovtsov & P. Jackson (Basingstoke: Palgrave Macmillan), 84–103.

Judt, Tony. 2007. *Postwar: A History of Europe since 1945* (London: Pimlico).

Koskenniemi, Martti. 2001. *The Gentle Civilizer of Nations: The Rise and Fall of International Law 1870–1960* (Cambridge: Cambridge University Press).

Leerssen, Joep. 2015. *Spiegelpaleis Europa: Europese cultuur als mythe en beeldvorming* (3rd ed. Nijmegen: Vantilt)

Leerssen, Joep. 2016. 'Imagology: On Using Ethnicity to Make Sense of the World', *Iberic@l: Revue d'études ibériques et ibéro-américaines*, 10: 13–31.

Mbem, André Julien. 2008. *Nicolas Sarkozy à Dakar: Débats et enjeux autour d'un discours* (Paris: L'Harmattan).

Merkl, Peter H. 2005 *The Distracted Eagle: The Rift between America and Old Europe* (London: Routledge).

Popper, Karl. 1978. 'Three Worlds' (The Tanner Lecture on Human Values, University of Michigan, 7 April 1978), online at https://tannerlectures.utah.edu/_documents/a-to-z/p/popper80.pdf (last accessed 29 September 2019).

Rigney, Ann. 2005. 'Plenitude, Scarcity and the Production of Cultural Memory', *Journal of European Studies* 35.1/2: 209–26.

Sojcher, Frédéric. 1996. *Cinéma européen et identités culturelles* (Bruxelles: Université de Bruxelles).

Sorlin, Pierre. 1991. *European Cinemas, European Societies 1939–1990* (London: Routledge).

Taguieff, Pierre-André, 1994. *Sur la Nouvelle Droite. Jalons d'une analyse critique* (Paris: Galilée).

Villepin, Dominique de. 2003. 'Discours prononcé à l'ONU lors de la crise irakienne, 14 février 2003', online at Wikisource, fr.wikisource.org/wiki/Discours_prononc%C3%A9_%C3%A0_l%27ONU_lors_de_la_crise_irakienne_-_14_f%C3%A9vrier_2003 (last accessed 17 September 2019).

CHAPTER 6

Rock, Mirror, Mirage: Europe, Elsewhere

Lucia Boldrini

ZERO – [Untitled, for lack of words]

I received Vladimir Biti's invitation to take part in the conference 'The Idea of Europe: The Clash of Projections' on 24 June 2016, the day after the referendum in which 51.9% of British voters chose to leave the European Union. I was in shock, nauseous, unable to speak. How could I even reply to such a kind invitation?

Some will say that I'm dramatizing – after all, it wasn't like the break-up of the ex-Yugoslavia, with its war and genocide; after all, like many Europeans, I too have often been fiercely critical of the European Union. But Europe is also what enables me to be critical of Europe[1] (see, I too slide from geographical denomination to political and economic entity, I who have often been irked by the conflation of the two): as a flawed, imperfect solution that struggles to stay faithful to the principles of its visionary early proponents (such as the too often forgotten Altiero Spinelli and Ernesto Rossi who, prisoners of Fascism in 1941 on the island of Ventotene, wrote the manifesto that envisaged the unity of Europe in order to supersede the nationalisms that had led to war and totalitarianism, and as a path to global egalitarianism[2]), it still remains better than

---

1 Rodolphe Gasché notes that 'at the same time that European values have served to justify and occlude the exploitation and humiliation of much of the rest of the world, these very concepts and ideas have also made it possible for Europe to question its own traditions and the crimes that have been committed in their name. Undoubtedly, this unique feature of critical self-evaluation is repeatedly celebrated by all the grand discourses on Europe; thus, it should also be subject to some suspicion [...] Yet the fact remains that there is such a tradition and such a culture in Europe.' (Gasché 2009, 7)
2 See e.g.: 'E quando, superando l'orizzonte del Vecchio continente, si abbraccino in una visione di insieme tutti i popoli che costituiscono l'umanità, bisogna pur riconoscere che la Federazione Europea è l'unica concepibile garanzia che i rapporti con i popoli asiatici e americani si possano svolgere su una base di pacifica cooperazione, in attesa di un più lontano avvenire, in cui diventi possibile l'unità politica dell'intero globo.' (Spinelli and Rossi 2017, 25) ['And when, as we transcend the horizon of the Old continent, we embrace in one common vision all the peoples that make up humankind, we will have to acknowledge that the European Federation is the only conceivable guarantee that a peaceful cooperation can occur with American and Asian people, while we await the more distant future when global political unity may become possible.'] Translations are mine.

the alternative of no Europe. But my dismay, my inability to speak or think, was also an emotional reaction to an event that denied my being who I was where I legally was. I had been part of a shared 'we'. Suddenly, I wasn't.

Over two years later,[3] as the UK parliament is in chaos over what form Brexit should take, as populism in Europe brings back the conditions that Spinelli and Rossi thought a European federation could overcome (their internationalism set against those 'who will, albeit involuntarily, play into the hands of reactionary forces by letting the incandescent lava of popular passions set in the old moulds and the old absurdities resurface'[4]), my thoughts are still fragmented; emotion still affects thought; 'Europe' still feels broken. This article will, by necessity, bear the signs of that (first-person, singular, plural) fragmentation from which it arises. Much has been written by philosophers, historians, sociologists on 'Europe'. But fragmented, struck dumb, I sought writers and artists whose work reflects, and reflects on, their experience of the shifting boundaries of 'Europe', of the clashing projections that arise from its name and constructions – not to find answers, necessarily, but to find different perspectives, articulations, what may force a double-take or a re-think. For convenience, these fragments will be numbered and titled, but sequence does not always signal logical consequence.

ONE – Utopia, Lollipop, Alibi

In the introduction to her collection of essays *Café Europa*,[5] Slavenka Drakulić writes that, on re-reading her pieces, she was surprised and troubled to realize that she had used 'us' and 'we' more often than she normally would, as if she were speaking for all of the people of Eastern Europe (1999, 1). And yet,

---

3   This article was completed in December 2018; as I revise the proofs, the UK has indeed left the EU, and the distress of Brexit has been blunted by the tragedy of Covid-19. I have been tempted to revise the article in this light, but decided to leave it as it was written, as a document of a state of mind brought about by that particular historical moment. The issues raised by that moment have not gone away, and may in fact become all the more acute as countries re-emerge out of lockdowns with shattered economies and potential new nationalisms, while having to confront the racist legacy of colonialism and of the slave trade, newly raised by Black Lives Matter.
4   '[Q]uelli che [...] faranno, sia pure involontariamente, il gioco delle forze reazionarie lasciando solidificare la lava incandescente delle passioni popolari nel vecchio stampo, e risorgere le vecchie assurdità [...]' (Spinelli and Rossi 2017, 25).
5   'Introduction: First-Person Singular' (Drakulić 1999, 1–5). Originally published in English in 1996, the book collects essays written between 1992 and 1996.

she writes, she hates this first-person plural pronoun that reeks of the mandatory collective existence that communism imposed, depriving individuals of their 'I' – almost literally, physically *reeks*: 'I can smell the scent of bodies pressed against me in a 1 May parade, or at the celebration of Tito's birthday on 25 May, the sweaty armpits of a man in front of me, my own perspiration [...] I can feel the nausea [...]' (2). That is, she adds, why testimonial journalism – when the eye witness can only speak as an 'I' and not as a 'we' – was a rare genre in the Yugoslavia in which she grew up (2). But that collective, 'hideous' first-person plural repels her also because she had seen first-hand, as an eye witness, how dangerous it can be when it becomes infected by nationalism, forcing individuals into a 'we' that had never existed:

> The war in the Balkans is the product of that 'us', of that huge, 20 million-bodied mass swinging back and forth in waves, then following their leaders into mass hysteria. [...] Those who used 'I' instead of 'we' in their language had to escape. It was this fatal difference in grammar that divided them from the rest of their compatriots. (3)

Personal pronouns, we know from Benveniste, are shifters: their meaning changes depending on who uses them. This is more than a grammatical point. For Drakulić,

> in Eastern European countries, the difference between 'we' and 'I' is [...] far more important than mere grammar. 'We' means fear, resignation, submissiveness, a warm crowd and somebody else deciding your destiny. 'I' means giving individuality and democracy a chance. (4)

To me, the 'we' that I felt I lost on 23 June 2016 was not authoritarian: it was the sign of a shared imagination, a shared history (including a shared history of war, totalitarianism and violence to be overcome) and a shared future. A flawed history, yes; and yes, a distant and ever receding, utopian future; but one in which individuals could participate because of our multiple, intertwined histories and differences, not despite of them. This imperfect 'we', in progress, shaped by centuries of encounters, clashes, and transformations, would not erase but would instead accept difference, the multiplicity of the identities that gather within it.

But why does Drakulić, who decries the totalitarianism of what 'we' meant for her, for the people of Eastern Europe, continue to use this first-person plural pronoun in her essays?

> Because a common denominator is still discernible, and still connects us all, often against our will. It is not only in our communist past, but also the way we would like to escape from it, the direction in which we want to go. It's our longing for Europe and what it stands for. Or, rather, what we imagine Europe stands for. (4)

In the essay that gives the name to the collection, 'Café Europa', Drakulić notes that in Eastern Europe, many shops, restaurant, bars, hotels have Western sounding names:

> In using such as name as Europa, there is an assumption that everyone knows what we mean by Europe. One thing is sure: it is no longer the name of an entire continent. It describes only one part of it, the western part, in a geographical, cultural, historical and political sense. Europe has been divided by the different historical development of its component parts, communism and most of all by poverty. (11)

Poverty: it is not by chance that the areas of the UK that most heavily voted to leave the European Union tended to be the most deprived, the worst affected by de-industrialisation and by the austerity that followed the 2008 financial crash. Drakulić is part of the elite that can travel, speak, be heard, for whom globalisation means larger horizons, not lower pay – so am I. In Tahar Ben Jelloun's 2006 novel *Partir (Leaving Tangier)* the young Moroccan protagonist, Azel, who dreams of reaching Europe, wishes that he may be a crate in which goods are transported – not *in* a crate, but the crate itself: his dream is that he could be delivered to Europe, 'a land of prosperity and freedom',[6] but the point is that, because of EU policies, he would have much more freedom as merchandise than as a human being. The use of the first-person plural is troubling because it assumes a right to speak for those whose life experiences we cannot claim to share. By not discriminating ('discriminate': 'make or see a distinction; differentiate') the 'we' becomes discriminatory ('make a distinction, esp. unjustly'). It is the inability to discriminate within that 'we' ('observe distinctions carefully; have good judgement') (Fowler and Fowler 1990) that allows populism to construct a different, exclusionary, discriminatory, nationalist and nativist 'we'; and *we* have allowed it.

> So, what does Europe mean in the Eastern European imagination? [...] It is something distant, something to be attained, to be deserved. [...] It

---

6 Ben Jelloun 2009, 25; 'une terre de liberté et de prospérité' (Ben Jelloun 2006, 46).

offers choice: from shampoo to political parties. [...] It is a promised land, a new Utopia, a lollipop. [...] Europe is the opposite of what we have. (Drakulić 1999, 12)

As I write in England in 2018, when an equally mythical 'Europe' has become the scapegoat and the alibi (Latin for 'elsewhere') – as if Great Britain, by voting to leave on 23 June 2016, had drifted further apart, geologically, from what Valéry had called in 1919 'a little promontory on the continent of Asia'[7] – these twenty-year-old words make me smile bitterly.

TWO – Leaving: Rock, Mirage

For some, of course, *leaving* means coming.

Tahar Ben Jelloun's *Partir* opens with the striking image of young Moroccans dreaming of Europe, attracted by the mirage of the twinkling lights across the Strait of Gibraltar:

> In Tangier, in the winter, the Café Hafa becomes an observatory for dreams and their aftermath. [...] Leaning back against the wall, customers sit on mats and stare at the horizon as if seeking to read their fate. They look at the sea, at the clouds that blend into the mountains, and they wait for the twinkling lights of Spain to appear. They watch them without seeing them, and sometimes, even when the lights are lost in the fog and bad weather, they see them anyway.[8]

For many, as we know far too well from the news, the dream turns into nightmare. 'As if in an absurd and persistent dream', the protagonist, Azel

> sees his naked body among other naked bodies swollen by seawater, his face distorted by salt and longing, his skin burnt by the sun, split open

---

7 'Will Europe become *what it is in reality* – that is, a little promontory on the continent of Asia?' (Valéry 1977, 102); 'L'Europe deviendra-t-elle *ce qu'elle est en réalité*, c'est-à-dire: un petit cap du continent asiatique?' (Valéry 1957, 995)
8 Ben Jelloun 2009, 1. 'À Tanger, l'hiver, le café Hafa se transforme en un observatoire des rêves et de leurs conséquences. [...] D'autres, assis sur des nattes, le dos au mur, fixent l'horizon comme s'ils l'interrogeaient sur leur destin. Ils regardent la mer, les nuages qui se confondent avec les montagnes, ils attendent l'apparition des premières lumières de l'Espagne. Ils les suivent sans les voir et parfois les voient alors qu'elles sont voilées par la brume et le mauvais temps.' (Ben Jelloun 2006, 11–12)

across the chest as if there had been fighting before the boat went down. [...] He knows that there, in this specific circle, a fluid boundary exists, a kind of separation between the sea and the ocean, the calm, smooth waters of the Mediterranean and the fierce surge of the Atlantic. He holds his nose, because staring so hard at these images has filled his nostrils with the odour of death, a suffocating, clinging, nauseating stench. When he closes his eyes, death begins to dance around the table where he sits almost every day to watch the sunset and count the first lights scintillating across the way, on the coast of Spain.[9]

The Pillars of Hercules, this most mythical of boundaries of the Mediterranean, between the known and the unknown worlds, the permitted and the forbidden, acquires again mythical status, this time as forbidden boundary – a Schengen boundary – between North and South.

For the young Moroccans and Sub-Saharan migrants that long to leave, the Rock on the North side promises the solidity and safety of the idea of Europe: a mirage, a broken promise.

THREE – Otherwhere

Youssouf Amine Elalamy's 2000 novel *Les clandestins*, translated as *Sea Drinkers*,[10] is the story of fourteen characters who seek to cross the Strait and try to reach Spain at night; their drowned bodies are swept back by the currents and the waves onto the African shore, 'scattered on the sand' like 'strange fish'.[11]

> Fish so big one might have said they're people, God have mercy, that looks like people, Almighty God, they look like people, yes, they are people! Woe to us, they are our people!

---

9   Ben Jelloun 2009, 2–3. 'Comme dans un rêve absurde et persistant, Azel voit son corps nu mêlé à d'autres corps nus gonflés par l'eau de mer, le visage déformé par l'attente et le sel, la peau roussie par le soleil, ouverte au niveau des bras comme si une bagarre avait précédé le naufrage [...] Il sait que là, dans ce cercle précis, existe une frontière mobile, une sorte de ligne de séparation entre deux eaux, celles calmes et plates de la Méditerranée et celles véhémentes et fortes de l'Atlantique. Il se bouche le nez car, à force de fixer ces images, il a fini par sentir l'odeur de la mort, une odeur suffocante qui rôde, lui donnant la nausée. Quand il ferme les yeux, la mort se met à danser autour de la table où il a l'habitude de s'installer tous les jours pour regarder le coucher du soleil et compter les premières lumières qui scintillent en face, sur les côtes espagnoles.' (Ben Jelloun 2006, 13–14)
10 Elalamy 2008; English translations in this article are amended.
11 'éparpillés sur le sable, d'étranges poissons.' (Elalamy 2011, 23)

Everywhere, bodies had washed up on the beach. There were black ones, there were white ones. The sea had not discriminated. They all had their eyes eaten out.[12]

Among the bodies washed ashore is that of Little Zouheïr, his body full of words, of sentences that he has never told, and will now never tell.

We all remember the photos, splashed on the front pages of newspapers across Europe at the beginning of September 2015, of three-year-old Aylan Kurdi, washed up on a beach after his family had tried to take him away from Syria to the refuge of Europe. The image of a three-year old child, dead, alone on a sandy beach was capable of eliciting a sufficiently emotional reaction. We do not often hear of the hundreds of children that have died since, or died before; another shipwreck is no longer news, unless the number of the dead reaches a new record and is sensational enough, unless a particularly moving photograph is capable of occasioning our pity. Texts like Ben Jelloun's *Partir* or Elalamy's *Les Clandestins* bring us back to the news that we no longer read.

A photographer, in *Les clandestins*, takes photos of the bodies. Some days later, a French weekly magazine prints the headline over one of the photos:

WHAT A PRETTY LITTLE BEACH![13]

On the island where the body of little Aylan washed up on the beach, some tourists had complained of their holidays being spoiled by migrants; others simply ignored or coexisted, on their 'pretty Turkish beach', with those stories of death and desperation.[14]

I am reminded, a little incongruously, of W. H. Auden's poem 'Good-bye to the Mezzogiorno' (1958):

> Out of a gothic North, the pallid children
>   Of a potato, beer-or-whiskey

---

12 Elalamy 2008, 94. 'Des poissons si gros que l'on eût dit des hommes, que Dieu nos protège, ça ressemble à des hommes, Dieu Tout-Puissant on dirait des hommes, mais oui, ce sont des hommes! Malheur à nous, ce sont nos hommes! Un peu partout, des corps avaient échoué sur la plage. Il y en avait de noirs, il y en avait de blancs. La mer ne semblait pas avoir fait la différence: tous avaient les yeux dévorés.' (Elalamy 2011, 23)
13 Elalamy 2008, 131. 'UNE SI JOLIE PETITE PLAGE!' (Elalamy 2011, 102)
14 See e.g. the articles in the *Metro* (Willis 2015) and in the *Daily Mail*. The title of the latter is worth quoting: 'By day a tourist paradise, by night a migrant hell: The pretty Turkish beach where people smugglers send families to their deaths.' (Reid 2015)

> Guilt culture, we behave like our fathers and come
> Southward into a sunburnt otherwhere. (Auden 1979, 239, ll. 1–4)

The 'sunburnt otherwhere' of the Greek islands is 'other' enough for tourists from the north to go and get some sun on their 'pallid' skin, but not so 'other', for those tourists and journalists, that it should be allowed to be full of swarthy, sunburnt migrants, reminding us of other wars and poverty. No double-take here, no demand to reconsider the colonial assumptions inherited from 'our fathers', no acceptance of the responsibility for those whose history *we* have contributed to setting on this course.

FOUR – Who Are You?

In the essay 'People from the Three Borders', Drakulić writes about Istria – 'the most western part of Croatia, the most southern part of Slovenia and the most north-eastern part of Italy' (1999, 162) – and about the new state border that appeared between Slovenia and Croatia.

The question at the Croatian border, 'have you anything to declare' (161), is for Drakulić equivalent to asking 'who are you?', or rather, 'are you Croat' – and more specifically, 'Are you a proper Croat? Are you patriotic enough – that is, are you a nationalist?' (161–62).

People here have always mixed, Drakulić writes. Istria is the home of 10 different Slavic dialects and four of Italian origin (162); people regularly entertain parallel conversations in different languages (162–63). Drakulić narrates how, when reporters in 1994 interviewed inhabitants of Croatian border villages that had been annexed overnight by Slovenia, the people told the Croat reporter that they were Croats, the Slovene reporter that they were Slovenes, and the Italian reporter that they were, of course, Italians (163). The problem, she comments, was with the either-or question: they saw no need to choose (163): 'The journalists saw the villagers' nationalities as political categories; the villagers were talking about their own identity, of which their nationalities were only one aspect.' (163). I am somewhat sceptical of Drakulić's reading: there is more than a trace of defiance in the villagers' attitude, of showing how easily the 'foreigner' can be fooled, be told what they want to hear (because the Italian from Italy, the Slovenian from Slovenia, the Croat from Croatia are *not us*). Drakulić optimistically ignores this, she is possibly even blind to it; the message for her is that 'Istrianism' means 'the enlarging concept of identity, as opposed to the reducing concept of nationality' (164). These words sound almost quaint today, when the notion of 'identity' is shrinking and identitarian politics seems to be less concerned with acquiring rights than with claiming exclusivity, denouncing appropriation, when nativists of all stripes strut on world stages and claim to put their nation(ality) 'first'.

In the same essay, Drakulić tells the story of a friend who, on a weekly shopping trip to Trieste, produced, at each border (Croat, Slovene, Italian), the passport that corresponded to that border (168). But what her friend dreamed of was a single passport – a European Union passport that would make obsolete all the fears and tensions that force one to declare him- or herself as a citizen of a particular place, and thereby risk being hated by those that cook a different food, have a different inflection, or different memories: '"Imagine," he says to me, "one day perhaps only a few years from now, both Slovenia and Croatia will become members of the European Union [...] I dream about that day, when nobody will hate me because of the food I prefer, my memory, or the language I speak."' (169). Europe, for Drakulić and her friend, would be Istrianism (an ideal, optimistic Istrianism, without the blind spot) on the larger scale.

Croatia is now the most recent member of the European Union. Living in Brexit Britain – a country that has chosen the past over the present under the guise of a fake promise to 'take back control of our borders' – these words, spoken from a part of Europe that is still, today, struggling with many of the same issues as it did over two decades ago when Drakulić wrote her essay, cause another bitter smile. But they do raise the important issue of the relationship between identity, nationality and place: there isn't a single answer to that triangulation, and however much I may decry the (nationalist) attachment to an exclusionary national identity, at the same time I must recognize that such emotional attachment is just as powerful as my attachment is to the idea of Europe as my (ideal, imperfect) larger home. My European cosmopolitanism – aware, or so I like to think, of the opposite pitfalls of nationalism and globalization: the nationalism that excludes, and the globalisation that condemns Azel to wanting to be a crate – is not superior to the national attachment of others whose experiences have been different from mine. It is our fault – the fault of cosmopolitan Europeans – that we haven't been able to tell a different history, construct a different narrative, make that 'we' welcoming not just of the external others, but of the internal selves that perceive themselves to be exiled from it.

FIVE – Walking into the Frame

Among the best-known works of Lebanese-born, British-Palestinian artist Mona Hatoum are her maps. The most famous is possibly *Present Tense* (1996), made of 2,200 blocks of olive-oil soap from Nablus, on which are drawn the boundaries of the territories that would have been under Palestinian self-rule had the 1993 Oslo Accords been implemented. The solubility of soap, the fact that it can dry up and shrink, makes those imaginary boundaries materially unstable in this map too (Tate 2011). Historically, in fact, many of them never existed as boundaries, they were always ever in the imagination, shifting, though some have been sometimes marked by walls. The map that most fascinates me, however, is called, simply, *Map* (1999). It is made of glass marbles, laid out on the floor of the gallery in the shape of the continents – the floor is the sea, the oceans. As visitors walk into the frame and among the continents, the vibrations of their steps cause the marbles to move, making the boundaries of the lands unstable, shifting.[15]

As we enter the world, our presence destabilizes any boundary. There is danger involved – it is 'treacherous' – yet the alternative is to not-visit the exhibition, avoid movement, eschew life. With another leap, I am reminded of Primo Levi's anti-fascist elegy of zinc in *Il sistema periodico* (*The Periodic Table*), first published in 1975. Levi notes the different reaction of zinc to acid depending on its purity – it dissolves when impure, it resists attack when it is pure – and draws from it 'two conflicting philosophical conclusions: the praise of purity, which protects from evil like a coat of mail; the praise of impurity, which gives rise to changes, in other words, to life'. The latter is not only a parable for the rejection of Fascism, which forbids 'Dissension, diversity', 'wants everybody to be the same' (Levi 1986, 33–34), but also a reminder that, as a Jew, Levi himself was the racial impurity that fascism wanted to expunge.[16]

SIX – Bitter Sugar

Drakulić asks, 'Is anyone today able to say where Europe, and all it stands for, begins, and where it ends?' (1999, 13) – and when? Surely it is both less and more than Valéry's small promontory off the Asian continent. Curtius, who

---

15   Hatoum has commented: 'Because of my background, I am acutely aware of questions of national borders and territories. I come from an embattled area which has been infinitely dissected by a ludicrous amount of borders [...] As a reaction, I made a map which denies all political borders. But this map is so unstable that even the geographical delineation of the continents cannot be fixed, since the simple movement of those walking across the floor will shift parts of it and threaten to destroy it. At the same time, it renders the floor surface treacherous for viewers as it destabilizes the surface they walk on. So there is this double aspect of fragility and danger.' (artdaily.com)

16   '[D]ue conseguenze filosofiche tra loro contrastanti: l'elogio della purezza, che protegge dal male come un usbergo; l'elogio dell'impurezza che dà adito ai mutamenti, cioè alla vita. [...] il dissenso, il diverso [...] il fascismo [...] vuole tutti uguali.' (Levi 1997, 768)

is concerned with literature, attributes to Goethe the distinction of being the last European;[17] for philosophers, 'Europe' starts about then.[18] In a useful summary of the history of 'Europe' in her review of Jacques Derrida's *The Other Heading*, Margaret Heller (2008, 95) refers to Martin Lewis and Kären Wigen's observation that 'Europe', favoured by humanists, started replacing 'Christendom' in the early modern period. But where is the temporal or spatial border when what the border should keep separate is already mixed – has been mixed historically, socially, culturally, genetically, politically? This is not to make facile assumptions about the desirability of fluidity and the deplorability of the restrictions that borders impose. When European powers expanded colonially and imperially, the lines of Europe's own borders, never clear, were further smudged, both geographically and in the histories that would ensue; of course, so were those of the lands that were conquered.[19]

The violence of that smudging of borders is inscribed everywhere, including in the beauty of our landscapes and buildings. British-Nigerian poet Patience Agbabi wrote the poem 'The Doll's House' (2013) after a visit to Harewood House, in the north of England, built in the eighteenth century with the proceeds of the sugar trade from plantations in the West Indies, where thousands of slaves worked. The dramatic monologue, written in Chaucer's 'rime royale', is spoken by the daughter of the House's cook, Angelica, who takes the listener on a tour of a replica Harewood House confected 'out of sugar-flesh and -bone'. The tour begins 'below stairs, where you'll blacken your sweet tooth, | sucking a beauty whittled from harsh truth'. The furniture of the bedroom is 'all carved from sugarcane; | even the curtains that adorn its frame' are 'drizzled with tiny threads of spun "white gold"'. In the library, 'burnt sugar' 'turned sweet to bitter', a 'secret passage' becomes the 'Middle Passage' (Agbabi 2013, lines 3, 13–14, 53–54, 56, 59, 62–64).

---

17   'To see European literature as a whole is possible only when one has acquired citizenship in every period from Homer to Goethe'; 'The founding hero [...] of European literature is Homer. Its last universal author is Goethe.' (Curtius 1953, 12, 16); 'Die europäische Literatur als Ganzes zu sehen, ist nur möglich, wenn man sich ein Bürgerrecht in allen ihren Epochen von Homer bis Goethe erworben hat.' 'Der Gründerheros [...] der europäischen Literatur ist Homer. Ihr letzter universaler Autor ist Goethe.' (Curtius 1948, 20, 24)
18   Rodolphe Gasché for example notes that '"Europe" has been something like a philosopheme since at least the eighteenth century', though he also argues that 'it is in phenomenological thought in particular that Europe is explicitly discussed as either a concept or an idea – in other words, as something that is clearly of the order of the philosophical.' (2009, 17)
19   This concerns both state frontiers, modified or imposed by wars and colonial expansion, and cultural borders, which have no clear line and are in constant transformation. On the differences and relationships between 'frontier' and 'cultural border', see Leerssen (2006, 175–77).

Nationalism and the Europeanism that harps on the 'Christian roots of Europe' want to stop, now, any diluting or contaminating of 'indigenous' traditions. Drakulić in her description of Istrian people; the British-Palestinian Lebanese-born Hatoum in her 'map'; the British-Nigerian Agbabi in her poem; Levi in his celebration of zinc: they all expose the short-sightedness of any idea of solid borders, of purity, of national rootedness as the mark of identity, when the smudging of those borders, the evolution of traditions through constant encounters, clashes, equivocations, exploitations, has not only already been happening for centuries but is intrinsic to the European expansion over other territories, and thus both to European identity as a whole and to that of individual European colonial powers.

SEVEN – Elsewhere

At the start of his 1990 essay 'Europe in Ruins' ('Europa in Trümmern: Ein Prospekt'), Hans Magnus Enzensberger describes scenes of abject poverty, violence and destruction in Luanda, Beirut, El Salvador, Sri Lanka – 'Reports from the Third World, the kind we read every morning over breakfast' (Enzensberger 1994, 77) – only to reveal, immediately after, that in fact he'd used the names of 'Third-World' places, but the descriptions were of European cities at the end of the Second World War: Rome, Frankfurt, Athens, Berlin. Yes, this was Europe only 45 years earlier. The double-take thus forced on the readers highlights how amnesiacly close we are to disaster. This 'pile of ruins' (77) is no otherwhere.[20]

Later in the essay, Enzensberger describes American journalists' eye-witness accounts of Europe in the immediate aftermath of the war. Martha Gellhorn, who visited the Rhineland in April 1945, wrote that, whoever she spoke to, they'd say that the Nazis had always been in the next village, never here. She 'was incensed, indeed staggered by the statements of Germans she met':

> No one is a Nazi. No one ever was. There may have been some Nazis in the next village, and as a matter of fact, that town about twenty kilometres away was a veritable hotbed of Nazidom. [...] Oh, the Jews? Well, there weren't really many Jews in this neighbourhood. [...] I hid a Jew for six weeks. I hid a Jew for eight weeks. (I hid a Jew, he hid a Jew, all God's

---

20   'Berichte aus der Dritten Welt, wie wir sie jeden Tag zum Frühstück lesen können'; 'ein Trümmerhaufen' (Enzensberger 1997, 35).

chillun hid Jews.) We have nothing against the Jews; we always got on well with them.[21]

No one was responsible, responsibility was always somewhere else.

EIGHT – Immaculate Conception

In his *Panfleto desde el planeta de los simios* ('Pamphlet from the Planet of the Apes'), published in 1995, the Catalan writer Manuel Vázquez Montalbán surveys European culture and politics from a post-1989 perspective; mirrors have broken into a myriad fragments;[22] what has happened, he asks, to the democratic imaginary?[23] Europe's self-image is built on myths, and it is these myths that have brought us to the Eurocentrism of a European Union which, having privileged its markets, lacks a centre that can hold it together and lead to a different, emancipatory future.[24]

---

21 Enzensberger 1994, 80–81. 'Erbittert, ja fassungslos reagiert die Amerikanerin Martha Gellhorn, als sie im April 1945 ins Rheinland kommt, auf die Äußerungen ihrer deutschen Gesprächspartner: "Niemand ist ein Nazi. Niemand ist je einer gewesen. Es hat vielleicht ein paar Nazis im nächsten Dorf gegeben, und es stimmt schon, diese Stadt da zwanzig Kilometer entfernt, war eine regelrechte Brutstätte des Nationalsozialismus. [...] Oh, die Juden? Tja, es gab eigentlich in dieser Gegend nicht viele Juden. [...]. Ich habe sechs Wochen lang einen Juden versteckt. Ich habe acht Wochen lang einen Juden versteckt. (Ich hab einen Juden versteckt, er hat einen Juden versteckt, alle Kinder Gottes haben einen Juden versteckt.) Wir haben nichts gegen Juden; wir sind immer gut mit ihnen ausgekommen."' (Enzensberger 1997, 38)

22 'Los espejos se han roto, los imaginarios se han esfumado' (Vázquez Montalbán 2000, 12) ['the mirrors have broken, the imaginaries have vanished']. All translations are mine. Later in the pamphlet, Vázquez Montalbán recalls the European distorting 'mirrors' described by Josep Fontana in his book *The Distorted Past: A Reinterpretation of Europe* (1995), including the barbarian mirror, the Christian, the feudal, the rural, the savage, that of progress, etc. (Vázquez Montalbán 1995, 106).

23 '¿[Q]ué habéis hecho del imaginario democrático?' (13).

24 See e.g., 'La justificación de la hegemonía y bondad europea procede de la suma e interacción de mitos como la bondad original indoeuropea, la razón generando virtudes privadas y públicas, todo lo que ha conducido a un eurocentrismo. Eurocentrismo hecho añicos en cuanto de simple mercado económico común se ha tratado de llegar a la propuesta de esa tercera vía diferente y emancipatoria.' (106) ['The justification of the European hegemony and goodness derives from the sum and the interaction of myths such as the Indo-European original goodness, reason that generates private and public virtues – all that has led to Eurocentrism. Eurocentrism shattered into pieces as soon as, starting from the simple common economic market, it tried to reach the proposal of a third way, different and emancipatory.']

This pamphlet, which echoes Spinelli and Rossi's Manifesto in its utopian idealism despite its cynical, often dejected tone, is still surprisingly current today. Vázquez Montalbán accuses intellectuals of having become part of the professionalization of politics, of having been too close to the prevailing ideas and policies, and thus having served as the echo of power rather than the thorn in its side (he includes himself in this category of failure).[25] Because of this, he argues, we have lost the memory of the past and the vision of the utopian future that we wanted to build. Utopia, no matter how impossible, is necessary as there can be no future without it; but we have failed to lay the foundations for it.[26]

We should have started teaching the necessity of Europe, Vázquez Montalbán writes; we should have created a common imaginary; instead the building of Europe was left to the markets, which have created social inequalities and disaffection, while the cultural unification hasn't gone much further than the Eurovision song contest (109).[27]

---

25 See the chapter '¿Y qué decir de los intelectuales?' (31–48) ['And what about the intellectuals?'], in particular: 'Este presupuesto es aplicable a los dos posibles ejercicios de sabiduría, para movernos en los esquemas clásicos del terreno del saber y en el de la opinión, es decir, en el del filósofo, el historiador o el científico y en el del propagandista, sea sofista, literato o creador de opinión, territorios en los que me inscribiría a mí mismo para ayudar al lector a que abandonase toda esperanza de estar recibiendo sabiduría.' (33) ['This assumption can be applied to the two possible forms, to stay within the classical schemes, of the exercise of knowledge: the terrain of knowledge and that of opinion, that is to say, that of the philosopher, the historian and the scientist, and that of the propagandist, be it the sophist, literary person or opinion-maker, domains in which I will include myself, to help readers abandon any hope that I can teach them anything.']

26 '[N]o interesa salvar la Memoria ni la Historia [...] ni repensar la realidad para acceder a un futuro diferente' (42) ['there is no interest in saving Memory or History [...] nor in re-thinking reality to bring about a different future']; 'Se desacredita al mismo tiempo la memoria y la utopía, [...] el descrédito de la memoria significa que es innecesario recordar las causas de los actuales efectos. [...] Acusan: se han sacrificado toneladas y toneladas de carne humana en nombre de la utopía, en nombre del futuro perfecto. Pero esta condena de las utopías, de esa *conciencia moral del mañana*, oculta que sin ellas no se habría progresado' (71–2) ['Both memory and utopia are discredited [...] The discrediting of memory means that it is unnecessary to remember the causes of the current effects. [...] They accuse: tons and tons of human flesh have been sacrificed in the name of utopia, in the name of the perfect future. But this condemnation of utopias, of the *moral conscience of tomorrow*, conceals that without them there would have been no progress.']

27 'Tal vez a fines de los años cuarenta y comienzos de los cincuenta hubiera sido conveniente iniciar la pedagogía pública de la necesidad de Europa, necesidad derivada del miedo a la reproducción de las causas de las guerras mundiales y a la expansión del bloque comunista a costa del resto de Europa diezmado por las destrucciones. Hubiera fraguado entonces un compartido imaginario europeo, entre el miedo y la esperanza, [...] mientras

In a striking and very disturbing image, Vázquez Montalbán compares Europe to a young woman whose repeated pregnancies due to repeated rapes are explained again and again as an Immaculate Conception:[28] not unlike the Nazis being always in the next village, in not wanting to face up to the unsavoury reality that we created or are complicit with, we find miraculous explanations that absolve us of responsibility. Thus, when Vázquez Montalbán says that the necessity of Europe should have been taught at school, he doesn't mean, to use Agbabi's image, a sugary model of Europe blind to the origins of that sugar: this imaginary, he argues, needs to be aware that Guernica, Sarajevo and Buchenwald are on our conscience, as are imperialism, conquest and extermination. Making this a political electoral programme would destroy any party or politician that proposed it, and therefore it will never be proposed;[29] yet it would be necessary in order to build a Europe that approaches that impossible necessary utopia.

---

se construía una Europa de los estados mercaderes, preludio de una Europa de los mercaderes a secas. [...] no se emprendía un esfuerzo cultural serio para crear una consciencia europea' (108) ['Perhaps in the late 'forties and early 'fifties it would have been advisable to start teaching the necessity of Europe, a necessity stemming from the fear of repeating the causes of the world wars and the expansion of the communist bloc at the expense of the rest of Europe, decimated by the destruction. We should have shaped then a shared European imaginary, between fear and hope, [...instead] we built a Europe of merchant states, a prelude to a Europe just of the merchants. [...] no serious cultural effort was made to create a European consciousness.']

28 'Algo así como una doncella que sólo tuvo embarazos a causa de violaciones, pero que de hecho sigue siendo la *Inmaculada Concepción*' (105) ['a bit like a young woman who gets pregnant repeatedly because of being raped, but who in fact continues to be the *Immaculate Conception*.']

29 'Se precisa, pues, un imaginario que nos recuerde cuantos Guernikas, Sarajevos y Buchenwalds llevamos sobre nuestra mala conciencia y cual ha sido nuestro papel imperialista depredador y creador de desquites que ocultamos en nuestra falsa conciencia. Consciente de las dificultades de todo tipo que hay para proponer este tipo de imaginario, que llevaría al descalabro electoral a la formación política que lo asumiera en su programa y al fracaso personal a todo eurócrata que se empeñara en sustituir los espejos deformadores por espejos necesarios, me temo que seguiremos autoengañandonos [...]' (112) ['We need, therefore, an imaginary that reminds us of how many Guernicas, Sarajevos and Buchenwalds we carry on our bad conscience, and of how our imperialist predatory role created recriminations that we hide in our false conscience. I am aware of all the difficulties that there would be in proposing this type of imaginary, which would lead any political party that adopted it as its programme to electoral defeat and any Eurocrats who committed to replacing the deforming mirrors with necessary mirrors to personal failure, and I fear that we shall carry on deceiving ourselves.']

NINE – Not Yet

We thought 'the idea of Europe' would grow on us, Vázquez Montalbán says, but it didn't – quite the opposite.[30] Vázquez Montalbán's words remind me of the nineteenth-century Italian writer and politician Massimo d'Azeglio, famously supposed to have stated in 1861 that 'fatta l'Italia, bisogna fare gli italiani' ('we have made Italy, now we must make the Italians'). The historian Christopher Duggan (2009) has argued that although these words are usually assumed to signal the political necessity of amalgamating fragmented, diverse peoples on the Italian territory, what d'Azeglio meant was in fact the need to emancipate Italians from the decadence of their character due to centuries of subjection to despotism and to the Church, due to corruption – in order to make people better citizens and individuals, free from vices such as cowardice, dishonesty, irresponsibility.[31] In this sense, what d'Azeglio meant would be less a desire for overcoming historical and cultural differences than an echo of the descriptions offered by Montesquieu about a century earlier, or by Mme de Staël in 1800, in their writings about divisions and differences between the peoples and the cultures of Europe and the moral and temperamental inferiority of the people of the South by comparison with those of the North.[32]

---

30 '[...] se pensó que el mercado generaría los contenidos doctrinales de una "idea de Europa" [...] y un supermercado europeo daría origen a esa consciencia pública necesaria. No ha sido así. Al contrario. El Mercado Único ha generado sectores nacionales agraviados [...]' (108–09) ['we thought that the market would generate the doctrinal contents of an 'idea of Europe' [...] and a European supermarket would deliver the necessary public awareness. It wasn't so. Quite the contrary. The Single Market generated grievances in national sectors.']

31 Duggan's article anticipated part of his contribution to a debate held in Trieste on 29 May 2009 on 'Costruzione dell'identità italiana' ['the construction of Italian identity'] with Ernesto Galli della Loggia and Piero Peluffo.

32 See e.g., when Montesquieu writes in De l'esprit des lois that 'C'est que les peuples du nord ont et auront toujours un esprit d'indépendance et de liberté que n'ont pas les peuples du midi' (Montesquieu 1976, vol. 2, 718) ['The fact is that the peoples of the North have and always will have a spirit of independence and liberty that is lacking in the peoples of the South']; or when he says that the people of the North 'ont peu de vices, assez de vertus, beaucoup de sincérité et de franchise' (477) ['have few vices, enough virtues, much sincerity and frankness'], but if we approach the South we depart from morality itself as 'des passions plus vives multiplieront les crimes' ['the most lively passions multiply crimes']. Translations are mine. For her part, in 1800 Mme de Staël (1991, 203) wrote that the greatest progress of literature and of the soul was achieved when 'les Peuples du Nord' ['the Peoples of the North'] brought about the fall of the Roman Empire and embraced Christianity, which was 'nécessaire aux progrès de la raison' (165) ['necessary to the progress of reason']. Translations are mine. On this, see also Dainotto (2007, 143–59); Boldrini (2013).

Neither the amalgamation of Italians nor the making of us Europeans into better citizens has quite worked yet. (You will notice that hopeful, idealistic 'yet' I added there – though I do so with another bitter smile as I think of the nationalist rhetoric of the current Italian government, whose most vociferously right-wing partners used to just as vociferously preach the break-up of Italy and the secession of the rich and virtuous North from the inferior, poor, immoral South).

D'Azeglio's perspective on Italians is echoed by those who, like Vázquez Montalbán, see how we have made Europe but have failed to make the Europeans. The European centre does not have enough hold, and has lost one piece. The fear is that it may lose others, but a hopeful question – possibly a misguidedly idealistic question – arises: if it is true that the European Union grows through its crises, might the loss of Britain help make the Europeans at last? Might the willing, wilful giving up of the rights of citizenship by one part of the communion lead Europe to realize that European Union citizenship should mean much more than the sum of the parts, and envisage a form of citizenship able to both reflect and transcend, in the most advanced democratic experiment yet, the links to its component nation states: open, that is, not only to the Italians, the Germans, the Poles, etc. – i.e., those who acquire it by already being part of one of the parts – but also, for example, to British individuals who choose to retain it,[33] or to the immigrants that may not be Italians or Greek, or Spanish, or French, but may be Europeans by virtue – *by virtue* – of their having chosen to participate, actively, freely and willingly, in the social life of Europe?[34]

TEN – Who Is the Real European?

The novel *Scontro di civiltà per un ascensore a Piazza Vittorio* (*Clash of Civilizations over an Elevator at Piazza Vittorio*), published in 2006 by the Algerian writer Amara Lakhous, gives us more evidence, if we needed it, that d'Azeglio's words haven't been fulfilled yet. The novel is set in Rome, in an apartment block inhabited by immigrants from various continents and Italians from different parts of Italy. Amedeo is being accused of the murder of one of the building's inhabitants, but no one believes this: he is loved by everyone, he

---

33 This is not to suggest that citizenship can be bought like a gym membership: British citizens are already EU citizens, and the British government's interpretation of the vote to leave the EU seems, at present, to be moving towards one of the most astounding acts of withdrawal of rights that a modern state has ever imposed on its own citizens.

34 On the notion of 'European citizenship' and the aspiration for the European Union to be a 'democratic laboratory', see Balibar (2004).

helps everyone, he is kind, polite, well educated, intelligent, respected, speaks excellent Italian, reads the quality newspapers, knows every corner of Rome and its history perfectly, even better than the taxi drivers. Towards the end, we discover that Amedeo's real name is Ahmed, and that he left Algeria after his fiancée was killed in the civil war.

Lakhous breaks up the very notion of an Italian identity against which that of the migrant is measured, and exposes the hypocrisy of any notion of the superiority of the 'native'. The representation of the migratory experience focuses, significantly, as much on the new global migrants as it does on the Italian history of internal migration and regional differences, making a mockery of the xenophobic rejection of the foreign immigrant in the name of an Italianness that is shown to be non-existent, or at best very fragile. The Neapolitan concierge Benedetta is despised by the Professor from Milan; those from the South despise those from the North, and viceversa; and they all despise or mistrust the foreigners, whom they understand only through their prejudices (they eat dogs, they are ignorant, they are poor...). The polite, well-educated Amedeo is seen as the best, the most integrated, the least despicable Italian of them all – as Benedetta says, 'if Signor Amedeo is a foreigner, then who is the real Italian?' (Lakhous 2008, 34).[35]

Who is the real European?

As we see with Amedeo / Ahmed, the truest meaning of Italianness / Europeanness may best reside in those that arrive into it seeking integration, not in those that already assume, unthinkingly, their belonging to it.

ELEVEN – Europe Doesn't Exist: We Know Because We Live There

So many different Europes, all of them projections, all of them elsewhere, otherwhere, alibis, someone else's fault and responsibility, rocks that attract like a mirage, rocks against which the dreams crash and sink... We must ask ourselves, how do we dialogue with those – both inside and outside – that have seen the idea Europe become a distant ivory tower, or a fortress,[36] that

---

35 '[S]e il signor Amedeo è forestiero [...] chi sarebbe l'italiano vero?' (Lakhous 2006, 44). English translation slightly amended.
36 Enzensberger reflects on the return of the concept of 'Fortress Europe': 'A slogan copyrighted by none other than Joseph Goebbels has reappeared in public debate: 'Fortress Europe'. It once had a military meaning; it returns as an economic and demographic concept. Under these circumstances a booming Europe will do well to remind itself of a Europe in ruins, from which it is separated by only a few decades' (Enzensberger 1994,

excludes them? with those, both inside and outside, who have been excluded from the gains of an open, global market, and who thus seek to leave it, or enter it? What emotional connection can there be with and within this Europe, what shared narrative? Vázquez Montalbán writes: we have to accept that Europe doesn't exist: we know it because we live there.[37]

Who is this 'we', who belongs to it? The use of the first-person plural pronoun is not just a matter of grammar. As we – each one of us – enter into its frame, its borders slightly shift. Because it is a shifter, it is not fixed, its referent does not exist as an absolute. Its usefulness is in its capacious contingency, its ability to mean, each time, something or someone different. 'We' is always in-progress. 'We' demands care, entails a responsibility: care for and responsibility towards those that it claims to represent.

The difference between democracy and populism (both vesting power in the people: Greek *demos*, Latin *populus*) is in what notion of 'we' they are prepared to accept. Populism conceives 'we', 'the people' in absolute terms. It would fix the borders and the meaning of 'we'; it defines itself against 'others'; it grounds the idea of 'the people' in an origin that excludes those that do not share it. In the name of that origin it erases history and silences memory. Democracy's conception of 'we' is, or at least should be (it is often not the case), different; among its difficult but necessary duties is the inclusion and protection of minorities against the tyranny of the majority, as Tocqueville warned nearly two centuries ago in *Democracy in America*. Populism decrees that 51.9% is equivalent to 'the will of the people' – a 'people' conceived as having single 'will' – and that the other 48.1%, plus all those that did not vote (including those that could not), no longer have a say; they have no home: they are 'citizens of nowhere';[38] therefore they have no protection, no rights. In its totalizing, its maths yields less than the total. Democracy, to be

---

99); 'Schon taucht in der Diskussion ein Slogan auf, dessen Copyright kein anderer als Joseph Goebbels für sich in Anspruch nehmen kann: das Schlagwort von der 'Festung Europa'. Was damals militärisch gemeint war, kehrt wieder als ökonomisches und demographisches Konzept. Unter diesen Umständen wird ein Europa im Wohlstand gut daran tun, sich an ein Europa in Trümmern zu erinnern, von dem uns nur ein paar Jahrzehnte trennen.' (Enzensberger 1997, 54)

37   '[H]emos de asumir que Europa aún no existe, y lo sabemos porque vivimos en ella' (Vázquez Montalbán 2000, 112) ['we have to assume that Europe does not yet exist, and we know it because we live there']. Vázquez Montalbán is paraphrasing Georges Arnaud's words about Guatemala in his 1950 novel *Le salaire de la peur* (*The Wages of Fear*).

38   In her speech to the Conservative Party Conference in October 2016, British Prime Minister Theresa May said, 'But if you believe you're a citizen of the world, you're a citizen of nowhere. You don't understand what the very word "citizenship" means' (May 2016).

democratic, would contain, care for, 51.9% *plus* 48.1% *plus* all those who did not vote or could not vote, including the children whose future it is the custodian of, but which it does not own. Its maths yields more than the sum total. Recognizing that Europe doesn't exist, that it is a shifter, always in-progress, means recognizing that its idea cannot be founded on a callous 'will of the people'[39] that wants 'everybody to be the same', that silences and expunges (the step is a short one) those who think differently, who like a different food or have different memories. A community built on a totalizing, absolute 'will of the people' would again and again relegate Spinelli and Rossi to their prison on an island, Levi to the *Lager*, Drakulić (and me) to waves of nausea, Azel to his nightmares. Yet a community that does not recognize the disenfranchisement of large swathes of its citizens, made citizens of nowhere by their inability to influence or resist the local effects of global events (Marsili and Milanese 2018, 3–5) is equally callous.

Addressing these problems is the difficult task of politics. As Cassirer remarked in 1944, however, 'The great political and social reformers are indeed constantly under the necessity of treating the impossible as if it were possible'; utopia is nowhere, but 'just such a conception of a nowhere has stood the test and proved its strength in the development of the modern world [...] The ethical world is never given; it is forever in the making' (Cassirer 1972, 61). The 'symbolic construct' of Utopia (62) – what Vázquez Montalbán (2000, 72) calls 'the *moral conscience of tomorrow*' so tightly intertwined with the memory of the past – also needs literature, the arts, acts of imagination and of representation; it needs us to learn to read and to tell, with care and better than we have done, the stories and the histories of the contingent, everchanging but capacious 'we' that has emerged from, and that continues to be shaped by, our encounters, exchanges, conflicts, similarities and divergences; of the emotional bonds that these encounters, and sometimes clashes, engender; of our responsibility to engender them; of how we always, inevitably, cause the 'we' to shift because we cannot but walk into the frame.

The task of bringing Europe into existence, of *being there* even when we'd like it to be elsewhere, is, to coin a phrase, infinite. That Europe doesn't exist is not its weakness, it must be its strength.[40]

For an extended discussion of the tensions between cosmopolitanism and citizenship, between globalization, Europe and the nation state, see Marsili and Milanese (2018).

39 As Albert Weale shows in his recent discussion of this concept, 'Any pervasive myth is dangerous in a democracy; the myth of the will of the people is particularly dangerous.' (Weale 2018, xii)

40 My warm thanks to Sergio Graziosi, Josh Cohen and Chris Baldick for their thoughts on the draft of this paper.

Works Cited

Agbabi, Patience. 2013. 'A Doll's House', *The Poetry Review*, 103.1.
artdaily.com. 'Palestinian Artist Mona Hatoum at MOCA LA', http://artdaily.com/news/5259/Palestinian-Artist-Mona-Hatoum-at-MOCA-LA [last accessed 6 December 2018].
Auden, W. H.. 1979. *Selected Poems* (new ed. E. Mendelson; London: Faber).
Balibar, Étienne. 2004. *We, the People of Europe? Reflections on Transnational Citizenship* (trl. James Swenson; Princeton, NJ: Princeton University Press).
Ben Jelloun, Tahar. 2006. *Partir* (Paris: Gallimard).
Ben Jelloun, Tahar. 2009. *Leaving Tangier* (trl. Linda Coverdale; London: Arcadia).
Boldrini, Lucia. 2013. 'The Uncertain Mediterranean Borders of Comparative Literature', in *IV Uluslararasi Karşilaştirmali Edebiyat Bilimi Kongresi, 'Kültürler ve Değerler Buluşması' / IV International Comparative Literature Congress, 'Meeting of Cultures and Values', Bildiriler / Proceedings*, ed. Adnan Karaismailoğlu & Yusuf Öz (Kırıkkale: Kırıkkale Universitesi Yayilari), 441–454.
Cassirer, Ernst. 1972. *An Essay on Man: An Introduction To a Philosophy of Human Culture* (New Haven, CT: Yale University Press).
Curtius, Ernst Robert. 1948. *Europäische Literatur und lateinisches Mittelalter* (Bern: Francke).
Curtius, Ernst Robert. 1953. *European Literature and the Latin Middle Ages* (trl. Willard R. Trask; London: Routledge and Kegan Paul).
Dainotto, Roberto M. 2007. *Europe (in Theory)* (Durham, NC: Duke University Press).
Drakulić, Slavenka. 1999. *Café Europa: Life after Communism* (London: Penguin).
Duggan, Christopher. 2009. 'Il significato di "Fatta l'Italia, bisogna fare gli italiani"', *Il Piccolo*, 24 May, http://ricerca.gelocal.it/ilpiccolo/archivio/ilpiccolo/2009/05/24/NZ_26_PIED.html [last accessed 6 December 2018].
Elalamy, Youssouf Amine. 2008. *Two Novellas by YAE: A Moroccan in New York; and Sea Drinkers* (trl. John Liechty; Lanham: Lexington Books).
Elalamy, Youssouf Amine. 2011. *Les clandestins: roman* (Vauvert: Au diable vauvert).
Enzensberger, Hans Magnus. 1994. 'Europe in Ruins', in *Civil War: From L. A. to Bosnia* (London: Granta), 73–99.
Enzensberger, Hans Magnus. 1997. 'Europa in Trümmern. Ein Prospekt', in *Zickzack. Aufsätze* (Frankfurt /Main: Suhrkamp), 33–54.
Fowler, H. W., & F. G. Fowler. 1990. *The Concise Oxford Dictionary of Current English* (8th ed.; Oxford: Clarendon Press).
Gasché, Rodolphe. 2009. *Europe, or the Infinite Task: A Study of a Philosophical Concept* (Stanford: Stanford University Press).
Heller, Margaret. 2008. 'Derrida and the Idea of Europe', *Dalhousie French Studies* 82: 93–106.

Lakhous, Amara. 2006. *Scontro di civiltà per un ascensore a piazza Vittorio* (Rome: Edizioni e/o).

Lakhous, Amara. 2008. *Clash of Civilizations Over an Elevator in Piazza Vittorio* (trl. Ann Goldstein; New York: Europa Editions).

Leerssen, Joep. 2006. *National Thought in Europe: A Cultural History* (Amsterdam: Amsterdam University Press).

Levi, Primo. 1986. *The Periodic Table* (trl. Raymond Rosenthal; London: Abacus).

Levi, Primo. 1997. *Il sistema periodico* (*Opere*, 1; Torino: Einaudi).

Marsili, Lorenzo & Niccolo Milanese. 2018. *Citizens of Nowhere: How Europe Can Be Saved from Itself* (London: Zed).

May, Theresa. 2016. 'Full Text: Theresa May Conference Speech', https://blogs.spectator.co.uk/2016/10/full-text-theresa-mays-conference-speech/ [last accessed 6 December 2018].

Montesquieu, Charles de Secondat baron de. 1976. *Oeuvres complètes* (ed. Roger Callois; 2 vols; Paris: Gallimard).

Reid, Sue. 2015. 'By day a tourist paradise, by night a migrant hell: The pretty Turkish beach where people smugglers send families to their deaths', *Daily Mail*, 3 September, https://www.dailymail.co.uk/news/article-3221686/By-day-tourist-paradise-night-migrant-hell-pretty-Turkish-beach-people-smugglers-send-families-deaths.html [last accessed 6 December 2018].

Spinelli, Altiero, & Ernesto Rossi. 2017. *Il manifesto di Ventotene* (Milano: Mondadori).

Staël, Anne-Louise-Germaine de. 1991. *De la littérature considerée dans ses rapports avec les institutions sociales* (ed. Gérard Gengembre & Jean Goldzink; Paris: Flammarion).

Tate. 2011. 'Mona Hatoum: Studio visit', *Tateshots - 29 September*, https://www.tate.org.uk/art/artists/mona-hatoum-2365/mona-hatoum-studio-visit [last accessed 6 December 2018].

Valéry, Paul. 1957. 'La Crise de l'esprit', in Id., *Œuvres* (ed. Jean Hytier; 2 vols; Paris: Gallimard), 1: 988–1014.

Valéry, Paul. 1977. 'The Crisis of the Mind', in *Paul Valéry: An Anthology*, ed. James R. Lawler (London: Routledge & Kegan Paul), 94–107.

Vázquez Montalbán, Manuel. 2000. *Panfleto desde el planeta de los simios* (Barcelona: Mondadori).

Weale, Albert. 2018. *The Will of the People: A Modern Myth* (Cambridge: Polity).

Willis, Amy. 2015. 'British tourists are complaining about refugees ruining their holidays to Kos and making them feel "awkward"', *Metro*, 28 May, https://metro.co.uk/2015/05/28/unsympathetic-british-tourists-complain-refugees-are-making-their-holiday-to-kos-awkward-5219529/# [last accessed 6 December 2018].

CHAPTER 7

You Say *Liberté, Égalité, Fraternité?* Japanese Critical Perceptions of the Idea of Europe: A Preliminary Reflection for the Regeneration of Universal Humanism

Shigemi Inaga

1   Preliminary Observations

1.1   *From Conceptual Impasse to Mutual Dialogue*
If the reader is interested in the ideas of Europe that Asians have concocted, I would strongly recommend reading their travel writings. I am not making this proposal out of nationalistic patriotism. And yet the lack of bilateral balance in the flow of information should be mentioned: European literature is fully accessible in Japanese translation but not vice versa.

It should not be forgotten that many Europeans have left writings on the Rest of the world. These European observations have served as the basis for descriptions in fields ranging from the natural sciences to humanities (like *Der Kosmos* by Alexander von Humboldt). In the case of Japan, we can easily establish a list from Saint Francis Xavier (1506–1552), or Luís Fróis (1532–1597), Engerbert Kempfer, Franz von Siebold, B.H. Chamberlain, and Lafcadio Hearn up to Roland Barthes and Maurice Pinguet (Saeki and Haga 1987). Natural history, as well as geography and ethnography, have since developed into modern academic disciplines, and Western methodology is predominant today, especially in social sciences. Area studies and cultural anthropology are no exception. Most cultural theories are European or Western products and it is rare that the non-European reflections on Europe have been seriously taken into account (Le Pichon and Eco 2011).

This lack of reciprocity has been questioned. Naoki Sakai has vehemently criticized the basic distinction between Western *humanitas* and non-Western *anthropos: humanitas*, originating from Europe, has subordinated the Rest of the world as *anthropos*. Non-Europeans (from Asia, Africa, and South America) serve as the suppliers of primary data for the benefit of Western theories, which claim the status of *humanitas*. The West (*humaine*) consumes the raw (i.e., *sauvage*) materials supplied by the Rest (Sakai 2001). In the post-colonial context, this dichotomy has not been overcome; on the contrary, the hegemony of European scientific methodology has been reinforced by the Westernized immigrant intellectuals. These *aussereuropäische* émigré academics, coming from the Rest of the world, now represent (by way of their intoxication to) Western scholarship, occupying core or marginal positions in many European and American universities.

1.2 Crisis of the European Model

The European style educational system has almost completely seized the entire surface of the human habitable zone on the earth, suffocating so-called non-European traditional cultures (in the name of 'human rights', preventing child abuse, etc.). In parallel, cultural anthropology has lost its conventional 'fields' of research in the last 40 years. English or American language(s) have triumphed as the only 'officially recognized working' language(s) (of hegemonic importance), especially in natural sciences: other European languages (including French or German) have lost their 'civil rights', while other 'minor' non-European languages are literally on the edge of extinction (made to survive perhaps only by the discipline of area studies, in the category of *anthropos*).

To what extent is Europe responsible for this English-American linguistic imperialism? I ask this question because some scholars, like Geoffrey Barraclough, strongly oppose the idea of including Britain and the US among the European cultural legacy (Barraclough 1963; Barraclough and Kimura 1977). Let us also add, however, that the current linguistic neo-colonialism by English-American languages is doomed to decline sooner or later: before the mid-21st century the Spanish speaking population of the United States will outnumber English speakers; and statistically speaking, at least in non-academic fields, Chinese and Spanish enjoy a much greater numbers of users than the official language of the former British Empire.

1.3 Toward a Methodological 'Clash of Projections'

Yet the geographical 'territorial issue' of linguistic occupation is not my main concern here. Let me mention Sir George Sansom to explain my intention. This British scholar and diplomat is known for having written one of the best accounts of Japanese cultural history for European readers (Sansom 1931). The merit of his writing consists of its treating Japan not as an isolated case in a far off place, but as an important organic part of the entirety of World History. His comparative approach not only allowed him to make Japan accessible to a Western (or at least English and French) readership, but it also enabled Japanese readers to better understand the particular qualities of British (in particular) and European culture and society (in general). Characteristics of each culture cannot be revealed without mutual elucidation between the observer and the observed. And yet European culture tended to believe in the universal validity of its own criteria when judging other cultures in reference to European standards considered superior, absolutely rational and ultimately relevant.

The reverse tendency of ego-centrism among the Non-Western Rest was no less harmful. In Japanese studies, the controversy around Ruth Benedict's *The Chrysanthemum and The Sword* is a typical case (Benedict 1946). Based upon interview records of Japanese prisoners of war during the Second World War, the author, an American cultural anthropologist, proposed the idea of Japan as 'the culture of shame', as opposed to the 'culture of sin' (in the model of Judeo-Christian value judgment). This classical book became a famous / infamous bestseller in post-war Japan: Many Japanese nationalists took 'shame culture' as a proof of Japan's moral inferiority. They felt hurt by the American author (and ashamed). They saw her book as asserting the existence of an ethical problem in Japanese culture and of a deficiency rooted in the country's shame culture. This (tautological) reaction is itself a sort of *amour propre blessé*, or a wounded self-respect.

Yet, it is well known that Clifford Geertz, in his *Works and Lives: The Anthropologist as Author* (1988) reversed this negative perception of the 'shame culture' (Geertz 1988). At the outset, he writes, the Japanese 'shame culture' looked strange and unfamiliar to him, but the reading of Ruth Benedict's entire book finally convinces him of the relevance of the moral judgment based on the feeling of 'shame'. Whereas, upon finishing the book, he could no longer feel at ease with the Judeo-Christian moral code; he had already lost his naive conviction in the guilt and punish model; his spontaneous reliance on the European and Western 'guilty consciousness' as a self-evident and universal moral code had been collapsed.

Similar reciprocal 'deforming' mirror effects of finding an incommensurable chirality (to use an optical metaphor) in encounters with other cultures are not rare. Eminent Europeans have often experienced this uneasy sense of identity crisis in their encounters with Japanese culture. João Rodrigues (1558/60?–1633/4), a Portuguese missionary to Japan, is one of the first cases (Inaga 2008). He tried to understand Japanese language grammar according to the Latin template of declension. But in doing so he found it simply impossible; the Japanese language cannot be reduced to the 'Catholic' i.e. universal code of Latin. This brought him to discover new grammatical categories such as the particle. Two and a half centuries later, Percival Lowell, the famous American astrophysicist and diplomat found a 'reversed world of humpty-dumpty' when he disembarked at Yokohama Bay at the end of the

19th Century. Such experiences have been so frequently repeated by each generation of Euro-American travellers that Claude Lévi-Strauss, in his final book, *L'Autre face de la lune* (2011) composed a succinct genealogy of the Western idea of Japan (Lévi-Strauss 2001). He characterized it as the 'opposite-reversed land' of Europe. Yet I wonder if his vision was not a typical European projection? Lévy-Strauss's theory of complementarity between the West and the East may well be subscribed to the general strategy of *apprivoiser l'Autre* or taming the Other by boxing it into one's own categories. In so doing, the clash of mutual projections is 'adequately' neutralized and domesticated for 'appropriate' arrangement (Inaga 2013).

With this preliminary observation in mind, let me now examine some of the 'ideas of Europe' left by Japanese intellectuals in their encounters with it. Nevertheless, let me declare in advance, to avoid useless misunderstanding, that privileging Japan as an exception is not my intention. I would not want to repeat what has often happened in the case of infamous *Nihonjin-ron*, or discourses on Japanese-ness.[1] I also have to confess the limitation of my own approach: even by limiting myself to Japan, developing a full anthology of Japanese travel writings in Europe would be out of the question (Ōkubo 2008). The following are just three typical but extremely personal case studies ranging through three generations, so as to examine Japanese reactions to three fundamental ideas of Europe that were elaborated in the French Revolution, namely *liberté*, *égalité* and *fraternité*.

2   Three Cases in Question

2.1   *First Case Study: Mori Ōgai and Questioning the Idea of* Fraternité

Let us begin with the third idea: *fraternité*. Mori (Rintarō) Ōgai (1862–1922) was one of the first Japanese medical students to stay in Europe. He was sent to Prussia by the Japanese Army in 1884 at the age of 23 and stayed there until 1888. *Mori Ōgai Gedenkstätte* is located in the city of Berlin. He is now remembered as a prolific writer and translator of many European works of literature into Japanese via German original or translations (Goethe, Shakespeare, Oscar Wilde, Ibsen, H.C. Andersen, Schnitzler, Zola, Maupassant, D'Annunzio, Hofmannsthal, Dostoevsky, and Gorki, to mention just a few). And yet he finished his official career at the top rank of medical doctor and inspector general in the Japanese Army. During his mission in Prussia as a military attaché, the

---

1   See the exceptionally original article on Nihonjin-ron in Wikipedia ('Nihonjinron', n.d.).

young Ōgai took part in a conference of the International Red Cross held in Karlsruhe in September 1887.[2]

On the fourth day of the conference, one issue came up in discussion, namely: if a war were to break out outside of Europe, should each branch of the European Red Cross be mobilized for assistance? The question was raised from the Dutch delegation. The supposed 'war', it was assumed, could not be other than a clash between European colonial military powers entering into combat with one another, inevitably involving colonized local rebels. At this occasion, the young Japanese officer got permission to speak and gave his opinion as follows. Firstly, as the issue was concerned only with the European branches, Japan had to step back from the decision-making and abstain from voting. This is of course common sense reasoning in itself, and does not constitute any protest. And yet it also implicitly pointed out the inadequacy of Europeans' grasp of the subject, for they unthinkingly overlooked the presence of non-European membership and representatives. Japan's abstention amounts to an indirect objection to the violation made against the spirit of Red Cross. Mori's voice made it clear to the European members that the issue constituted an imminent threat to the principle of fraternity among the Red Cross constituents. The supposed idea or ideal of 'equality' among members was called into question.

Secondly, Mori also made Japan's position clear: it was not Mori's or Japan's intention to propose a modification of the relevant clause, but in principle the issue should have been presented as follows. If a war were to break out in one continent, the Red Cross branches in other continents would be mobilized to offer assistance. Having said this, Mori added: Japan takes it for granted that the Japanese Red Cross would act to provide necessary assistance if a war were to break out on a continent other than Asia, including, obviously Europe. The minutes of the meeting, kept in French, show that at this statement by Mori, a 'bravo' rose up from the audience (Kobori 2013, 158). In the following session, Mori also made it clear by presenting as proof a printed booklet that the Japanese Army had already distributed to its members with the Japanese translation of the Geneva Convention of 1864 (dealing with the treatment of the prisoners) even though other European nations who had signed it earlier had not yet distributed the document to their militaries. Mori somewhat proudly noted in his diary that the Russian representative, 'Usfaitcheff' (*sic*) gently touched Mori's shoulder and expressed his 'happy amazement'. From then on the European delegates' attitude toward Japan improved remarkably (Kobori 2013, 157–8).

---

2   For biographical details, see Kobori 2013. The anecdote that follows here is on pp. 157–158

Obviously the young Mori, only 26 years old, must have made his statement out of racial and ethnical indignation, feeling implicit discrimination against his nation. The unconscious European ego-centrism was revealed by this young participant from Asia. His rational statement, despite its barely concealed resentment, gained general approval, for it was stated in full respect of the moral spirit which the International Red Cross had been supposed to incarnate: the universal fraternity or brother-sisterhood. Mori's statement, made as a modest contribution by a non-European member, was to be put into practice by the Japanese army as its basic moral spirit during the First World War. The Japanese Red Cross – and especially its mobilized nurses with self-sacrificial devotion – was highly appreciated as having played an exemplary role in the assistance of wounded soldiers. By this time Mori had become one of the most important individuals in the whole military medical rescue operation. It is also well known that the Japanese military discipline in the occupation of the capital Yanjing in China during the so-called 'Boxer Rebellion' (1899–1901) was highly praised. Furthermore, during WWI, the treatment of the German prisoners sent from Qingdao to Japan was exceptionally well regarded by the foreign press.

Naturally the question comes to mind: why was it not so in the Second World War? Why was the Geneva Convention systematically neglected during battles in China and the Pacific Ocean, 20 years after Mori's retirement and death? When and why did the Japanese Army go wrong? One may be horrified by the fact that the atrocities committed by the Japanese Army in China as well as in the Pacific during WW2 can be located in the mechanical extension of the principle that Mori clearly stated at the Karlsruhe International Red Cross Conference: that Japan is entitled to manage according to its own will any war so long as it occurs in Asia. This historical irony also reveals another hidden egocentricity inherent in the benevolent action of the Red Cross movement.

2.2 Second Case Study: Takeyama Michio, and Questioning the Idea of Égalité

Europe claims and promotes the idea of equality; and yet the case of Mori's intervention exposed its limit as well as the logical incoherence in its practical application. In fact, many non-European elites and intellectuals could not help feeling that the principle of equality is applied only to European and Europeanized citizens, but not to the 'coloured people'. The case of Takeyama Michio (1903–1984) epitomizes this pattern – yet in an unexpected way and with a self-conscious insight.

One of Takeyama's great-uncles was an eminent early figure in the field of German literature in Japan, though his glory was eclipsed by the return of Mori

Ōgai to Japan. Takeyama himself was also an exceptionally talented intellectual from the privileged elite. He was appointed associate professor at Tokyo High School immediately after his graduation from the Tokyo Imperial University in 1926. The following year he embarked for Europe and stayed there until 1930. During his time in Europe, he travelled to Spain. It was only after Japan's defeat in World War II that he published an essay on his Spanish experience.[3]

The essay begins with a rather shocking statement: 'What surprised me in Europe is the fact that counterfeit money was in every country'. Takeyama and his cousin were easy victims. If they were not so frequently duped in Germany and France, they noticed that in Spain they were ideal targets. In the countryside they were about to buy a mantilla, but when his cousin put 5 huge silver five-peseta coins on the table, something unexpected happened. The shopkeeper (a lady of a certain age; her gender cannot be overlooked in this cultural and historical context) gazed at the coins, and then all of a sudden screamed. People around them got angry and furiously accused the Japanese tourists of treachery. About twenty coins of the five-peseta they had received previously in exchange turned out to be fake money. The two Japanese gentlemen cleverly learned a lesson from this 'surprisingly' unpleasant incident, and took caution not to receive any more fake coins. Still, how to get rid of the doomed fake 20-odd coins before leaving Spain remained their obsessive concern.

Several times they tried to 'cheat' the Spanish merchants or tried to pay with the dubious coins for the entrance of a bullfight; of course every attempt stupidly and miserably failed; the local people were shrewder than the naïve tourists. They once lost their reservation at a hotel as the room had been changed without their being notified. Despite the cancellation, a hotel boy chased after them to ask for a tip. They handed him the ill-fated coins. The next day the boy waited for the two Japanese at the entrance of a new hotel. Obviously, his aim was to ask to change the counterfeit to the genuine currency.

It so happened that it was not until they took the international train for France that they could pay farewell to the wicked coins. The chance for liquidation finally came when they were to pay their bill in the dining car. The payment was to be made by dropping the coins in a silver bowl that the chief server carried by hand. The bowl was already full of silver coins glittering in a gorgeous fashion. The Japanese took mischievous courage in pouring the dubious coins into this bowl. The chief server, while gazing at the coins with the effigy of the Crown Prince, did not say anything. He might have noticed the nature of the wicked coins by their clinking sound. Maybe the dignity of his

---

3   For Takeyama's biography, Hirakawa 2013. The anecdote that follows here is in Takeyama 2017, 15–34.

profession prevented him from complaining to his foreign customers despite his concealed scepticism. In any case, now that the coins were deposited in the bowl, no one could discern who contributed the genuine coins and who mixed in the illegal coins.

Takeyama's cousin said, 'Et voilà,' and the chief servant graciously saluted the guests and left them to move on to his subsequent duty. The two Japanese men, upon returning to their third class compartment, could not help exclaiming 'bravo!' with delight at their success. But at second thought, Takeyama murmured that they had committed the crime of taking lunch without payment. To this his cousin furiously reacted by saying, quite theoretically: 'We have just returned the counterfeit coins to the Spanish National Railway. This means that we have had the Spanish government compensate. It is simply logical and absolutely normal that the government pay back the damage their people caused to foreigners'. Yet, they could not entirely forget the bad aftertaste of a guilty consciousness their 'success' had left behind. And so they concluded their ill-natured adventure with the following sore remark: 'Fake or forgery should be accomplished with an utmost dignity and noblesse'.

Generally speaking, at border crossings, tourists have to declare taxable assets. They might end up paying the tax with counterfeit money like that foisted on Takeyama. Whether beneficial or harmful, forgery constantly changes its physiognomy. And nobody can be a better eyewitness of this unexpected metamorphosis than the foreign tourist from far away. The reality of frequent treachery and prestidigitation are shamelessly pressed upon foreigners, for they are the best targets and the easiest victims to be cheated. From this experience it seems that our Japanese professor learned how to pay cultural tax at the inter-cultural border crossing. The idea of equality, proclaimed as a European ethical code, reveals itself as unfortunately deceptive, when it is confronted with the economic reality such as the circulation of the counterfeit money. It is from beneath the counterfeit currency that the truth manifests itself.

Money transactions reveal the hidden side of so-called hard currency. The counterfeit coins flooding the black market epitomize the behaviour of the soft currency that surreptitiously sustains the market economy as a whole. A similar counterfeit transaction can easily happen so long as border control is practised amidst unequal power relations. In other words, authority is inevitably destined to create counterfeiters and outlaws, simply because they are indispensable so as to maintain the established social order.

Let us remember that Takeyama remained one of the rare breed of 'conservative' intellectuals; throughout the Cold War he was a staunch anti-communist, basing this opposition to totalitarian hegemony on the same logic as his rejection of Nazism during the period when Japan concluded the Anti-Comintern Pact with the Third Reich of Nazi Germany in 1936 against the Soviet Union. Takeyama had the insight to perceive what kind of 'fakes' had been concealed underneath the specious regimes of National Socialism and Stalinism.

Let me also recall one more fact. The film *The Harp of Burma*, directed by Ichikawa Kon, received the San Giorgio Prize at the Venice Film Festival in September 1956, a few years after Japan's independence was restored following the 1945 defeat. Michio Takeyama was the author of the novel on which the movie was based. It tells the story of a Japanese ex-soldier musician who remains in Burma after Japan's defeat; he becomes monk so as to console the souls of the unknown dead whose bodies have been left and scattered in the battlefields. Takeyama, who had lost many of his students mobilized in the war, borrowed a *Märchen* narrative while intending to show through fiction that there had been the possibility of reconciliation between the British and Japanese armies to put the war to an end.

The novel had been published in 1948 despite the strict censorship under the US military occupation on matters related to war. While the Japanese staff members of the American GHQ classified Takeyama's printed proof as inadequate, the American CIE officers removed the prohibition and allowed the publication. Was it a simple coincidence that Takeyama published his Spanish essay shortly after this incident? Was there not a hidden connivance between the two? Censorship is a form of gate-keeping at a checkpoint. There, egalitarian principles can be easily curtailed. But curiously enough, just as the counterfeit money was miraculously rehabilitated at Takeyama's border crossing, his own fiction narrative of the war was also saved from self-imposed Japanese censorship. In both cases, thanks to the implicated gatekeepers, the precarious nature of the egalitarian principle was shown while revealing inherent and concealed social crisis. The truth reveals itself through the compensation of the fake manipulation under the threatening risk to equality.

2.3 Third Case Study: Kudō Tetsumi and the Idea of Liberté

During the Cold War period, when Takeyama was regarded by the left wing as an opinion leader among conservative liberals, the idea of liberty was highly respected in the Western bloc. 1961 and 1962 saw the coup d'état in Korea, the Cuba Missile Crisis and the independence of Algeria in 1962. In 1963, South Vietnam also experienced a coup d'état, a prelude to the Vietnam War. The Mediterranean Sea was set on alert by the Cyprus Crisis of 1963–64. It was during this crisis-ridden period that Kudō Tetsumi (1935–1990) arrived in Paris (1962). Japan had also experienced a major crisis in 1960: the Japan-U.S. security treaty had provoked massive protests.

Kudō was already famous in Japan for his provocative performances at the Yomiuri Independent annual art exhibitions. He was greeted in Paris by sensational frenzy, but not without provoking instinctive disgust and aversion. Take the case of *Love* (1964). Kudō explains his bizarre 'work' as follows:

> Two huge heads make a 'love affair' in an electric circuit. Their body is degenerated into quasi-extinction and only the head skulls have evolved. Their kissing lips are already half rotten; or rather the pair of lips no longer exists but as contact points for an electric discharge. The touching lips emit the message 'JE VOUS AIME' through Morse code. [...] Here we see the hideous reality of sexual intercourse: your voice, your attitude, your caresses, your smell, your sweat and moisture... all are transmitted to your body through dot-dash signals so as to create effects – just like galvanic skin response. Undoubtedly, your body at the moment is nothing but an integrated electric circuit (before the IC was invented); everything is in degeneration except for the huge head containing the brain. Why? Because the skull containing brain is the symbol of the electric circuit.[4]

This was Kudō's response to W.A.L. Beeren, curator of the Amsterdam Municipal Art Museum. While rescuing Kudō from miserable poverty in Paris, Beeren gently protested against Kudō's work by the need of 'We Europeans' to 'retain something of human noblesse'. This was enough for Kudō to burst into a fit of rage. Or more precisely, his enemy (i.e. 'Mr. Beeren' in particular and 'Europeans' in general) had just been caught in a trap Kudō had carefully laid. Beeren wondered if *Love* represents an 'atomic catastrophe with human bits and

---

4   Our retranslation from a Japanese translation of the 'original' English made by Nakahara Yūsuke (1968, 143). The published English version reads as follows:

> Two big heads? Those two enormous head, which expose electric circuits are sitting and talking 'love'. Their bodies are in a state of degeneration; only their heads seem to develop. They are kissing with their rooting mouths—no, their mouths are connected by electric contact parts. They say 'JE VOUS AIME' in Morse code. (...) when you are having sex; the voice, the caresses, the atmosphere, the smell, the heat, and the humidity... all of these convey a kind of signal to your body, a signal that achieves an effect. There's no doubt about it: your body is a mass of circuits at that time—that is, everything degenerates at that moment, except the big head that is a symbol of the electric circuit.

> This English version was originally published as Kudō Tetsumi, 'Dear Mr. Beeren (Dear Europeans)', and distributed in Kudō's Exhibition catalogue held at the Galerie 20, Paris, in 1965. It was reprinted in Kudō and National Museum of Art 2013, 153.

pieces left over', and asked Kudō, 'Do you want to collect us like scalps? But why in such clinical fashion? Don't be angry, but I cannot help thinking of the Nazis who made human-skin lampshades'.

To this Kudō, with an affected sarcasm, cynically and provocatively riposted:

> 'Human *noblesse*?' Let me herewith diagnose your disease as a kind of nostalgia. I do not want to deny your Christian tradition, your human *noblesse*, because shock treatment can sometimes have disastrous effects. But, gradually, you should try to think them as mere commodities – like stockings, ice cream, or instant coffee. They are as noble as Christian tradition and human *noblesse* – useful and convenient, too, aren't they? [...] 'Melting human beings?' Your 'human *noblesse*' is melting away and only the skin is left. But this is not 'murder' as you put it. It was not melted by chemical weapons. It is a necessary phenomenon; it begins to melt, it is molten, and it is reborn as a new transparent body (organism)'. (Kudō and National Museum of Art 2013)

In the subtitle of the text we read 'Dear Europeans'. Obviously this text was addressed to all Europeans. What was, then, Kudō's message to 'Europeans'? Kudō strongly felt that he had been deceived. He had naively believed while in Japan that the idea of liberty and freedom in expression was unconditionally respected in Europe. In reality, however, he found Europe bound to the idea of 'human noblesse', which he found hypocritical. In reality, human dignity had been threatened (during WWII and the following Cold War crises). And yet, by crudely revealing this plain fact of decaying humanity by way of artistic expression, Kudō had to face harsh criticism and instinctive repugnance from European intellectuals.

If so, intentionally provoking repugnance by way of artistic expression then became a convenient and useful weapon for Kudō: by transgressing the implicit moral code of 'human noblesse', Kudō successfully dis-covered, laid bare, the trauma in the depth of the European psyche. The idea of *liberté* was in fact *l'autre face* (the other hidden side) of a Judeo-Christian God. *Liberté* is guaranteed only at the cost of total surrender to God. Kudō continues:

> I can understand you Europeans creating God in your own image. But I think it's high time God was sold in the automats, neatly wrapped in small plastic bags. Anyway, your opinion is to me nothing more than a guinea-pig reaction. Please don't misunderstand me. I don't think of you alone as guinea-pigs [for scientific experiments] – all people to me are guinea-pigs to a doctor. (Kudō and National Museum of Art 2013).

3 Humanism in Question

3.1 Decomposed Humanism

Kudō did not come to Europe to learn the idea and ideals of humanism in Art. On the contrary, he claimed himself to be an outrageous and childish suicide-attack commander. To throw the Fine Arts as an institution into commotion and disturbance, or even into a delusion, was his only objective. Yet destruction was not the aim; rather, his raison d'être in Europe was not to 'provoke' but to provide a cure, a remedy to the disease of 'human dignity and noblesse' by which Europe was completely 'contaminated' in Kudō's eyes and perception. Of course this was by definition 'outrageous', i.e. excessive and beyond his position or status, and Kudō himself was well aware of his 'measureless' ambition (ambition démesurée). His dream was to be integrated into Europe as a kind of retro-virus, so as to dismantle and regenerate the Idea of Europe from within.

At a public lecture in Japan, Kudō gave the following explanation of his *Human Dwarf Tree Ningen Bonsai*:

> To explain it to the Japanese, one should say; to make a good career you should be moulded into a good form under the constraint of the wire rope like this 'bonsai'; this is the only way to compete with foreigners [i.e. Europeans]. To explain the same human dwarf tree to Europeans, one should modify the logic and say: despite the constraint of the chains and wire rope, life searches for its emancipation. We can understand in this way the human dignity and noblesse (Kudō 1982, 120).

This remark caused laughter among the Japanese audience.

Here is a lucid comparison of the Idea of Humanity. Sociologically speaking, while European individualism is born from the resistance to constraint, the Japanese collectivism consists of 'killing' egocentrism in the same way as 'cultivating' and 'taking care' of the dwarf tree. Both have their merits and demerits: on the one hand Europe is affected by the disease of deformity (the idea of liberty and freedom creates a hideous freak), whereas on the other hand, Japanese society hampers the freedom of/to deformity. Kudō, as an alienated exile and absolute outsider, does not belong to any side. And yet his existence is only tolerated in Europe, and never 'in Japan', he adds, 'where even the freedom of provocation is not allowed'.[5] This was why he fled Japan and stayed in Europe.

---

5   Kudo 1976; the original Japanese text is in Tetsumi Kudō and National Museum of Art 2013, 415.

3.2   Toward a Philosophy of Impotence

His confrontation with Europe as an idea led him to a kind of pessimistic defence of life through interminable germination by way of electronic, genetic and organic devices. Foreshadowing synthetic biology, which emerged only after Kudō's premature death at the age of 55 (in 1990), Kudō searched for possible ways of survival for beings that are not worth living. This severe anti-humane biology in search of an 'inhuman' sterile beauty is at the core of Kudō's so-called *philosophie de l'impotence*.[6]

According to Kudō, this 'philosophy of impotence'[7] was born under the American 'nuclear umbrella' provided by the U.S.-Japan Security Treaty, which is commonly referred to by the abridged Japanese term 'Anpo'. In other words, 'impo' results from 'ampo,' if one can use a play on words. It is true that Japan enjoyed the idea of 'liberty' under the American military occupation, but the very idea of liberty was the cause of Japan's cultural impotence! Japanese culture was thus 'domesticated' or rather literally 'castrated' by the Idea of Europe.

4   In the Guise of a Conclusion

We can certainly detect here, in Kudō's extravagant endeavour and his almost insane serenity, the ultimate state of a 'clash of projections' which crisscrossed around the 'idea of Europe'. This clash occurred within the evolving 'mutual perceptions' of Europe and Japan found in the last 100 years. What began with Mori Ōgai's logical protest regarding a violation to the idea of *fraternité* (1880s) was followed by Takeyama Michio's self-conscious questioning of the idea of *égalité* (1930–40s), and *liberté* in artistic expression led Kudō Tetsumi to dismantle the idea of *humanisme* from within Europe (1960–70s).

What these three anecdotic samples suggest is this. – In a sense, Europe remains invisible so long as it is observed from within; it is rather in its interaction with its outside strangers who are crossing its contact zones or borderlines

---

6   My interpretation of Kudō is developed in Inaga 2017, 229–60, esp. 253, where I analyse the text quoted from Kudo 1976. Cf. also Lyotard 1988.

7   The term 'impotence' (combining French *impuissance* and *impotence*) is usually pronounced in Japanese as 'Impotenz' by using the German term, implying its strong Freudian connotation. 'Castration' on the other hand, is translated by using Chinese characters as *kyosei* 去勢 (psychoanalysis) or *danshu* 断種 (biology). In this feeling of impotence, one may detect a typical amalgam of Buddhist 'resignation' and *Gelassenheit*, which Walter Benjamin could not attain in his self-imposed hesitation (and deliberate lack of determination) to leave Europe on time under crisis. See Vivian Liska's thoughtful chapter in the present volume.

that the intrinsic possibility of Europe as an idea reveals itself in terms of its universal crisis.

Works Cited

Barraclough, Geoffrey, and Kimura Shōzarō 木村尚三郎. 1977. *Bunmei ni totte no henkakuki* 文明にとっての変革期 [A Transition Period in Civilizations] (Tokyo: Nippon Hōsōkyōkai)

Baraclough, Geoffrey. 1963. *European Unity in Thought & Action* (Oxford: Blackwell)

Benedict, Ruth. 2005 [1946]. *The Chrysanthemum and the Sword: Patterns of Japanese Culture* (Boston: Houghton Mifflin)

Geertz, Clifford. 1988. *Works and Lives: The Anthropologist as Author* (Stanford: Stanford University Press)

Hirakawa Sukehiro 平川祐弘. 2013. *Takeyama Michio to Shōwa no jidai* 竹山道雄と昭和の時代 [Takeyama Michio and the Shōwa Era] (Tokyo: Fujiwara Shoten)

Inaga Shigemi 稲賀繁美. 2016. *Sesshoku zōkeiron* 接触造形論 [In Search of Haptic Plasticity: Souls Touching Each Other, Forms Interwoven] (Nagoya: Nagoya Daigaku Shuppankai)

Inaga, Shigemi. 2001. 'Mediators, Sacrifice and Forgiveness: Laurens van der Post's Vision of Japan in the P.O.W. Camp', *Japan Review*, 13: 129–143

Inaga, Shigemi. 2008. 'Japanese Encounters with Latin America and Iberian Catholicism (1549–1973): Some Thoughts on Language, Imperialism, Identity Formation, and Comparative Research', *The Comparatist*, 32: 27–35

Inaga, Shigemi. 2013. 'Fracturing the Translation or Translating the Fracture? Questions in the Western Reception of Non-Linear Narratives in Japanese Arts and Poetics', *Comparative Critical Studies*, 10: 39–56

Kobori Keiichirō 小堀桂一郎. 2013. *Mori Ōgai: Nihon wa mada fushinchū da* 森鴎外-日本はまだ普請中だ [Mori Ōgai: Japan is still under construction] (Kyoto: Mineruva Shobo)

Kudo, Tetsumi. 1976. 'Entretien avec Kudo' (Paris: Galerie Beaubourg)

Kudo Tetsumi 工藤哲巳 et al. 1982. 'Kūkan no hyōgen soshite / arui wa hyōgen no kūkan' 空間の表現そして/あるいは表現の空間 [Expression of the Space and/or Space of Expression]. *Gendai shisō* 現代思想 [La Revue de la pensée d'aujourd'hui], July

Kudo, Tetsumi, and National Museum of Art. 2013. *Your Portrait: A Tetsumi Kudo Retrospective*. Osaka: National Museum of Art

Le Pichon, Alain, and Umberto Eco, eds. 2011. *Le Renversement du Ciel-Parcours d'anthropologie réciproque* (Paris: CNRS Éditions)

Lévi-Strauss, Claude. 2001. *L'Autre face de la lune* (Paris: Seuil)

Lyotard, Jean-François. 1988. *L'Inhumain: Causeries sur le temps* (Paris: Galilée)

Nakahara Yūsuke 中原佑介; 1968. 'Erosu no geijutsuka tachi (4) Kudo Tetsumi' エロスの芸術家たち(4)[Artists of Eros (4) : Kudo Tetsumi] 工藤哲巳, *Bijutsu techō* 美術手帖 [B.T.], May

'Nihonjinron'. n.d. In *Wikipedia: The Free Encyclopedia*. <https://en.wikipedia.org/> [accessed July 2017]

Ōkubo Takaki 大久保喬樹. 2008. *Yōkō no jidai: Iwakura shisetsudan kara Yokomitsu Riichi made* 洋行の時代－岩倉使節団から横光利一まで [The Epoch of "Going Abroad": From the Iwakura Mission to Yokomitsu Riichi] (Tokyo: Chūō Kōron Shinsha)

Saeki Shōichi 佐伯彰一 & Haga Tōru 芳賀徹, ed. 1987. *Gaikokujin ni yoru nihon ron no meicho: Goncharofu kara Pange made* 外国人による日本論の名著—ゴンチャロフからパンゲまで [Masterpieces on Japan by Foreign Authors: From Goncharov to Pinguet] (Tokyo: Chūō Kōronsha)

Sakai, Naoki et al. 2001. 'Introduction', in *Traces 1: Specters of the West and the Politics of Translation*, ed. by Naoki Sakai and Yukiko Hanawa (Hong Kong: Hong Kong University Press)

Sansom, George. 1931. *Japan: A Short Cultural History*. (London: Cresset Press and New York: D. Appleton). Japanese translation: Sansom, George. 1996. *Seiō sekai to Nihon* 西欧世界と日本, trl. Hirakawa Sukehiro平川祐弘, Haga Tōru 芳賀徹, and Tada Minoru 多田実. 2 vols (Tokyo: Chikuma Shobo; repr. 1995 in 3 vols)

Takeyama Michio 竹山道雄. 2017. 'Supein no nisegane' スペインの贋金 [The Counterfeit Money in Spain] (1950), in Takeyama Michio serekushon 竹山道雄セレクション, vol. 3 *Bi no tabibito* 美の旅人 [Traveller in Search of Beauty], ed. by Hirakawa Sukehiro 平川祐弘 (Tokyo: Fujiwara Shoten), 15–34.

CHAPTER 8

East Looks West and West Looks East: Images of Russia

Aage Hansen-Löve

1   Presuppositions and Preconceived Opinions

The bad thing about prejudices is not so much that they are 'wrong' in that they fail to hit the mark, but because they *do*. They aim precisely at that blind spot which shields our own identity from an alien one, and they fuse this spot with the blurred image of an different culture that turns into a black hole threatening to absorb everything around it.

The beauty of preconceptions – especially the intercultural ones – is that they have little to do with facts, but a lot with projects, which is to say with culture in an interactive sense. Or, put more precisely, culture may also be said to grow out of the continuous recycling of these prejudices and very often belated or clearly fantastical judgments about other cultures. We look towards the alien, the foreign, the other so as not to discover our own culture in it, and we look towards our own culture so as not to have to see the different one.

When in the course of the following remarks I refer to the images of Russian culture, this is to be borne in mind. It would make little sense, by contrast, to view culture as merely a collection of historical, positive Facts (with a capital 'F') that objectively criticize this culture of prejudice or empirically refute it. For there remains the undeniable phenomenon that cultures are vast accumulations of projections and interpretations and are themselves hardly interested in the facts that are extracted from archives by studious historians and scholars – or slavists – as we can see from very current discussions on true facts and pure inventions.

Prejudices themselves are central facts of every culture and belong to the crucial factors guiding its internal and external self-reflection. What I am interested in here is the elaborate and highly effective feedback relations governing cultural attributions.

The radical postmodernist concept of 'inventing' our cultural or natural environment by dint of projections (as opposed to the reconstruction of historical or empirical 'actualities' remains a crucial problem in cultural studies. Perhaps the 'invention' of Russia is a 'invention' of the West – or vice versa.

2 What Makes Russia Special...

The special thing about Russia is that everyone – including the Russians themselves – assumes that Russia is something specific, something highly exclusive. In the following remarks I would like to expound upon a series of special features ascribed to Russia. The only thing really specific to these features are however not so much particular characteristics and attributes, but rather the strategies deployed, in Russia or the 'West', to define its own uniqueness and exceptionality.

Perhaps this special quality can ultimately be reduced to a specifically apocalyptic intonation (in the sense of Kant or Derrida). This 'tone' can sometimes be heard as a whisper and often as a roar in the vast torrent of discourse on and from Russia. It underscores a narcissism celebrating Russia's unique, privileged status even as this Russia undergoes total self-annihilation. Ultimately, this originary, privileged image of Russia would have to be reduced to that very tone of voice which articulates it in the first place.

3 Russia as Tabula Rasa without History and Without a Face: The Leibniz Project

There is no doubt that Leibniz, at the end of the 17th and the beginning of the 18th century, created a vision of Russia for Peter the Great that made history by arguing that Russia had no history. (Diderot or Voltaire later did the same for Catherine the Great). Accordingly, Leibniz conceived Russia as the construction site par excellence for a rationally planned ideal state, because it represented for him a total *tabula rasa*. He saw Russia without history, without a destiny and ruled by an 'oriental despotism' which, if fortunate enough to enter into ties with the rational spirit of the Enlightenment, would be able to bring forth a realm of reason *ex nihilo*.

Actually, the situation was the exact opposite of what Leibniz presumed. Not only did Russia have a history (spanning, in Leibniz's time, almost 8 centuries) and a complex culture, but it had rather too much of both. Apart from this it also had a geography, which led to the impression that Russia's natural landscape could take the place of history – as per the oft-cited remark that Russia had no history, but rather merely a lot of geography.

That is why in Russia, quality is transformed into quantity. Russia's endless space and chaotic lack of structure, its broad plains and flat topography, were praised by nineteenth-century Russian Slavophiles to be a mark of quality, even though it could succeed at best *ex negativo* as an aesthetics of the sublime: provoking both attraction and repulsion, as do the icy wastes of the polar regions or the watery depths of the oceans. Or as Immanuel Kant has it in his *Kritik der Urteilskraft:* 'Daher haben die Schriftsteller, welche die weitläufige Größe des russischen Reichs erheben wollten, es schlecht getroffen, daß sie es als ungeheuer betitelten; denn hierin liegt ein Tadel: als ob es, für einen einzigen Beherrscher, zu groß sei'.[1]

Proceeding from a total lack of knowledge about its subject matter, Western Europe constructed an image of Russia as something totally unknowable. The ethnocentric heroes of European culture transformed the vast, historically rich black earth of the East into the fruitless field of their own projections. Since no one in Europe knew anything about Russia (or wanted to know anything), *anything* became possible: the radiant glow of Enlightenment or the heart of darkness...

What the Europeans discovered was not the barbaric land of the Scythians, but rather an empty field full of people who provided the ideal object for an externally applied act of projection. Leibniz saw in Peter the Great, because of his spectacular trip to Europe in 1697, someone who had led his country out of 'barbarity'; he also shared the Tsar's notion that such a barbaric land must ideally be revolutionized from above because it was not yet burdened with the vices and problems peculiar to Europe.

The thing most urgently needed, in Leibniz's view, was the founding of an Academy which would provide standards for organizing that vast country. For Leibniz, then, the notion of a tabula rasa was an entirely positive one, if one takes into account his plans for reeducating the country.

'Because in this kingdom', Leibniz writes to the Tsar,

> for the most part everything pertaining to learning is new and so to speak written upon blank paper, it is possible to avoid the countless mistakes that have taken hold gradually and imperceptibly in Europe; we know that a palace that is built entirely new will turn out better than one built over the course of many generations [...] [Hence] it is better in my view to do much good for the Russians than little good for the Germans and other Europeans.[2]

---

1 Kant 1977, 569, as quoted in Hansen-Löve 1991, 166. 'For that reason writers wishing to emphasize the Russian empire's far-flung expanse erred in calling it prodigious; for this implies a reservation, as if it were too large for any single ruler' (ed.'s trl.).
2 Letter to Peter the Great, 16 January 1712, as quoted in Richter 1946, 124.

4 The Chaadaev Complex: A Complaint List

Before Russia could utter its first words, it had been wiped out of existence: erased, a nothing, without a homeland, and dangling, as it were, in thin or somtimes very thick air.

In his famed *Philosophical Letters* (1829–1831),[3] which were originally written in French to a female acquaintance, the Russian philosopher Peter Chaadaev delineated an image of Russia which most of his contemporaries, including the czar, regarded as catastrophic. This made him in the eyes of many into a forerunner of the so-called Westernizers, i.e., the left-wing social revolutionaries critical of Russia. In my opinion, however, Chaadaev is better viewed as the inventor of a distinctive flipping technique, which begins with the paradoxical veneration of the negative and deficient and ends with the triumph of lack and want.

Because of his merciless conclusions, Chaadaev was declared insane, personally placed under house arrest by the Tsar, and forced to undergo daily examinations by a doctor. Today, however, his ideas have experienced a not entirely unexpected renaissance, so that it is well worth going through his list of complaints once more:

1. The isolation argument. Chaadaev thought that Russia had become disconnected from the mainstream of European history, had isolated itself totally. Russia, in Chaadaev's view, had been shut out of the family of nations, for the Russians 'were born into the world as bastards, without inheritance'.
2. Chaadaev's second thesis was that Russia is a product of plagiarism. 'We [the Russians] are the first to discover truths, ones that have been already used up in other places [...] We belong neither to the West nor to the East [...] Because we exist apart from time, we were left untouched by the universal education of the human race.' 'We completely lack inner development and natural progress. Each new idea replaces an old one without leaving a trace, for new ideas do not proceed from old ones, but rather appear to us from God knows where. We have nothing new to offer. We exist in a state of general standstill.'
3. Chaadaev's next point was that Russia lacks qualities and is alien even to itself. Russia has nothing of its own and has no history: 'We have nothing individual [...] we have not acquired anything from traditional ideas.' In this way the history of the others lies in Russia's future. 'We move in time

---

3 The paraphrases included here are after the Russian edition, Chaadaev 1906.

so strangely that with each step forward the past instant disappears forever.' And: 'we are alien to ourselves.'
4. Last but not least, Chaadaev thought Russia to be an enormous void: 'At present, in any case, we are a gap in the moral order of the world. I cannot cease being amazed at this unusual emptiness and isolation of our social existence.'

The famed journalist Astolphe de Custine took up Chaadaev's image of Russia in his *La Russie en 1839*. Essential here is that Custine's treatise stripped Chaadaev's notions of all messianistic exaggerations; it set the tone for a distorted and disdainful image of Russia that lasted through the nineteenth century and well beyond. Many of the notions expressed in Custine's letters can be shown to have been taken directly from Chaadaev's writings and may well even have been obtained from Chaadaev personally.

But what a difference in the French adaptation of Chaadaev's ideas! Whereas the Russian exposed the historiosophical potential of Russian impotence, the Frenchman confined himself (as would many others in his wake) to the endless recycling of seemingly identical judgments. For the Frenchman Custine, the country's total barrenness and uniformity – the favoured starting-point for later Slavophile hymns to the steppes – leads to the spectre of a natural disaster area: everything is monotonous, barren, sad. Nomadic, restless Russians roam across this barren plain: a nomadic folk (the image will be no different in postmodernism) entrapped in a kind of endless forest of cobwebs. Custine definitively and irreversibly transformed the Russians into a projection based on a mixture of half-truths and strange observations: 'They are not an original, but a reflected source of light. They are not born, but appear.' 'They have no reality, neither a good one nor a bad one.' 'These erratic heads can bring forth nothing but dust and smoke, chaos and nothingness.'

5   The Culture of Misunderstanding as a Pingpong Policy

The fascinating thing here is not so much the fact of these obvious and everything but politically correct misunderstandings from a today's point of view, as it is hard to imagine any cultural interaction without them. The point was and is that not just Europe in the era of restoration or even reaction in the early nineteenth century conceived of the Russians in this way, but that the Russians immediately started believing it themselves. From this one can deduce several rules organizing this merciless and merry interaction between the two cultures:
1. Cultures like nothing better than to import externally produced negative images of themselves, i.e. ones that are formed outside of a culture and

then consumed within it. The politically motivated notion of the East, the Orient, of Asia, and of barbarians that had been cultivated for centuries in Europe was transferred to Russia – quite oblivious to whether there was any factual reason for it or not. The main thing, however, was that these projections were eagerly adopted by the Russians themselves, i.e. they assimilated foreign and alien projections and blended them together with homegrown images of their own selves.

2. Cultural misunderstandings are also often likely to be exported, i.e., they are first produced inside a culture and then consumed a second time outside it. This applies to the majority of Russian stereotypes, from the Russian soul to its wide-open spaces, to Mother Russia, a womb with a masochistic or schizoid nature, etc. etc.

There are two ways we can track the pingpong ball of 'zero culture' as it passes back and forth between East and West. Either we can follow the way the Russians serve it – flat and hard – across the net (later the Iron Curtain) to Europe, or we can begin with how the West picks up the ball and serves it back. The question here is not *who* began (or stopped); the question is: *what game* is being played and what happens when the play turns serious and the pingpong ball turns into a missile.

The main strategy of self-characterization is here not only the masochistic inferiority complex, but also the countertendency to revalorize the negative characteristics into positive ones.

In some degree the actual politics of today's Russia is not far away from this tradition. Because of that there was no official interest in Moscow some years ago to celebrate the centenary of Russian Revolution. For the Kremlin it would be much more attractive to solemnize the Congress of Vienna. But that's another story. Another dimension of actual history.

6 Paradoxes of Russian Self-Interpretations

6.1 *The Self-Orientalization of Russia, or 'We Are Exotic'*

Russia's struggle against 'Western' Enlightenment, i.e. against the ideas of revolution as well as against rationalism and materialism, required a countermodel that the Russians at the beginning of the nineteenth century believed to have found in a make-believe or Quasi-Orient. Our own culture – so their reasoning – is the alien culture of the others. Hence we are not only the East of Europe, but also the Orient, Asia, an exotic world that allowed even the century-long reign of the Mongols to appear in a positive light.

No less unhistorical and ornamental in nature was also the idealization of Muscovite culture of the fifteenth and sixteenth centuries: like the Gothic for

German romanticism it acted as a heroic backdrop against which the renaissance of Russianness in the spirit of pan-Asianism could stand forth.

6.2 Russian Apocalypse Now and Forever

There are serious students of Russia who claim that Russian culture is fixated on disaster and even postulate a specifically Russian tendency towards things apocalyptic. Here, too, Dostoevsky, that skilled creator of Russia concepts, propagated a Russian trademark responsible for infusing much of the discourse on Russia with the apocalyptic intonation mentioned earlier.

Thus in Dostoevsky's *The Possessed* the folk enthusiast Shatov arrives at the following paradoxical insight into the essence of Russia. In his view, the inner force driving the folk forward is 'the force of an untameable wish to arrive at the end and at the same time to negate that end.'

6.3 The Russian Idea – A Salvation for All

The tenet that a nation becomes one only after it has formed an idea of its own self is derived, as is well known, from the Romantic philosophy of history and German idealism. This notion arrived in Russia only after a certain delay, in the 1830s, but when it did, it hit home all the harder. Soon the much-discussed *idée russe* became a cultural export article, much like the *ballets russes* or Fabergé eggs, which – as the name indicates – were 'laid' by a French firm located in the country's capital.

Whatever one can say about the 'Russian Idea,' one thing is certain: nothing certain can be said about it, except that it is synthetic, all-inclusive and – particularly for everyone else in the world – holds forth the promise of salvation.

As so often was the case, Dostoevsky's notion (or rather that of Versilov, protagonist of *A Raw Youth*) was propagated to suggest that the Russians were the better Europeans because they were the better Germans, Englishman or Frenchman:

> Only to the Russian, even in our day, has been vouchsafed the capacity to become most of all Russian only when he is most European, and this is true even in our day, that is, long before the millennium has been reached. That is the most essential difference between us Russians and all the rest, and in that respect the position in Russia is as nowhere else. I am in France a Frenchman, with a German I am a German, with the ancient Greeks I am a Greek, and by that very fact I am most typically a Russian. [...] Only Russia lives not for herself, but for an idea, and, you must admit, my dear, the remarkable fact that for almost the last hundred years Russia has lived absolutely not for herself, but only for the other States of

Europe! And, what of them! Oh, they are doomed to pass th[r]ough fearful agonies before they attain the Kingdom of God. (Dostoevsky 1916: 464–65)

7 Russia as a Phantasm of the West after 1900

7.1 *Entirely Alien*
'The categories of Western thought' as Oswald Spengler was convinced, 'are as foreign to Russian thinking as they are to that of China or Greece'. In Spengler's view, the Russians are – for better or for worse – the 'Barbarians of Europe', which is to say a people without culture, modern analogue to 'the Carthaginians of Roman times with their half-Classical style'. (Spengler 1926, 2: 170)

For Spengler, 'Mother Russia' is profoundly everything: organic, shaped by instinct, magic and mythical. It is not by accident that we encounter remarks of this kind in his prophecies of decline, when we encounter Russia in Spengler's work mainly in the margins, as a peripheral but nonetheless exciting phenomenon. Russia forces itself upon us by its irrational foreignness, its hostility towards civilization and its anti-rational, archaic character. But we have to admit that the same characteristics formed the basis of a cult of Russia around 1900. We only think in this context of Rilke's Russia enthusiasm and his almost blind travellings in his beloved dreamland around 1900.

7.2 *Even so, Salvation through Russianness*
Russia accordingly provides us with a premonition of the future: it anticipates the salvation of Europe and is as Spengler says, the 'arriving apocalypse'. Already Nietzsche saw in Russia 'the only force that today has any staying power in its body, which can wait, which can still hold forth something of promise – Russia is the opposite of miserable European particularism and enervation [...] The entire West no longer has those *instincts* [...] out of which the future arises' (Nietzsche 1919, 8: 151; my trl.).

In this way impotence and inferiority flips over into potency, indeed into prepotency. In 'Germany', by contrast, we find the 'will to power' especially in the German North (*Jenseits von Gut und Böse*). For Nietzsche, however, this power has been weakened by the general malaise and 'degeneration' of civilization (the buzz word popularized by Max Nordau).

Salvation from this danger arises in the East, 'in that enormous middle empire where Europe, as it were, flows back into Asia, in Russia. In this regard Egon Friedell in his *Kulturgeschichte der Neuzeit* even goes so far as to claim an immense superiority of the Russian over the European. Here we also have the paradox figure of revaluating the obviously evil and sick characteristics into ideal ones, saving Europe and the whole mankind.

8 Russia Is Its Own Psychopathology

In his fascinating book *Eros of the Impossible* (1996, new ed. 2018), Alexander Etkind sets forth a compelling description of Russian reader response to Freud and to Freud's own reader response to Russia. In this point of view the boundaries between Russianness and Judaism merge due to their position of alterity in the context of European civilization.

In the case of Freud, we find a fatal identification of Russians with the psychopathological narcissist, who for his part bears traces of the artist-genius. Here, Lou Andreas-Salomé's interpretation of Russia in Freud's categories was not without influence on Freud himself, whose own highly stereotyped image of Russia was in keeping with the thinking of his day. Freud, in any case, left out none of the then-current cultural cliches about Russia; he himself disposed over an impressive stock of patients from that world, not the least of which was the famous 'Wolfman', Sergej Pankeev.

From this point of view, the feminine, the Russian, and the narcissistic character were one and the same; as Etkind notes, for Lou Andreas-Salomé the 'play with national stereotypes was an important part of Russia's charisma and something that helped make it irresistible to Western intellectuals' (Etkind 2018, 138). As such, nationality could not only be interpreted as a kind of 'psychic process', but Russianness could also be identified with the erotic and with the anima of the West (playing the role of the animus). Nolens volens Russia took on the role of the West's 'unconscious', as Boris Groys would also later confirm.

Freud also seemed to have assumed that Russia and the Russians had a profoundly split, ambivalent being, which – contrary to the case of Westerners – was 'unusually close to the unconscious'.

9 Russia is Literature: Russia is Dostoevsky and Vice Versa

In this sense Russia is identified with its own literature, which Egon Friedell – flipping from negative to positive – declares without a trace of envy to be 'the most modern literature of the nineteenth century'.[4] By the way the same can

---

4 This and the next quotations are my trl. of Friedell 2016 2: 358–362.

be said about Russian avantgarde literature and Painting, about which Egon Friedell oder Hugo von Hofmannsthal had no idea.

But that is not the least of it. In Russia, Friedell opines, 'everyone is an artist', which is why 'the art of the novel and the theater have developed there in a way otherwise not achieved in Europe'. 'Because the Russian is so subjective' [meaning: unconscious, irrational, feminine, archaic, un-European], 'thinking is transformed for him directly into poetry'.

Put in plain language, if that is at all possible in the face of such arguments, this means that in Russia everyone is a poet, Russia is its own poetry, poetry is the negation and overcoming of reality, Russia is unreal, or is its own unreality, and that Russia does not exist – outside of poetry about Russia. Or philosophical letters. At this point we remember the famous sentence in de Custine's characteristics of Russia: 'The philosopher in Russia is a figure of pity; the poet must and can enjoy it there'.

In this sense Russia has not only a great literature but, in a sense, *is* literature. As a student of Russian literature I am not totally against this definition. Maybe Russia is not more than a rumor that one can visit only in one's imagination. But also these trips require a lot of papers and you have to get a visa. Or a vis-à-vis serving as a mirror, where you can discover your alter ego. In this sense – everybody is a Russian. Or – a Berliner. Or an European.

10 Concepts of Russian in Post-Soviet Conceptualism

In a dialogue, 20 years ago, between the installation artist Ilja Kabakov and the cultural critic Boris Groys, we find the following memorable reflection, which in a wondrous way carries our topic *ad absurdum*:

> *Kabakov:* The less attention the West pays to Russia, the more Russia disappears – it's as if it were not there at all.
> *Groys:* You mean that Russia is simply a ghost that in reality doesn't exist? That Russia is nothing but the fear of Russia itself?

Boris Groys – in a much more radical way than the other Moscow Conceptualists of the 1970s – reveals himself here to be a master of flipping from negative to positive. Groys does this by appropriating the blind spot of the Russian idea completely and thus absolutizing the Chaadaev complex, which he however at the same time leads *ad absurdum* in postmodern contexts.

Groys' Russia has managed to achieve something of its own after all: Russia has now become the ideal object of desire, it has become the true realm of the postmodern and thus once more has its own history – and our own – ahead of it. Groys writes:

> Russia has indisputably defined itself [...] throughout its entire history through reference to the West – the occasional reference to the East is actually more for purposes of Romantic self-stylization [...] Russia has always considered itself to be opposed to the West, whereby it itself employs certain elements of Western culture. Russia namely has no cultural tradition which would be 'different' [from the Western one], as is the case with Chinese culture. Rather, Russian culture always invents itself anew as the 'other' of the West by adopting and transforming the oppositional, alternative currents of Western culture—and then directing them against the West as a whole. (Groys 1995, 8; my trl.)

In this sense Russia is not the Other of the West in substance, but rather its 'alternative', which demands a 'higher degree of universality' than the West. With Groys, the only Russian mark of quality is now the primeval Russian urge (already formulated by Dostoevsky) to 'take things to their limits' – a self-issued license, as it were, to be as radical as possible.

From this point of view Russia has nothing that is genuinely its own, but it has it more radically so than anyone else – one need recall the European imports ranging from Peter the Great's reforms to Lenin's version of Marx and Stalin's national variant of Communism.

> The Russians are the pagans of modern Europe, the ones who actually carry out Europe's alternative ideologies. [...] These strategies of appropriating alternative western currents with the goal of radicalizing them and turning them against the West as a whole characterizes not only the governmental and political history of Russia, but also its purely cultural history [...] Russia was and remains a threatening place for the West. [.] [Russia] adopts Western ways in order to combat them all the more [...] In doing so the Russians have long been aware *what* an effect their country has on the West—and they exploit this effect very consciously. (Groys 1995, 10–11; my trl.)

Works Cited

Chaadaev, Pyotr Yakovlevich. 1906. *Filosofskie Pis'ma* (Kazan: Gran). Online at https://new.runivers.ru/lib/book4759/59280/

Custine, Astolphe de. 1843. *La Russie en 1839* (Paris: Amyot). Online at https://gallica.bnf.fr/ark:/12148/bpt6k828082.image

Dostoevsky, Fyodor. 1916. *A Raw Youth* (trl. Constance Garnett; London: Heinemann)

Etkind, Alexander. 2018 [1996]. *Eros of the Impossible: The History of Psychoanalysis in Russia*. (London: Routledge)

Friedell, Egon. 2016. *Kulturgeschichte der Neuzeit* (2 vols.; Altenmünster: Jazzybee)

Groys, Boris. *Die Erfindung Rußlands* (Berlin: Hanser).

Kant, Immanuel. 1977. *Schriften zur Anthropologie, Geschichtesphilosophie, Politik und Pädagogik* 2 (Werkausgabe XII; Frankfurt/Main: Suhrkamp).

Hansen-Löve, A.A. 1991. 'Zur Typologie des Erhabenen in der russischen Moderne', *Poetica* 23.1–2: 166–216.

Hansen-Löve, A.A. 1999. 'Zur Kritik der Vorurteilskraft: Rußlandbilder', *Transit: Europäische Revue*, 16: 167–185 (long version of this article)

Nietzsche, Friedrich. 1919 *Götzen-Dämmerung* (Werke, vol. 8; Leipzig: Kröner)

Richter, Liselotte. 1946. *Leibniz und sein Rußlandbild* (Berlin: Akademie-Verlag)

Spengler, Oswald. 1926 *The Decline of the West* (trl. C.F. Atkinson, 2 vols.; New York: Knopf)

PART 3

The Heterotopias of Europe

∴

CHAPTER 9

On the Margins of (the Idea of) Europe: A Tale of Two Galicias as Constructive Comparativism

César Domínguez and Nikol Dziub

'To be sure, there will always be historians ready to leap to the defence of the diehard thesis', Marcel Detienne (2000/2008, 22–23) claims, 'that only that which is comparable can be compared'. Among comparative disciplines, comparative literature has painstakingly pursued the identification of sameness out of comparable objects which are either genetically or typologically related. The field of genetic relations supported the idea of European literature as a body of particularities transcended by an overarching umbrella of commonality (*unitas multiplex*), whereas the field of typological affinities paved the way for inter-civilisational comparability between Europe and, mainly, the Far East (East/West Studies). In contradistinction, Detienne (2000/2008, 23 and 24) advocates a 'constructive comparativism' that aims at 'adopting as its field of exercise and experimentation the entire gamut of cultural representations among the most distant societies of the past as well as those closest to hand'.

Though Detienne's arguments originated from within the discipline of social and cultural history in 2000, similar arguments have been put forward more recently by literary comparatists to overcome Eurocentric principles of comparison and test the very limits of comparability. With the exception of Susan Stanford Friedman, who examines 'the dynamic pull between commensurability and incommensurability' within comparisons, rather than being restricted to 'a static list of similarities and differences' (Friedman 2013, 507), other interventions by Aamir R. Mufti (2005) and Natalie Melas (2007) are circumscribed to the intersection of orientalism and postcolonialism. Interestingly, this circumscription is productive also for our case study, as justified below, though it needs to be qualified in accordance with our geopolitical coordinates.

The aim of our essay is to initiate an experiment in constructive comparativism by resorting to two *prima facie* incomparable objects, namely, Western European Galicia and Eastern European Galicia. With an intermittent history of independence and annexation to other kingdoms in the Iberian Peninsula, the kingdom of Galicia was administered within the Crown of Castile (1490–1715), and later the Crown of Spain (1715–1833), to be divided into four provinces (La Coruña, Lugo, Orense and Pontevedra) during the 1833 territorial division of Spain and later to be acknowledged as an 'autonomous community' and a 'historic nationality' by the 1978 Constitution. Eastern European Galicia, in turn, once the kingdom of Galicia-Volhynia and later a crown land of Austria-Hungary, ceased to exist as a geographic entity in 1918, when the Austro-Hungarian Monarchy was dissolved. The region now straddles the modern-day border between Poland and Ukraine.

Though both regions were part of the Habsburg Monarchy – Western European Galicia from 1516 to 1700 and Eastern European Galicia from 1772 to 1918 – and share the same name, there seems not to be any further firmer ground for comparison.[1] Simultaneous mentions of both regions in scholarship categorically aim to avoid confusing one with the other. To our knowledge, Karolina Golemo's 2015 article is the only piece of scholarship that attempts to trace socio-cultural connections between both regions, such as instances of dual Galicianism (e.g., Sofía Casanova Lutosławska, Gosia Trebacz[2]), a shared diasporic history (with the Americas as main destination) and the presence of St. James's Way in both landscapes. 'Symbolic parallels aside', Golemo (2015, 39) concludes, 'real palpable premises for similarities do exist'. Rather than similarities, Golemo's examples are cases that aim to promote a mutual deeper connection between both regions, such as the 2000 agreement between Kraków and Lugo as sister cities[3] and Marco Gallego's 2004 documentary *A outra Galicia* (The Other Galicia) and the 2011 docufiction *A maleta de Sofía* (Sofía's Suitcase).[4]

Rather than looking for 'real palpable premises for similarities', as Golemo does, our experiment in constructive comparativism consists of maintaining sameness and difference in tension and examining the politics of comparison

---

1. Both regions have the same name in English (Galicia), Polish (Galicja) and Ukranian (Галичина), whereas Western and Eastern Galicia are called, respectively, Galicia/Galitzia and Galiza/Galitsia in Spanish-Castilian and Galician. Most scholars have concluded there is no common etymological root for both names. Larry Wolff (2010, 1), however, makes the following connection: 'At the beginning of the [eighteenth] century there had been an old Habsburg province of Galicia in northern Spain, but it was taken, along with Spain, by the Bourbons in the War of the Spanish Succession. The name was therefore available in 1772, serving as the Latin form of the medieval Rus principality of Halych'.
2. Sofía Casanova (1861–1958) was a Western European Galician journalist and writer who, in 1887, married the Polish philosopher and writer Wincenty Lutosławski. As a result of having only daughters, Casanova was repudiated by her husband, which led her to live in poverty in both Galicias. Gosia Trebacz is a contemporary painter from Krákow who lives in A Coruña and considers herself doubly Galician.
3. 'Although the city was in Galicia for a relatively short period, Kraków became the natural depository and reserve of Galician myth in post-war Poland' (Purchla 2014, 90).
4. Both *A outra Galicia* and *A maleta de Sofía* recreate the life of Sofía Casanova Lutosławski.

(cf. Friedman 2013, 507 and 500) of these two distant regions. One – Galiza/ Western European Galicia – exists in maps; the other – Galicja-Галичина/Eastern European Galicia – even though it does not exist in current maps, is still alive as a symbol of linguistic and ethnic variety. To allow for the beginning of comparison, we have selected the most internationally acclaimed contemporary writers of both regions, Manuel Rivas for Western European Galicia and Andrzej Stasiuk for Eastern European Galicia, and, more specifically, two literary works that have not been translated into the other Galician writer's native language – *En salvaxe compaña* (literally, 'In Wild Company', translated as *In the Wilderness*) and *Opowieści galicyjskie* (*Tales of Galicia*). Coincidentally, both works were published in the early-mid 1990s.

Needless to say, neither of these two works nor their authors have been compared so far. The reason for our choice lies in wondering in which ways the work by the Eastern European Galician writer can inform us about Western European Galicia and, conversely, in which ways the work by the Western European Galician writer can inform us about Eastern European Galicia.[5] Surprisingly, Stasiuk said in an interview that he was not interested at all in Western Europe, including Spain: 'I haven't been to France or Spain and I've never thought about going there. I am simply interested in our part of the world, this central and eastern reality. My God, what would I be doing in France?' (qtd. in Rychlicka 2009, 55). A Western European Galician reader, in turn, may be attracted to the Spanish-Castilian translation of Stasiuk's work due to the 'odd' spelling of the region (Galitzia instead of Galicia) and wonder which Galicia these tales are about.[6]

According to Detienne (2008, 26), incomparability is a provocation that results in the disintegration of a familiar category. What this familiar category might be is unknown to us at the beginning of the experiment, and this essay is hence an exercise of reconstruction. Such reconstruction involves disentangling what a comparative reading illuminates about the other work. The essay

---

5 *Opowieści galicyjskie* has been translated into Spanish-Castilian, but not into Galician. Conversely, *En salvaxe compaña* has been translated into neither Polish nor Ukranian and, therefore, the Eastern Galician reader may only read Rivas's novel in translation into English, French or German.

6 Golemo (2015, 24) claims that 'if we were to ask a Spanish passerby what *Galicia* is and where it is located, he would not hesitate to answer that *Galicia* is a Spanish region'. Such claim is justified for our corpus on the grounds of a review of *Cuentos de Galitzia* – the Spanish-Castilian translation of *Opowieści galicyjskie* – tellingly titled 'A outra Galitzia' (The Other Galicia). Furthermore, the Western Galician blogger Mariña Pérez Rei claims that 'Galitzia comparte con Galicia a proximidade toponímica, ese elo que nos rescata do esquecemento no aceno dun nome' (<http://cafebarbantia.barbantia.es/?p=266>; Galitzia shares with Galicia the toponymic proximity, a link that rescues us from oblivion by the gesture of a name).

is divided into three parts. The first two parts are brief, for they only provide the key contextual and literary aspects of *En salvaxe compaña* and *Opowieści galicyjskie*, respectively. In the third part we aim to discuss the abovementioned disintegrated familiar category in relation to the position of both Galicias within Europe. Some concluding remarks will follow.

1   *En salvaxe compaña*: A Tale of Western European Galicia

Manuel Rivas is the most renowned narrator of contemporary Galician literature, both nationally and internationally (*cf.* Vilavedra 2012). His novel *En salvaxe compaña* was originally published in Galician in 1993 and translated into Spanish-Castilian by its author one year later, when the original text was awarded the Galician Premio da Crítica. It is set in Galicia in a period between the Spanish Civil War and 1991. This spatial and temporal specificity is challenged, however, by the interference of a double-sided underworld and, consequently, a double-sided afterlife. The double-sided underworld is made of, on the one hand, the vanished kingdom of Galicia (the 'reino soterrado'/'buried kingdom', as it is called in the novel (Rivas 1993/2008, 60 and 2003, 49)). This kingdom fell when García II, king of Galicia and Portugal, was imprisoned in 1071 until death by his brothers Sancho II, king of Castile, and Alfonso VI, king of León.[7] On the other hand, there is the underworld of the most concrete location of the novel, Arán, that is, the 'parroquia defunta'/'deceased parish' (Rivas 1993/2008, 80 and 2003, 67) made of 'un camposanto. Ósos e máis ósos'/'a graveyard. Bones and more bones' (Rivas 1993/2008, 137 and 2003, 121).[8] Both underworlds interact with the real Arán, in which the human characters cohabitate with King García II and his warriors, which have been transformed into crows, as well as the deceased members of the parish, which have been transformed into several other animals.

This multifaceted space is built upon the amalgam of Galician folklore and literary traditions, including the stories about King Arthur and his army, transformed into mosquitoes, who await for the end of their enchantment in the Galician lake of Antela, the Santa Compaña (Holy Company – a procession of souls that are in torment), and the pilgrimage to San Andrés de Teixido, a sanctuary which a person must visit while alive or transformed into an animal

---

7   For a historical account of King García II, see Portela Silva 2001. For the role of this king in literature, see Méndez Ferrín 2007.
8   The choice of Arán as the locale of the novel is reminiscent of the Aran Islands, the mythical repository of Irishness, in accordance with other Celtic references made by Rivas.

once dead (for these folkloric traditions, see Vaqueiro 2011). In terms of temporality, therefore, the past of both the vanished kingdom and Galicia during the Civil War and its aftermath, the present set in the 1990s, and the future of the to-be-returned king and the end of purgation coexist and rewrite each other.

By mixing fact and fiction, their meanings are interrogated and their hierarchies deconstructed in order to highlight how they were produced. The late parish priest of Arán, Don Xil, claims he has never heard of a Galician king, for 'non había máis reis que os das Españas'/'there were no other kings than those of Spain' (Rivas 1993/2008, 34 and 2003, 25). This emphasises the one-sidedness of official history, here a Spanish-Castilian-centric history, which has erased any trace of the vanquished García II in contrast to the overwhelming presence of the victorious Sancho II and Alfonso VI, the latter being known as *imperator totius Hispaniae* (emperor of all Spain). Unlike history, memory is malleable and shaped by context, so that a single event may simultaneously mean different – and even contradictory – things. Thus, for instance, the crows that fly over Arán are, for Misia, the incarnation of King García's warriors, whereas for Rosa, they are the deceased caused by a potato famine not long ago (Chap. 3), an interpretation the former character also accepts. It is precisely Misia, Don Xil's niece, who describes memory in the following terms:

> É unha dona misteriosa a memoria. Nós non escollemos os recordos. Eles viven a súa vida. Van e veñen. Ás veces, vanse para sempre. E hai recordos que se apegan a nós á maneira do lique á pedra. Son anacos de vida que non se esvaeron, que se alimentan do aire frío, que medran devagar na cortiza do tempo. (Rivas 1993/2008, 50)

> Memory is a mysterious lady. We do not choose our memories. They live their own life. They come and go. Sometimes they disappear for good. Other memories stick to us like lichen to a stone. They're bits of life that never fade, that feed on the cold air, and increase slowly on the bark of time. (Rivas 2003, 40)

Memory finds in literature one of its houses. It is in literature, and not in the 'pesadelo ao que chaman Historia'/'nightmare they call History' (Rivas 1993/2008, 24 and 2003, 16), that King García lives. Likewise, it is in literature where justice is restored. While Don Xil, who 'cando a guerra, [...] gobernaba vidas'/'during the war, [...] governed lives' (Rivas 1993/2008, 42 and 2003, 32), lives out his purgatory as a mouse, the bagpiper Arturo de Lousame, whose good conduct the parish priest had refused to confirm, taking him for an anarchist, lives out his as a cat. Such poetic justice is unrelated to either the Santa

Compaña or the pilgrimage to San Andrés de Teixido, two of the folkloric pillars of the novel.

As mentioned before, the story proceeds from the Civil War and its aftermath to the early 1990s. This period is embodied in the main character, Rosa, whom some references ambiguously present as the parish priest's daughter.[9] From her childhood to her adult life as wife and mother, Rosa's story may be read as a *Frauenroman* of liberation from male power, here represented by Don Xil and Rosa's husband – Cholo. On a different level, however, Rosa's story may be read as Galicia's (hi)story, with her rape by Cholo, 'trabada ao seu corpo, rendida, ben domada'/'stuck to his body, surrendered, under control' (Rivas 1993/2008, 24 and 2003, 16), reminiscent of the statement attributed to the sixteenth-century Spanish historian Jerónimo de Zurita about the 'doma y castración del Reino de Galicia' (taming and castration of the kingdom of Galicia).[10] This development ends with Rosa abandoning home with her children and her last visit to the *pazo*[11] (manor house) under the eyes of King García, who orders his army to fly 'A contravento!'/'Against the wind!' (Rivas 1993/2008, 190 and 2003, 170).

---

9   When Don Xil sees the fresco painting of the female allegory of vices discovered by young Rosa in the church, his reaction is described in the following terms: 'El mesmo, axitado nos adentros, notaba na punta da lingua o sabor salgado da pel da nostalxia, revivía as escenas da caída como se fosen o intre decisivo da existencia, e decatouse, foi só un escintileo feliz e doloroso como raiola que atina nos ollos, de que a nena, aquela nena prohibida, flor maldita, sementada no campo doutro, fora a súa única obra, a única pegada nun camiño sen volta'/'He himself, with his innards in turmoil, could feel the salty taste of the skin of nostalgia on the tip of his tongue, he relived the scenes of the fall as if they were the decisive moment of existence, and realized – it was only a happy and painful glimmer like a flash that reaches the eyes – that the girl, that forbidden girl, wretched flower, sown in another's field, had been his sole work, the single trace on a road without return' (Rivas 1993/2008, 17 and 2003, 9).

10   During the sermon on the fresco painting, Don Xil looks at Rosa, who wears a 'vestidiño azul de brancas grecas'/'blue dress with white motifs' (Rivas 1993/2008, 14 and 2003, 6), which happen to be the national colours of Galicia. Jerónimo de Zurita was appointed oficial chronicler of the Kingdom of Aragon in 1548. Though not exactly phrased this way in Zurita's 1562–80 *Anales de la Corona de Aragón* (Annals of the Crown of Aragon), the phrase 'doma y castración del Reino de Galicia' became central in the thought of Galician nationalists.

11   The Galician *pazo* is a symbol of the patriarchal rural power and history: 'Sentía xenreira por todo o que proviña daquela casa grande, fose como esplendor ou ruína, avoengo ou miseria, o maldito vicio da pedra zumegando historia, ese puto centro do universo'/'He felt anger towards everything that came from that large house, be it splendour or ruin, ancestry or misery, the cursed vice of the stone oozing history, that blasted centre of the universe' (Rivas 1993/2008, 145 and Rivas 2003, 128).

2 Opowieści galicyjskie: A Tale of Eastern European Galicia

In *En salvaxe compaña*, the fictional or literary universe seems to be a place where poetic justice reigns supreme. In *Opowieści galicyjskie* (Tales of Galicia) by Andrzej Stasiuk (published in 1995), fiction tries and fails to liven up reality. *Opowieści galicyjskie* forms a series of 15 stories, first published separately in *Tygodnik Powszechny* (The Catholic Weekly), but which however form a whole. In them, Stasiuk gives the floor to those whose voices usually are not heard, whose voices usually do not make or tell history. The reader, or rather the receiver[12], listens successively to the voices of Józek, Władek, Edek, Gacek, Kruk the blacksmith, Janek, Kościejny, Lewandowski, Roux the Sergeant, Maryśka... These voices appear one after another, and finally form the topography of a village lost in a ghostly and cryptic Galicia. The voices the receiver hears in Stasiuk's stories or tales are not the voices of the dead, or the voices of the undead, but rather the voices of the unliving. They dig a cave in a devastated collective identity, but they do not fill or inhabit it.

The Galician community as described in Stasiuk's stories or tales lives in an 'in-between' state, so much so that every story looks like a dysphoric tale, and the factual narratives look like fantastic nightmares telling the story of a dismembered reality. All the characters in the book live in their own otherwise uninhabited memories, they are survivors or relics. One of the keywords of Stasiuk's *Opowieści galicyjskie* is *ostatni* (last). The first character we meet when we read the book is the last employee of the Państwowe Gospodarstwo Rolne (the PGR, the State Agriculture Farm); and his tractor is the last tractor – and so on. Stasiuk's characters are strangers in their own 'country', in their own territory. The collective dimension of the Soviet era vanished, and only its material/materialist dimension remains. That is why Stasiuk develops a language made with material things and mechanical objects, whose decrepitude tells a deficient history.

Let us take the example of the naïve blacksmith Kruk. He is cut off from the post-Soviet Galicia because he still has the illusion that he lives in a utopian world, and because he is stuck 'w czasie, gdy język był tylko lustrzanym odbiciem świata i żył w absolutnej z nim zgodzie'/'in a time when language

---

12 The original title shows that Stasiuk considered his texts semi-fictional stories, or short stories based on geopolitical reality, rather than marvellous although dysphoric tales, but the slightly inaccurate translation – *opowieści* meaning 'short stories' – is interesting, for it suggests that Stasiuk is creating a fantastic post-historical folklore. Likewise, the Spanish-Castilian translation renders *opowieści* as 'cuentos' rather than 'relatos', a choice that in our context unintendedly connects Eastern European Galician to the rich marvellous tradition of Western European Galicia.

was only a mirror reflection of the world and lived in perfect harmony with it' (Stasiuk 1995/2012, 24 and 2003, 28). But in the new capitalist Galicia, words and objects function as Walter Benjamin's souvenirs (Benjamin 2002, 924), they are dead memories which build an empty or hollow language, and which dismember or disintegrate the causality of significance. Another interesting object is the swing: all of the village's children use it. This mechanical object and device is a counter-allegory of the Soviet era's collapse, and more specifically of the PGR's collapse. Stasiuk uses this childish and mechanical verticality in order to create a derisory counterpoint to the disintegration of Soviet Galicia.

One might also notice the way Stasiuk uses references to photography. Photography allows the writer to think of his own writing in (anti)temporal and (anti)historical terms. Photography, in Stasiuk's book, perpetuates empty traces of hollow objects: it generates an absurd temporality where repetition and tautology replace causality and testimony. In Stasiuk's Galicia, words, objects and photographs are vicarious: they are referentially empty, and refer to themselves or to anything/anybody. According to Roland Barthes, a photograph has no subjective power, but it ontologically and legally testifies to the past presence of what it captured: photography's effect 'is not to restore what has been abolished (by time, by distance) but to attest that what I see has indeed existed' (Barthes 1980/1981, 82). But in Stasiuk's Galicia, photography loses this power. Let us take the example of the faded wedding photo, where everyone may project the faces he wants to project.

> Widziałem tylko dwie plamy cienia w czarnej ramie. Ślubne zdjęcie. Musiałem sobie wyobrazić ich twarze. Nieruchome, płaskie, wygładzone retuszem projekty idealnego dostojeństwa. (Stasiuk 1995/2012, 60)
>
> I saw only two splotches of shadow in the black frame. A wedding picture. I had to imagine their faces myself. It was the model of ideal dignity, motionless, flat, smoothed by retouching. (Stasiuk 2003, 65)

This photograph, which should be both personal and foundational, is anonymous, and does not depict anything. Faces and names vanished, and the voices we hear in the book seem to come from what Jacques Derrida would have called a crypt – but from an empty crypt. History and memory are both obsolete here: history because the Galician world has come to an end, and because Galicia seems to be banned from the historical cause and effect chain; memory because the 'last' people or objects are not remnants, but ruins without any temporal background, and because photographs do not bear witness anymore to the past presence of an object.

So Galicia is a dismembered (temporal) territory. Another point we would like to mention about *Opowieści galicyiskie* is the importance, in the book, of something which is, literally, a 'commonplace': the 'bar'. A bar is, undoubtedly, what Michel Foucault (1984/1986, 25) would have called a 'heterotopia of deviation', one of those heterotopias 'in which individuals whose behaviour is deviant in relation to the required mean or norm are placed' (for an approach to Stasiuk's *Jadąc do Babadag – On the Road to Babadag* – in heterotopic terms, see Ivanov 2018). But, in Stasiuk's post-Soviet Galicia, the bar is not an 'other space', it is the Galician place *par excellence*. And this 'common place' is also a place cut off from the world, a place which annihilates both the village and the world. The bar is the matrix of a contamination process, which expresses itself through the literary device called hypallage. Alcohol deeply disturbs the causal chain in both the stories and history. The figures' drunkenness and incoherence contaminates their environment, and the whole Galicia, which is not a *topos* or an idea anymore, but the incoherent and disjointed raving of a few lost figures trapped in a space where the logical flow of thoughts has been disrupted, and where words do not match things anymore.

3   The Clash of Galician/European Projections

Both Rivas's and Stasiuk's Galicias are set in the early 1990s and, hence, are defined by a '*post-* atmosphere'. In the case of Western European Galicia, this is the aftermath of the entrance of Spain (and Portugal) into the European Economic Community, with the negative impact it had for the region in the short term. In the case of Eastern European Galicia, this was during the aftermath of, on one side of the border, the fall of the communist government in Poland and, on the other side, the independence of Ukraine. In both cases, identity conflicts came to the fore in regional, national and European terms, which have been dealt with by both writers in their fiction and nonfiction.

In his attempt to understand what the European Union is in terms of polity, the late sociologist Ulrich Beck, together with Edgar Grande, defined 'Europeanisation' in 2007 as the combination of three kinds of cosmopolitanism, namely, 'institutionalised cosmopolitanism', 'deformed cosmopolitanism' and 'cosmopolitan realism'. Whereas the first two kinds of cosmopolitanism are still valid today (institutionalised cosmopolitanism as the body of supranational institutions that stand legally above the individual member states; deformed cosmopolitanism as the kind of cosmopolitanism produced by these supranational institutions), eleven years later, cosmopolitan realism – the achievement of 'both national and European goals at the same time' (Beck and Grande

2007, 21) – has become obsolete. As proven by Brexit, 'the asymmetry of power and the egoisms of sovereignty' cannot 'balance each other out or be held in check through a kind of transnational social contract' (Beck and Grande 2007, 219). Europeanisation, therefore, is not an unstoppable project, as was believed in previous years.

Literature has been more realistic than sociology, even in times of the highest Europeanist euphoria. Notice in this regard that the works by Rivas and Stasiuk here analysed are set in the aftermath of the fall of the Berlin Wall, and yet they recreate a nightmarish Galicia inhabited by ghosts somewhere in Europe, but with no sign of Europe.[13] In *En salvaxe compaña*, ghosts include both the representatives of the independent kingdom of Galicia – King García and his 'exército de trobeiros, armados con arpas, cítaras e zanfonas'/'army of troubadours, equipped with harps, zithers and hurdy-gurdies' (Rivas 1993/2008, 21 and 2003, 12) – and the dead members of Arán, both groups transformed into animals. The connections of Western European Galicia with Europe have remained stuck in the past, when the 'buried kingdom' took its own decisions regarding dynastic alliances.[14] Similarly, in *Opowieści galicyiskie* there are the ghosts of Poland's communist past and the ghosts of those who, like Kościejny, walk beside the alive, all living in an 'odchodzącego świata'/'expiring world' (Stasiuk 1995/2012, 5 and 2003, 10). It is a Galicia in tension between the 'past' (the East, the Soviet Bloc, totalitarianism) and the 'future' (the West, Western Europe, democracy) and in search of a (Central) Europe of its own.

Though ghosts abound in both these works – and others – by Rivas and Stasiuk, they have not attracted critical attention. Hauntology, or ghost studies, 'has two distinct, related, and to some extent incompatible sources', the work of the psychoanalysts Nicolas Abraham and Maria Torok, on the one hand, and Derrida's *Spectres de Marx*, on the other (Davis 2005, 373). The main

---

13   In the early 2000s, when *Opowieści galicyiskie* was published, Poland was celebrating its entrance into the European Union as a 'return to Europe' (*cf.* Kato 2016, 92).

14   'O rei de Galicia non era moi de espada. Tiña por amigo o rei mouro de Sevilla, e tamén, ao norte, o rei normando. Este rei era pai dunha princesa fermosísima, moi loura e coa pel tan branca que cando bebía viño tinto víaselle baixar pola gorxa. Ía casar co rei de Galicia. Pero este foi feito prisioneiro e o rei normando morreu sen poder vir en axuda do galego'/'The king of Galicia was not very keen on the sword. He was friends with the Moorish king of Seville, and also with the Norman king to the north. This king was the father of an extremely beautiful princess, who was very fair and had such pale skin that when she drank red wine you could see it running down her throat. She was to have married the king of Galicia. But he was taken prisoner and the Norman king died before he could come to the aid of his Galician friend' (Rivas 1993/2008, 20 and 2003, 12). Besides the alliance with a Norman king, notice the alliance with a Moorish king and the caracterisation of king García as 'not very keen on the sword', which implicitly puts him in sharp contrast to the kings of Castile.

attraction of hauntology for literary critics is the topic of the secret,[15] which has a different status in each of the two sources (Davis 2005, 378). Such application is evident for the case of Western European Galicia in María do Cebreiro Rábade Villar's discussion of the work by Rosalía de Castro within the cracks and fissures between reality and the supernatural inhabited by ghosts. Danny M. Barreto (2011, 85) takes a step further and links the 'ghostly state of living death to which subjects are restricted' to 'a symptom of Galicia's cultural and political position within Spain as a stateless nation'. In the case of Eastern European Galicia, one may turn to Alexander Etkind's proposition on post-Soviet hauntology, even though his arguments are restricted to Russia.

The ghost occupies an in-between space, the interstice between presence and absence, life and death. In its territorial incarnation, Galicia – either Western European or Eastern European – is neither 'fully incorporated into the sovereign state nor entirely autonomous' (Barreto 2011, 385). *En salvaxe compaña* and *Opowieści galicyiskie* recreate a post-totalitarian Galicia in the westernmost and easternmost edges of Europe.

These post-totalitarian Galician *loci* look like heterotopias – spaces where the *heteroclite*[16] reign supreme. Michel Foucault claims that there are two kinds of heterotopias – 'heterotopias of crisis' and 'heterotopias of deviation'. Even though Foucault argues that heterotopias of crisis are persistently disappearing, we would say that Rivas's and Stasiuk's Galicias belong to this kind. If 'heterotopias of crisis' are places 'reserved for individuals who are, in relation to society and to the human environment in which they live, in a state of crisis: adolescents, menstruating women, pregnant women' (Foucault 1984/1986, 24), one may say that post-totalitarian Galicias are characterised as adolescent spaces. In the *Frauenroman* that *En salvaxe compaña* is, the novel begins with the discovery by young Rosa of the old fresco paintings in the church that show 'donas, que eran, as máis, de conto, fermosas, vestidas como raíñas'/'ladies, most of whom were out of story-books: they were beautiful, dressed as queens' (Rivas 1993, 11 and 2003, 3). The patriarchal power represented by the priest, however, obliges the reader to see them as 'pecadoras'/'sinners' (Rivas

---

15   In *En salvaxe compaña*, secrets, besides Rosa's being the daughter of the priest Don Xil, are everywhere. As Don Xil says, 'disto que oíches, nin chío, Matacáns [...] Son cousas de familia'/'Not a word about this, you hear me, Matacáns? [...] These are family matters!' (Rivas 1993/2008, 74 and 2003, 61). In *Opowieści galicyiskie*, Stasiuk (1995/2012, 80 and 2003, 86) imagines a secret passage leading to the 'other side'.

16   'That word should be taken in its most literal, etymological sense: in such a state, things are "laid", "placed", "arranged" in sites so very different from one another that it is impossible to find a place of residence for them, to define a common *locus* beneath them all' (Foucault 1969/2002, xix).

1993, 13 and 2003, 5). And the novel ends with Rosa leaving Arán and her home. In *Opowieści galicyjskie*, even elderly people go back to adolescence, because they live in a territory which is the result of the tormented fantasies of a collective puberty: 'No więc te stare kobiety i dzieciarnia stoją przed mapą nowego świata, którego kontynenty uporządkowano według pragnień poszczególnych części ciała, zachcianek i smaków'/'So those old women and little children stood before a map of the new world, whose continents had been laid out according to the desires of particular parts of the body, its whims and tastes' (Stasiuk 1995/2012, 17 and 2003, 21).

Another reason for considering that both Galicias are heterotopias lies in that Foucault (1984/1986, 26) says that 'heterotopias are most often linked to slices in time – which is to say that they open onto what might be termed, for the sake of symmetry, heterochronies'. And time, in Rivas's and Stasiuk's Galicias, is clearly 'out of joint' (Shakespeare, *Hamlet* I. 5). Actually, space and time are both out of joint. According to Foucault (1984/1986, 26), there are two types of heterochronies: there are 'heterotopias of indefinitely accumulating time, for example museums and libraries', and there are heterotopias which 'are not oriented toward the eternal', but which 'are rather absolutely temporal [chroniques]. Such, for example, are the fairgrounds'. But Foucault mentions also 'a new kind of temporal heterotopia' which 'has been invented: vacation villages, such as those Polynesian villages that offer a compact three weeks of primitive and eternal nudity to the inhabitants of the cities'. In such 'vacation villages', 'the two forms of heterotopias [...] come together', because everything works there 'as if the entire history of humanity reaching back to its origin were accessible in a sort of immediate knowledge' (Foucault 1984/1986, 26).

Rivas's and Stasiuk's Galicias resemble this last 'kind of temporal heterotopia' because their Galicias – being places where the causal logic of time is disrupted – are also places where one can experience eternity – of course a disphoric eternity – through the present. Galicia, either Western or Eastern, is a ghostly space, a kingdom of sentiments in Rivas's words, with a sovereign who is 'un pobre rei de corazóns'/'a poor king of hearts' (Rivas 1993/2008, 35 and 2003, 26), an 'odchodzącego świata'/'expiring world' (Stasiuk 1995/2012, 5 and 2003, 10) in Stasiuk's words, for which history is a nightmare and whose memory can only be retold *against the wind* by returned (Stasiuk's Kościejny) or to-be-returned (Rivas's King of Galicia) ghostly figures. Galicia is a *non-lieu*, with neither past (at least there are not traces of it in official history), nor future, for migration is the only way out.[17]

---

17 'Spiderman', one of the characters of *En salvaxe compaña*, explains his experience as immigrant in New York working in the construction of skycrapers this way: 'Alí, a aquela

Foucault, with his 1967 discussion of heterotopias, attracted attention to the in-betweenness of potentiality and actuality and, consequently, the concept of heterotopia might be the 'familiar category' waiting for disintegration upon a comparative reading of *En salvaxe compaña* and *Opowieści galicyjskie*. And yet there is something that still escapes from Foucault's formulation, namely, the uncertainty of a terrain where life and death (as symbolised by Rivas's and Stasiuk's ghosts) cohabitate and mix. Elizabeth A. Povinelli devoted her 2011 book *Economies of Abandonment* to 'those conditions in which a social project is neither something nor nothing' (Povinelli 2011, 8) and coined – upon Giorgio Agamben's concept of 'zone of indistinction' – the concept of 'zone of indetermination' to make reference to 'maximally intensified zones of oscillation' where 'new forms of life and worlds will emerge and the ways and the forms of a new politics must be thought' (Povinelli 2011, 10).[18] Furthermore, Povinelli (2011, 9) herself makes the connection between Agamben's zone of indistinction and Foucault's heterotopia explicit, as well as with Michael Warner's 'counterpublic', Charles Taylor's 'new social imaginary' and Nancy Frazer's 'subaltern counterpublic' (Povinelli 2011, 7).

In the last sections of *Homo Sacer*, Agamben (1998, 174) describes the concentration camp as a 'zone of indistinction' for it materialises 'the state of exception [...] in which bare life and the juridical rule enter into a threshold of indistinction'. Furthermore, Agamben claims that 'we find ourselves in the presence of a camp every time such a structure is created, independent of the kinds of crime that are committed there and whatever its denomination and specific topography' (Agamben 1998, 174), and includes within these zones of indistinction the stadium in Bari in which in 1991 illegal Albanian immigrants were herded and the *zones d'attente* in French international airports where foreigners asking for refugee status are detained.

Agamben's description of these zones of indistinction as areas in which the limits between life and death are uncertain is especially relevant for our reading of Rivas's and Stasiuk's works. But, how can we make the transition from Agamben's concentration camp as the paradigmatic zone of indistinction to

---

    altura, só esramos os indios e os galegos. Tiña de compañeiros uns de Carnota e tomabamos compango de chourizo, alí sobre Nova York'/'At that height, it's just the Indians and us Galicians. Some of my workmates were from Carnota and we'd share chorizo up there, over New York' (Rivas 1993/2008, 111 and 2003, 96). Stasiuk, for his part, describes Galicia as a 'centuries-old palimpsest created by a succession of migrating (or invading) cultures' (see the translator's notice in Stasiuk 2003, 134).

18   The concept of 'indeterminacy' has been previously defined by Povinelli (2002, 239) as 'the condition in which two incompatible translations (or "readings") are equally true interpretations of the same text'.

the Galician topography analysed here? Anthony Downey (2009, 118) takes a step in this direction when he claims that 'such zones [of indistinction] do not necessarily have to have a localised topography and can be national in their scope' as exemplified by modern-day Algeria and Tangiers. Though not explicitly stated, it is obvious that the liminality of these zones is related to their postcolonial past, precisely the overlooked factor that has been criticised in Agamben's argument. Agamben 'makes only swift and oblique reference to colonisation and to colonial prison camps', Simone Bignall and Marcelo Svirsky (2012, 1) argue, and, they add, 'nor does he engage with the broad field of enquiry defining postcolonial criticism, or with the thinkers and writers of the postcolony'.

As mentioned in the introduction, interventions by Mufti and Melas aimed at overcoming Eurocentric principles of comparison and testing the very limits of comparability are circumscribed within the intersection of orientalism and postcolonialism. And we add that this circumscription is productive also for our case study, though it needs to be qualified in accordance with the geopolitical coordinates of our corpus. While both the Iberian Peninsula and Eastern Europe have been constructed as oriental objects (*cf.* Domínguez 2006 and Todorova 2009), engagement with postcolonial criticism is stronger – though not exempt of controversy – in Eastern Europe than in Spain. Of the burgeoning field of postcolonialism in Central and Eastern Europe, we adhere to Janusz Korek's claim that 'the category of "Orientalism" could also be applied with some success to Western scientific discourses on the subject of Central and Eastern Europe' for, like Edward W. Said's 'East', Central and Eastern Europe have also been epitomised 'by sensualism, irrationality, traditionalism or conservatism, despotism, primitivism, compliance and femininity' (Korek 2007, 14). Furthermore, Korek (2007, 17) argues that the 'problems that faced Ukraine as a former Soviet republic at the time of the break-up of the USSR were structurally similar to those that faced Poland, which was a "satellite" of the Kremlin at the time of the decolonization of the Eastern Bloc'.

From our perspective, the (post)colonial status of the Galician topography makes possible to read it as a zone of indistinction[19] despite Agamben's scant attention to colonial issues (for a link between the concept of 'zone of indistinction' and Slav longing for sovereignty, see Biti 2018).[20] In fact, the presence

---

19   Interestingly, in his essay in *Moja Europa* Andrukhovych makes reference to Soviet forced labour camp deaths, purges, mass murders, and permanent places of residence (*cf.* Wierzejska 2015, 382), which are Agamben's zones of indistinction *par excellence*.
20   Neil Lazarus's 2012 article on approaching the literatures and cultures of the former Soviet bloc as postcolonial is tellingly titled 'Spectres Haunting: Postcommunism and Postcolonialism'. In the case of Western European Galicia, an approach to the region from the

of the colony is pervading in Foucault's elaboration on heterotopias and therefore makes more evident its absence in Agamben's formulation. In the case of Eastern European Galicia (and Central-Eastern Europe in general), Jagoda Wierzejska (2015) has analysed *Moja Europa* (*My Europe*, 2000), a collection of two essays by Yurii Andrukhovych ('Центрально-східна ревізія' – 'The Central-Eastern Revision', written in Ukrainian and translated into Polish by Lidia Stefanowska) and Stasiuk ('Dziennik Okrętowy' – 'A Logbook', written in Polish), and concluded that, although both writers recreate a vision of *their* Europe that goes beyond the colonial narratives of subordination and domination, in the end some of their tropes reveal the post-dependent condition of the (Galician) subject. In the case of Western European Galicia, in turn, Isabel Castro Vázquez has approached Rivas's works from the perspective of the concept of 'resiliencia' (resilience), which she defines as 'un comportamiento cultural que, a diferenza da resistencia, non busca un enfrontamento defensivo senón que pretende subsistir dentro dunha *realidade colonial* opresiva mantendo a maior fidelidade posible ao propio' (Castro Vázquez 2007, 15; emphasis added; 'a cultural behaviour which, in contrast to resistance, does not look for a defensive clash but rather aims to survive within an oppressive *colonial reality* being as faithful as possible to oneself').

4   Concluding Remarks

However controversial it is to look at Western and Eastern European Galicias through the prism of colonial problems, we claim that both *En salvaxe compaña* and *Opowieści galicyiskie* request such reading as a result of their textual construction of Galiza/Galicja as a zone of indistinction (our disintegrated familiar category), a 'temporal and spatial hiatus' (Downey 2009, 120) in which the Galician subject lives on the blurred threshold of life and death, presence and absence, and in a *zone d'attente*. Galiza and Galicja, like their inhabitants, are neither sovereign nor fully heteronomous. This does not mean that there is an exact correspondence in their construction as a zone of indistinction.

---

perspective of 'internal colonialism' may be traced back to Xosé Manuel Beiras's 1972 foundational book *O atraso económico de Galicia* (The Economic Backwardness of Galicia) and Francisco Rodríguez and Ramón L. Suevos's 1978 foundational book *Problemática nacional e colonialismo. O caso galego* (The National Problem and Colonialism: The Galician Case). For a recent discussion of Galician economy and politics in terms of internal colonialism, see Pablo del Valle 2017; and for the Galician literary field in the aftermath of the Francoist regime, see García Martínez 2017. For the role of the concept of 'internal colonialism' during the 1960s–1970s within the context of European integration, see Nagel 2011.

On the contrary, whereas in *En salvaxe compaña* the Others reincarnate in heroes to claim their importance (Castro Vázquez 2007, 16), in *Opowieści galicyiskie* Galicians are still non-Europeans, paying tribute therefore to the Orientalist discourse on the uncivilised periphery (Wierzejska 2015, 392).[21] The application of a (post)colonial prism must be sensitive not only to the distinct characteristics of both Galicias, but also to the differences of their textual construction by Rivas and Stasiuk, the tension between sameness and difference of constructive comparativism.

In this regard, we consider that the experiment in constructive comparativism we have carried out here represents an opportunity to further investigate the productivity of, on the one hand, comparing cultural representations of *prima facie* incomparable societies (Western and Eastern European Galicias) and, on the other hand, applying the (post)colonial prism *within* Europe, by which the critique presented to Agamben regarding his lack of engagement with colonialism is also extended. In short, Galiza/Galicja appears as an important testing ground for a different conceptualisation of Europe.

Works Cited

Agamben, Giorgio. 1998. *Homo Sacer: Sovereign Power and Bare Life* (trl. Daniel Heller-Roazen; Stanford: Stanford UP).

Andrukhovych, Yuri, and Andrzej Stasiuk. 2000. *Moja Europa. Dwa eseje o Europie zwanej Środkową* (Wołowiec: Czarne).

Andrukhovych, Yuri. 2017. 'The Central-Eastern Revision (Expanded Version 2005)', in *My Final Territory: Selected Essays* (trl. Mark Andryczyk and Michael M. Naydan; Toronto: University of Toronto Press). Orig. pub. 2000.

Barreto, Danny M. 2011. '*Ir de morto, ir de vivo*: Galicians in a State of Living Death', *Journal of Spanish Cultural Studies* 12.4: 385–399.

Barthes, Roland. 1981. *Camera Lucida* (trl. Richard Howard; New York: Hill and Wang). Orig. pub. 1980.

Beck, Ulrich, and Edgar Grande. 2007. *Cosmopolitan Europe* (Cambridge: Polity).

Benjamin, Walter. 2002. *The Arcades Project* (trl. Howard Eiland and Kevin McLaughlin; New York: Belknap Press).

---

21 The incommensurability between Western and Eastern Europe has been further explored by Stasiuk in his play *Noc* (*Night*), which was commissioned by the Schauspielhaus of Düsseldorf to celebrate the 2004 enlargement.

Bignall, Simone and Marcelo Svirsky. 2012. 'Introduction: Agamben and Colonialism', in *Agamben and Colonialism*, ed. Marcelo Svirsky and Simone Bignall (Edinburgh: Edinburgh University Press), 1–14.

Biti, Vladimir. 2018. *Attached to Dispossession: Sacrificial Narratives in Post-imperial Europe* (Leiden: Brill).

Castro Vázquez, Isabel. 2007. *Reexistencia. A obra de Manuel Rivas* (Vigo: Xerais).

Davis, Colin. 2005. 'Hauntology, Spectres and Phantoms', *French Studies* 59.3: 373–379.

Detienne, Marcel. 2008. *Comparing the Incomparable* (trl. Janet Lloyd; Stanford: Stanford University Press). Orig. pub. 2000.

Domínguez, César. 2006. 'The South European Orient: A Comparative Reflection on Space and Literary History', *Modern Language Quarterly* 67.4: 419–449.

Downey, Anthony. 2009. 'Zones of Indistinction. Giorgio Agamben's "Bare Life" and the Politics of Aesthetics', *Third Text* 23.2 (March): 109–125.

Etkind, Alexander. 2009. 'Post-Soviet Hauntology: Cultural Memory of the Soviet Terror', *Constellations* 16.1: 182–200.

Foucault, Michel. 1986. 'Of Other Spaces' (trl. Jay Miskowiec), *Diacritics*, 16.1 (Spring): 22–27. Orig. 1967.

Foucault, Michel. 2002. *The Order of Things: An Archaeology of the Human Sciences* (London: Routledge). Orig. pub. 1969.

Friedman, Susan Stanford. 2013. 'World Modernisms, World Literature, and Comparativity', in *The Oxford Handbook of Global Modernisms*, ed. Mark Wollaeger and Matt Eatough (Oxford: Oxford University Press), 499–525.

García Martínez, Pablo. 2017. 'Literatura heterónoma a la salida del franquismo: el caso del primer nacionalismo marxista gallego', *Journal of Spanish Cultural Studies* 18.2: 153–167.

Golemo, Karolina. 2015. 'On the Two Galicias: From Lesser Poland to the Outskirts of Europe, from the Atlantic to the Vistula River', *Sprawy Narodowościowe* n.s. 46: 23–45.

Ivanov, Sanja. 2018. 'Central European Heterotopias of Decay: The Poetics of the Real in Andrzej Stasiuk's *On the Road to Babadag*', *Central Europe*, 15 February https://doi.org/10.1080/14790963.2017.1412715.

Kato, Ariko. 2016. 'Rewriting Europe: The Central Europe of Yuri Andrukhovych and Andrzej Stasiuk', in *Perspectives on Contemporary East European Literature: Beyond National and Regional Frame*, ed. Kenichi Abe (Sapporo: Hokkaido University), 91–102.

Korek, Janusz. 2007. 'Central and Eastern Europe from a Postcolonial Perspective' (trl. Tadeusz Z. Wolánski), in *From Sovietology to Postcoloniality: Poland and Ukraine from a Postcolonial Perspective*, ed. Janusz Korek (Huddinge: Södertörns Högskola), 5–22.

Lazarus, Neil. 2012. 'Spectres Haunting: Postcommunism and Postcolonialism', *Journal of Postcolonial Writing* 48.2: 117–129.

Melas, Natalie. 2007. *All the Difference in the World: Postcoloniality and the Ends of Comparison* (Stanford: Stanford University Press).

Méndez Ferrín, Xosé Luís. 2007. 'A sombra literaria do rei Don García', *A Trabe de Ouro* 69: 33–44.

Mufti, Aamir R. 2005. 'Global Comparativism', *Diacritics* 31.2 (Winter): 472–489.

Nagel, Klaus-Jürgen. 2011. 'Entre la "independencia en Europa", una "Europa con cien banderas" y una "Europa de" o "con las regiones"', *Hermes: Pentsamendu eta historia aldizkaria* 37: 4–23.

Pablo del Valle, Javier de. 2017. 'La identidad en disputa: El nacionalismo y la tesis del colonialismo interno en Galiza' (master's thesis, Universidad Nacional de Educación a Distancia).

Portela Silva, Ermelindo. 2001. *García II de Galicia, el rey y el reino (1065–1090)* (Burgos: La Olmeda).

Povinelli, Elizabeth A. 2002. *The Cunning of Recognition: Indigenous Alterities and the Making of Australian Multiculturalism* (Durham, NC: Duke University Press).

Povinelli, Elizabeth A. 2011. *Economies of Abandonment: Social Belonging and Endurance in Late Liberalism* (Durham, NC: Duke University Press).

Purchla, Jacek. 2014. 'Galicia after Galicia, or: On the Uniqueness of the Myth of the "Vanished Kingdom"' (trl. Piotr Krasnowolski), in *The Myth of Galicia*, ed. Jacek Puchla and Wolfgang Kos (Kraków: International Cultural Centre – Wien Museum), 87–91.

Rábade Villar, María do Cebreiro. 2009. 'Spectres of the Nation: Forms of Resistance to Literary Nationalism', *Bulletin of Hispanic Studies* 86.2: 231–247.

Rivas, Manuel. 2003. *In the Wilderness* (trl. Jonathan Dunne; London: The Harvill Press).

Rivas, Manuel. 2008. *En salvaxe compaña* (4th rev. ed.; Vigo: Xerais). Orig. pub. 1993.

Rychlicka, Aleksandra. 2009. 'Central Europe Imagines Central Europe: The Construction of Regional Identity in the Works of Andrzej Stasiuk' (master's thesis, Utrecht University).

Stasiuk, Andrzej. 2003. *Tales of Galicia* (trl. Margarita Nafpaktitis; Prague: Twisted Spoon).

Stasiuk, Andrzej. 2012. *Opowieści galicyjskie* (Wołowiec: Czarne). Orig. pub. 1995.

Todorova, Maria. 2009. *Imagining the Balkans* (updated ed.; Oxford: Oxford University Press).

Vaqueiro, Vítor. 2011. *Mitoloxía de Galiza. Lendas, tradicións, maxias, santos e milagres* (Vigo: Galaxia).

Vilavedra, Dolores. 2012. 'Cartografiando la narrativa gallega contemporánea: la posición de Manuel Rivas y Suso de Toro en el sistema literario', in *Voces de Galicia. Manuel Rivas y Suso de Toro*, ed. Sadi Lakhdari (Paris: INDIGO & Côté-femmes), 20–41.

Wierzejska, Jagoda. 2015. 'Central European Palimpsests: Postcolonial Discourse in Works by Andrzej Stasiuk and Yurii Andrukhovych', in *Postcolonial Europe? Essays on Post-Communist Literatures and Cultures*, ed. Dobrota Pucherová and Róbert Gáfrik (Leiden: Brill–Rodopi), 375–397.

Wolff, Larry. 2010. *The Idea of Galicia: History and Fantasy in Habsburg Political Culture* (Stanford: Stanford University Press).

CHAPTER 10

United Europe and Disunited Yugoslavia

Damir Arsenijević

> The age demanded an image
> Of its accelerated grimace
> EZRA POUND, *'Hugh Selwyn Mauberly'*

∴

1   Let Me Tell You a Joke...

One of the humorous sketches of the Bosnian group *Top Lista Nadrealista* (The Surrealists' Top Chart), entitled *United Europe and Disunited Yugoslavia*, opens with Europe protecting itself from war-torn Yugoslavia with a huge concrete wall, topped with barbed wire, waiting until there is only one remaining living Yugoslav from the war. This last remaining Yugoslav is then welcomed into the European community. Portrayed as exhausted, dirty, and hungry, he is invited to join a feast. Whilst he is devouring the food that is lavishly laid out on the tables, the Europeans start fighting amongst themselves about the origins of the war in Yugoslavia. Then, we see a reporter standing on the ladder on the Yugoslav side of the wall who talks about the hundred-year war in Europe, monstrosities hitherto unseen, and who expresses pity that a peace initiative for a democratic solution to the war in Europe that Yugoslavia proposed has been turned down. When he climbs down the ladder, he pushes it to the ground lest some 'fool' from war-torn Europe climbs over into Yugoslavia.

Can we imagine an encounter between Europe and Yugoslavia in which the border between the two is not a wall with barbed wire – an encounter in which Bosnia and Herzegovina is not a vast space for the expelled, who are kept on hold outside of Europe, in a ghetto for refugees from Africa and the Middle East, or in a waiting room for those who have long sought an escape to Europe, only to find themselves a supply of cheap labour? In other words, can we fantasise a future for Europe that is not a hundred-year war, can we embark on imagining a hopeful scenario for a European future in which the ladder will be left standing on the wall in the expectation of a cross-over?

2 'They Migrate, We Flee to Seek Refuge': Governance through Insecurity

The railway station in Tuzla, late autumn 2018.

In a forgotten railway station, in a deserted waiting room (to where?), in the middle of nowhere, while at least geographically in the heart of Europe of the twenty first century, in the hilly Balkans, a man prays to Almighty Allah – for health? For an apartment? For a job? For peace? For bread? For justice? For love? For home? For a homeland? With his forehead he touches the ground of the waiting room, which, for dozens of years, was walked on by the feet of the people of a country that no longer exists: feet that moved towards a brighter future, feet that disappeared from that spot and were scattered in the universe as if they had never existed…A man prays before the pillar as if the pillar is a monolith where God lives. Is God really in that pillar, or has God ceased speaking about all things, people and phenomena? Or perhaps this man knows God is behind the pillar, bringing peace and salvation to him? Maybe beyond this pillar, beyond Bosnia, beyond intellect, beyond God, there is a sunny field and in this field await all the people whom this man has ever loved and everything else he has ever loved? (Duraković 2018)

A man prays in a deserted railway station in Tuzla, Bosnia and Herzegovina, in early December 2018. I received the photograph from a friend who brings food and clothes to refugees from Syria, Iraq, Afghanistan, or Pakistan, who are on their way through Tuzla to a place where they can attempt to cross the border into Croatia, into the European Union. When crossing into Croatia, they will try to escape Croatian border control guards who will, if they catch them crossing the border, beat them up, destroy their mobile phones, and send them back to Bosnia.

The *punctum* of the photograph bruises me. In the background of the praying man, but positioned above his figure, are the patched up, empty offices in the railway station and above these is a sepia wallpaper print of Tuzla's coal miners. The photograph is a holding frame for a catachrestic relationship between these disparate image components that speak of different temporalities – different layers of the past, present, and future that trigger temporal and spatial dislocation. Catachresis both hollows out and combines in the photograph all that which has been expelled. Therefore, the waiting room of the deserted railway station can simultaneously be a monument to the socialist past, the atopia of today's 'on hold'-existence in Bosnia and Herzegovina, and a makeshift prayer room. If this photograph were a written text, it would be a grotesque.

The man's expulsion from his home brings to the fore the expulsion of the Yugoslav socialist future by the so-called transition into capitalism, evidenced in the photograph by the makeshift railway station offices: their curtains, broken windows mended with parcel tape, leased out units, separated by different style doors and painted in a patchwork of colours, are the staples of transitional architecture. This temporal and spatial dislocation points to a range of different uncertainties and expulsions to which these different image components testify. And they all amplify the question: 'what are the spaces of the expelled?' (Sassen 2014, 221). If, as Sassen argues, expulsions are the structuring principle and the systemic dynamic of today's capitalist order, how can we transform what is left behind, the spaces of the expelled and those who are themselves expelled, into new and hopeful economies, histories, and communities (ibid, 222)? As in archaeological layers, high above us, the miners, captured and held in the wallpaper print, gaze into an imagined, prosperous future, but all they see, like Benjamin's *Angelus Novus*, is a pile of catastrophes.

I share the photograph with Ferida Duraković and Šejla Šehabović, two Bosnian women writers, and together we try to make sense of it, try to make sense of how the disparate image components have been sutured together to make the situation in the photograph appear natural. We are all struck by how this photograph speaks of the complete destruction of Yugoslavia, its political subject – 'the working people' (*radni ljudi*), and the larceny of the property that this political subject created for decades – socially-owned property (*društvena svojina*). Since the collapse of socialism, Bosnia and Herzegovina has been the victim of predatory international capital and local nationalist intentions to profit relentlessly from the natural and human resources of the country. These nationalists enlisted the working class in the war and genocide, stole the socially-owned property held in common, and dismantled the socialist-run industry that protected workers' rights. Now, they are selling off the country's natural resources – water and air, forests and land – for their own profit, eradicating entire ecosystems in order to build hydro-electric plants[1] or to use that land as a dumping ground for hazardous waste. This expels both the people and the land.

The insecurity created through such expulsions is described by Šejla Šehabović thus:

> On official holidays, along with the state and republic flags, we also waved the black, miners' flag. I played accordion in the school orchestra – during each performance, higher up on the podium, stood the men in black and green uniforms, they were tall and they sang with deep male voices. On their heads they wore black caps with the insignia of the crossed hammers, the symbol for mines which I had to draw on a map at school. That is what I thought about when I was doing my homework. They dig underneath our houses, underneath our streets, and come up into daylight to sing our songs with their deep voices. They taught me to love the city whose streets and houses built above the mine tunnels through which the men with deep voices walk. They taught me never to leave the city. Our roots are deep here, they said to me. Deep as the mines, strong as the men mining in the pits. We did not leave even when the war came. We grieved over our refugees more than we did over the dead. In the photograph of Tuzla railway station, destroyed by the transition, the symbols of my childhood, men in miner's caps, proudly looking into the future and believing in their strength – are faced with the biggest fear I was taught about: homelessness. In this photograph, the man who is carrying out a religious ritual has no home. The world is turned upside-down – men wander the surface of the earth, they swim or float, belonging to nobody. They pray to God, prostrate on the ground, but this ground offers them nothing. We do not know where they come from and they do not know where they are going. They migrate, we flee seeking refuge. (Šehabović 2018)

---

1 See https://www.theguardian.com/environment/2015/dec/11/major-banks-put-up-nearly-1bn-for-controversial-balkan-dams-says-report

Catachresis in the photograph also testifies to *governance through insecurity*, as a mechanism which seems to proffer a continuance of a minimum of social assurance whilst, simultaneously, wielding the constant threat of instability and conflict. Fear, anxiety, and hopelessness are mobilized by governance through insecurity to promote particularisation through enforced expulsions: of industry, of people, of ecosystems. This weakens the capacity for communal solidarity and emancipatory communal action (Lorey 2015). The photograph is a metonym for Bosnia and Herzegovina, because both function as a ghetto for the expelled. It also forces us to see the hopelessness of the predicament in which we live. To interrupt the governance of insecurity, we need the 'courage of the hopeless', a leap into 'refound causes, causes found again, causes that emerge at the site of something that never was – that never existed – but which we are nevertheless able to recognize'. (Zupančič 2018, 29)

3   The Remains of a Yugoslav Muslim – Governance through Trauma

Milica Tomić, *Sigurnost u putu* [Road Safety], 2008.

In the photograph, a woman holds a framed picture, in which we see three figures: the woman herself, a young man in uniform, and a young girl. This young man in uniform is the husband of the woman who holds the picture. This image of him in uniform is what she has left of him: him wearing the JNA uniform, the uniform of the Yugoslav People's Army, which killed him and buried him in a clandestine mass grave. The teenage girl in the picture is their daughter – she was only two when her father tried to escape into the woods. She and her mother were expelled from the region of Srebrenica by that very same army that went in pursuit of the young man.

This is the most beloved image the woman has of her husband, as she waits for him to be located, excavated, re-associated, identified, and then buried again. The event of the burial will mark the time when the family, as a family, will be together once again, when these two women are reunited with the remains of the husband and the father. Through a digitally manipulated collage that she had commissioned as a framed picture, a family is re-assembled: of him when he was in his late teens, of her and their daughter as they are now. This is the family brought together as it never was and never could be. Against the idyllic surroundings of the background setting, stand the cut-and-pasted figures, each drawn from their different place and time. The catachresis in the picture enables a patchwork of mourning to emerge. The catachrestic relationships between space and time, the figures and the idyllic surrounding, trace and circumscribe the woman's desire – the desire of the wife and the mother – to put together and recreate the destroyed family around the missing man. This is catachresis as *love after genocide*, which liberates and enables the woman to go beyond the 'law of the mass grave' (Arsenijević 2013). According to this law, in Bosnian society, the woman is supposed to be a perennially grieving and anonymous referent for her husband's loss. Defying her own anonymity and the anonymity of her husband – for he is an unidentified, missing person, robbed of his proper name – the woman embraces catachresis to name the unnameable and imagine the unimaginable. In creating her catachrestic commemoration, the woman gives the man and the family to loss in order to gain the world of signification. The photograph, in which the collage features, upholds such commemoration, as it is a pre-production photograph of Milica Tomić's art work *Sigurnost u putu*. In this work, Milica Tomić, in a conversation with women survivors, draws portraits of their missing male relatives from the women's stories of the men.

Through her catachrestic commemoration, the woman opposes governance through trauma, as it is currently imposed and enacted in Bosnia and Herzegovina. The mechanisms of so-called 'transitional justice' decontextualise and further depoliticise the political origins of the violence of war and genocide. The top-down transitional justice approach promotes multiculturalist politics as a panacea to counter the effects of war and genocide in Bosnia and Herzegovina. It uses political correctness as a tool to gag public expressions of grief, for fear of renewed animosity and violence. The problem with multiculturalist politics, however, is that it reduces social conflict to a friction between many identities, recasting cultural, religious and ethnic differences as 'sites of conflict that need to be attenuated and managed through the practice of tolerance' (Brown 2006, 15). In the discourse of tolerance, what is taken as a given is that each ethnic victim has her or his own micro-story, each ethnic group has its own destiny, and what is promoted as life is actually an image of lives led on parallel tracks, in a state of never-intersecting apartheid.

More importantly, this catachrestic commemoration rescues the executed Yugoslav Muslim from the ideological mechanism of ethnicization and re-signifies him in a haunting evocation. In the dominant commemorative regime, ethnic identity is installed as the only possible political identification and the loss from the war and genocide is reduced to the merely personal and familial. In Bosnia and Herzegovina, bodily remains are exhumed, counted, re-associated, managed, and consecrated as *ethnic* remains. The Scientist, the Bureaucrat, and the Priest form an alliance in order to produce a religious, ethnic victim – a religious Bosniak out of a Yugoslav Muslim – through: forensic science; multiculturalist post-conflict management with its politics of reconciliation; and religious ritual (Arsenijević 2011). In so doing, these three sets of vested interests assume the perspective of the perpetrator of the execution, in whose fantasy the Yugoslav Muslim had to be branded as an ethnic other in order to be executed. Therefore, in everyday life, the surviving ethnic victims can only mourn dead ethnic victims, and those who continue to profit from the wealth they amassed during the war and genocide remain in power. The dominant commemorative discourse depoliticises the demos itself, reducing the polis – the socio-political structure – to mere familial ties, to the oikos. Therein lies the ideological mechanism of the transition into capitalism: it is only through the war and genocide of the 1990s, which was carried out in order to destroy the political subjectivity forged in the anti-fascist revolution of World War II – that is the non-religious Yugoslav Muslim – that Yugoslavia could be obliterated and its socially-owned property could be privatised and looted. Therefore, in the violent transition, the diminution of that Yugoslav political subjectivity – from the political people as *radni ljudi* to ethnic groups – is kept and maintained through the local and international management of loss in post-war Bosnia and Herzegovina.

Governance through trauma produces a perpetual victim and the 'demoralized subject of human rights' (Pupavac 2005). Furthermore, governance through trauma is carried out in the context of the dominant revisionism, which is attempting to equate fascism with the communism of World War II. However, the transition into democracy in Yugoslavia not only leads nowhere but as Buden (2017, 350) claims: 'it has never occurred in the first place...the historical logic of the post-communist transition makes no sense whatsoever. Which, however, doesn't mean that it has no ideological function. Indeed, the logic of transition is grounded in a sort of negative continuity with the socialist past. Whatever conflict arises on the proclaimed path from communist totalitarianism to a full-fledged democracy, it is always blamed on the remnants of the communist past, which automatically makes the capitalist reality of the transitional process appear as a genuinely conflict-free condition in which interests, however disparate, never collide'. And those who have are surviving through the transition have become 'the waste – criminalized and ghettoized for there is still some value to be extracted from them' (Husanović 2015, 116).

Governance through trauma enables the ongoing extraction of value from the dead and the living. Juxtaposed to it is the catachrestic relationality in the framed picture that evokes the spectral remainder of the executions and brings it together with those who are deemed to be the waste of the transition – the woman and the daughter. Thus, the catachrestic relationality of the framed picture instigates a proper politicisation of the polis through profanation, in the Agambenian sense, as a return to common use of that which has been removed to the 'sphere of the sacred' but which is not a mere restoration of a 'natural use' of that which was removed. Profanation, for Agamben, is not limited to the abolition of the form of separation 'in order to regain an uncontaminated use that lies either beyond or before it' (Agamben 2007, 85). The activity that results from profanation becomes 'a pure means, that is, a praxis that, while firmly maintaining its nature as a means, is emancipated from its relationship to an end; it has joyously forgotten its goal and can now show itself as such, as a means without an end. The creation of new use is possible only by deactivating an old use, rendering it inoperative' (ibid., 86). Love after genocide pluralises commemorative discourses, enables the return of the proper name of the political subject to an anonymous victim, and enables the woman to mourn by signifying her loss beyond the dominant commemorative injunctions. It thus enables the construction of a new subject position after genocide by creating space and time for the expelled.

4 The Proletarian Lung: Governance through Poverty

This photograph shows the disintegrating and abandoned post-industrial remnants of former factories in one of the largest socialist Yugoslav mining and chemical industrial complexes in the city of Tuzla, Bosnia and Herzegovina. The two giant rusting spheres of the Chlorine Alkaline Power House (better known by its acronym, HAK) and the surrounding rusting pipes of its skeleton still hold more than 47 tons of stagnant, highly-flammable propylene oxide. This is a ticking bomb, surrounded by scattered, abandoned and corroding barrels, from which, slowly, over a quarter of a century, mercury, cadmium, and arsenic have been leaking into the ground. Around HAK, which has been privatised,

Chlorine Alkaline Power House, Tuzla, winter 2018.

stripped of assets, and subsequently abandoned, there are black rocks of carcinogenic toluene diisocyanate (TDI) waste protruding from the ground. In the vicinity of HAK, these rocks outline many of the unknown landfill sites of this hazardous waste. The accurate size and exact locations of these landfills are undocumented by the government or any other official environmental protection agency. Only the impoverished and unemployed former industrial workers go anywhere near the lethal remnants of HAK. They disassemble and pick through the site for scrap metal to sell. This work exposes them to toxic waste, which leads to high numbers of premature deaths among them.[2] These deaths happen either as a result of accidents, or through prolonged and imperceptible exposure to toxins, leading to slow deaths. This is 'unseen poverty' that testifies to human and ecological disposability through 'slow violence', which occurs gradually, out of sight, beyond media spectacle. (Nixon 2011, 4).

After targeting and executing the working class in the war and genocide in the 1990s, which was termed transition into capitalism, predatory capital targeted the factories, putting tens of thousands out of work, stripping factories of assets, taking out huge mortgages on them, and after turning them into post-industrial wastelands, subsequently abandoning them. This was called privatization. After extracting material value from these factories, the mercenaries of capital, supported by local ethno-nationalist elites, abandoned the toxic waste. Aldin Bejhanović is a metal picker who suffered a pulmonary embolism, caused by the toxic waste at HAK. He says:

---

2   Informative reports by investigative journalists of June 2018 reveal the extent of the damage. See https://www.cin.ba/en/otrovni-otpad-pod-nogama-tuzlaka/

> We removed gunmetal valves from pipes in manholes. There was work. But after some time we uncovered the barrels. They were stinking … They stank so strongly that it hurt my eyes. I couldn't take it … I stopped for a while, but later me, my dad, and a neighbour came back to cut out more pipes. And we found it there. We did not know that it was a poison. The place was not even marked.

He describes being poisoned thus:

> I felt out of breath when I bent down to pick something up, and I had put up with this for around two weeks. I thought it was cigarettes … When it grabbed me and threw me down and when blackness fell over my eyes, I couldn't get to my car. (CIN 2018)

Bejhanović's uncle was not so lucky: his lungs were burnt after he had inhaled poisonous gas from the pipes that he had cut and he quickly died from his injuries.

The 'proletarian lung' of the metal picker, whose lungs get burned by the left-over chlorine in the HAK pipes and who succumbs to his injuries and then dies, is the expelled organ that speaks of *governance through poverty*. His death is the toll extracted by the logic of predatory capitalism in Bosnia and Herzegovina today.

> The conditions under which labor power is sold in a capitalist labor market act on the individual's glucose cycle as the pattern of exertion and rest depends more on the employer's economic decisions than on the worker's self perception of metabolic flux. Human ecology is not the relation of our species with the rest of nature, but rather the relations of different societies, and the classes, genders, ages, grades, and ethnicities maintained by those social structures. Thus, it is not too farfetched to speak of the pancreas under capitalism or the proletarian lung. (Lewontin and Levins 2007, 37)

In the extractive logic of governance through poverty, pollution is weaponised. This logic operates under the guise of 'growth', which claims to offer jobs and economic security. Its mechanism is inclusion of citizens through exclusion. This may seem like a paradox: those who are on the margins of society are not peripheral, but central to this governance. In everyday life, it destroys and contaminates water, air, and land in Bosnia and Herzegovina and renders its people and land expellable and disposable through exposure to pollution. For 25 years, the tactics of governance through poverty have been used in the transition into capitalism to train the citizens of Bosnia and Herzegovina in the ways of humanitarianism and precarious living on meagre and irregular salaries and pensions. These tactics are heterogeneous, as ethno-nationalist elites distribute the political pressure resulting from social injustice, forcing a range of institutions – from education to health – to buffer societal discontent. The main aim of governance through poverty is to manage low-income populations and train them to become at least passive, and at best cooperative subjects of the market (Soss and Schiram 2011). At the core of this governance through poverty lies the creation and the promotion of what Wendy Brown calls 'sacrificial citizenship', as the valorisation of sacrifice for a greater good. Such driven sacrifice may come in the shape of enforced job cuts; indefinite lay-offs or unpaid 'leave'; wage freezes or years of unpaid salaries. Expelled and sacrificed, in governance through poverty, a citizen 'releases state, law, and economy from responsibility for and responsiveness to its own condition and predicaments, and is ready to sacrifice to the cause of economic growth and fiscal constraints when called to do so.' (Brown 2016, 12)

The number of deaths per head of population caused by air pollution rank Bosnia and Herzegovina as the second deadliest country in the world.[3] This is how the war-time logic of the 1990s extends into the present and creates a continuity between mass graves and hazardous waste. The post-industrial wastelands are contested sites around which simultaneously intersect the grief and anger caused by ecological accidents[4] and new anxieties around current and potential future investments in fossil fuels.[5] Slow violence creates casualties that are struggling to be recognised *in time* – they are *untimely* and invisible – as *toxic time* cannot be recognised in the regime of the sensationalist media. In addition to toxic time, toxic landscapes become a part of those who are expelled, as 'various toxins take up residence within the body, the supposedly inert 'background' of place becomes the active substance of self' (Alaimo 2010, 102). Our awareness of how our surroundings are integral to and inseparable parts of our bodies is the start of a different kind of materiality for the struggle for the commons. This struggle starts from the expelled poor – bodies and the environments; from the recording and sharing of the stories of the proletarian lung and proletarian cancer. This is the struggle to reclaim and fiercely defend both space and time as our commons against the slow, extractive violence exerted by governance through poverty.

---

3   These are the UN estimate of January 2018. See https://www.unenvironment.org/news-and-stories/story/coming-clean-air-bosnia-and-herzegovina
4   See http://ba.n1info.com/a277700/English/NEWS/Lukavac-citizens-concerned-about-pollution.html
5   See https://www.business-humanrights.org/en/bosnia-herzegovina-air-pollution-worsens-in-tuzla-while-govt-plans-for-more-coal-power

5 Conclusion: Protesting to Maintain Production

The February 2014 popular protests in Tuzla.

The photograph shows a moment from the popular protests in Tuzla, Bosnia and Herzegovina, which started in early February 2014. These protests had been foreshadowed by a range of site-specific protests, over previous years, which had focused, more diffusely, on voicing dissatisfaction and demanding accountability from those in power. The February 2014 protests marked a qualitative shift: moving beyond citizens solely *recording* social injustice towards the devising anew of citizen-led, collective approaches to decision-making about their future in popular assemblies, called plenums. Much of the previous pseudo-activity, involving, as it did, the recording of social injustice was supported, practically and financially, by the civil society scene and NGOs. This was a form of self-sabotage that was donor-driven and displayed a fascination with identity politics differences – whilst appearing actively to be seeking change, it was dedicated to keeping the status quo for the elites and oligarchs, completely neglecting the pursuit of socio-economic justice for people living in post-war Bosnia and Herzegovina. The language of the February 2014 protest was unambiguous – the banners read *'We are hungry in all three languages'*, *'Reverse corrupt privatisation'* and *'End nationalism'* – articulating clearly a set of newly identified priorities. In doing so, these protests asserted the democratic right to demand freedom, justice, and better life. In a powerful affirmation of the struggle for the common property that had been stolen from them all, the protests were also a practical site to forge and test new solidarities. Together with the workers from various factories and plants, the unemployed, students, war-veterans, and pensioners all came together to show that their disposable bodies still mattered in the fight against the post-war exhaustion – characterised by poverty and hunger.

The February 2014 protests were inspired by the struggle of workers of several privatised Tuzla-based factories who were being exposed to the most brutal extraction of labour. In late 2012, the workers of the DITA detergent factory in Tuzla, Bosnia and Herzegovina, set up barricades in front of their factory in order to prevent the wholesale asset stripping and the destruction of their place of work. Previously, protests against unjust and forced factory privatisations throughout Bosnia and Herzegovina had been easily dispersed and ignored. DITA workers employed new and unprecedented strategies and tactics. DITA stood amidst a bare landscape of a few scattered remnants of other closed-down factories. The workers of DITA were determined to prevent the closure and dissolution of their factory, which they referred to as 'home'. Exhausted by years of industrial action in pursuit of their claim for 44 unpaid monthly salaries and other remunerations that were owed to them – and far from the traditional model of strikes to halt production – the DITA workers, together with local activists, fought to keep production at their factory going. And the barricade at DITA was indeed productive: their demand for support for the protection of the factory as a productive entity was a genuine conceptual and organisational break-through. The DITA barricade was organised along the lines of the 1992–1995 wartime defense of Tuzla, in that the workers set up a base camp in front of the factory and put in place 24-hour guard duty. Their claim was axiomatic: 'we are not on strike, we are protesting to maintain production'. To be in 'protest to maintain production', amidst violent privatization, impunity, factory closures, and a corrupt judiciary, means to decolonise and reclaim the factory from the deadly grip of the triad of governance through insecurity-trauma-poverty. It also means to go a step further, and – in the face of the dominant resignation and cynicism – to reclaim the production of possibility itself. In their claim, DITA factory workers materialised a new subject position, which is continuing to show its relevance and will continue to produce its impact in and on the future. Coupled with their conception of the factory as 'birth home' or 'first home', which, from the current perspective of transition may seem to be residual and anachronistic, the DITA factory workers enabled the creative production of a different world beyond the new politico-economic dispensation ushered in and maintained by the ethno-nationalist oligarchies. Through everyday interventions that distract and insist on disinformation, the ethno-nationalist oligarchies shape the vocabulary of politics, economics, and culture – tactics through which they normalise social inequality. These agents of power and capital manipulate language in order to continue to extract value from political projects that were founded on concentration camps and mass graves. By conceptually re-framing the struggle for the commons, DITA workers rescued political imagination by producing new keywords and new methods to fight for a more just social transformation in Bosnia and Herzegovina today.

The February 2014 protests interrupted the triad of governance through insecurity-trauma-poverty that has, for almost a quarter of a century, invested into making impossibility seem convincing. The renewed enthusiasm, pride and sense of agency created in and by the protests was birthed out of the refusal to accept and inhabit a world where the currently dominant ethno-capitalist organization of life is presented as the only possibility. This is why both local and international forces mobilised, with great speed, to criminalise these protests and to brand them as 'terrorism'. The knowledge gained in and through these protests was that the right to violence itself had to be decolonised. This is the deep, re-claimed knowledge of war-time survival in the disunited Yugoslavia of the years between 1992 and 1995: to 'fire back when fired upon'; to stop counting the tally of human rights violations scored against you and to fight to survive, regardless of being branded a terrorist if you do so; against the predominant injunction to forget, to create continuity of your own knowledge of this survival and, generationally, to pass it on.

Generationally passing on this knowledge, the poet Šejla Šehabović remarks thus:

> In 2014, on the occasion of the opening of the renovated Vijećnica library and its accompanying jubilation in Sarajevo, I was interviewed for the BBC and I was asked, as a cultural worker, to comment on its inaugural programme., In the year that marked the anniversary of the outbreak of the First World War, I gave a statement about everything that was pertinent to the urban destruction that occurred during the war of the 1990s. Then I said to the reporters: 'I hope you are aware that, at this moment, while the symphony orchestra is preparing to give a recital, and the international invitees are taking their seats in the front rows, not even 20 metres away from there, just across the Miljacka river, a police squad is preventing hungry workers, who have organised a protest, from crossing the bridge. 'Let's not talk about it', said the interviewer, 'tell us more about the Vijećnica building'. At that point I knew that Europe had learned nothing. A few days later, on a Bulgarian National TV programme, I spoke about groups that organise actions concerning social justice in Bosnia and Herzegovina. The

interviewer asked me: 'Do you expect ethnic conflict in your country?' I replied: 'I don't know why I would expect people who are fighting corruption to initiate ethnic conflict?' The interviewer said: 'Let's end this interview.' That's when I knew that the desire for oblivion will end tragically. Then came the refugees and 'Europe' disappeared in a single summer. No, there are no students in the Sarajevo Vijećnica building, there is no 'library' there anymore, and nobody reads books in there any longer. To enter the beautifully painted interior, more opulent than can be recalled by any living reader, visitors have to buy a ticket, like you would for a museum or an art gallery, and, for an even more handsome sum, wealthy foreigners can use the building as a sought-after, fashionable wedding venue. In front of the entrance to it, on its steps, writers, who can still remember how they rescued books from the burning library, read poetry to those who pass by. The security guards, who do not let them enter the building, say 'I'm only doing my job'. (Šehabović, 2017)

Protesting to maintain production stands for a collective work on increasing our capacities for solidarity and for associating labour against social inequality. The totality of this knowledge is the ladder, left standing up against the wall on the territory of the disunited Yugoslavia, that is offered to Europe today.

Works Cited

Agamben, Giorgio. 2007. *Profanations* (New York: Zone Books).

Alaimo, Stacey. 2010. *Bodily Natures: Science, Environment, and the Material Self* (Bloomington: Indiana University Press).

Arsenijević, Damir. 2011. 'Gendering the Bone: The Politics of Memory in Bosnia and Herzegovina', *Journal for Cultural Research*, 15.2: 193–205.

Arsenijević, Damir. 2013. 'Love after Genocide' in *Moments: Eine Geschichte der Performance in 10 Akten (Moments: A History of Performance in 10 Acts)*, ed. Boris Charmatz et al. (Karlsruhe: ZKM), 472–479.

Brown, Wendy. 2016. 'Sacrificial Citizenship: Neoliberalism, Human Capital, and Austerity Politics', *Constellations*, vol. 23.1, 3–14.

Brown, Wendy. 2006. *Regulating Aversion: Tolerance in the Age of Identity and Empire* (Princeton NJ: Princeton University Press).

Buden, Boris. 2017. 'Afterword: And so They Historicized' in *The Cultural Life of Capitalism in Yugoslavia: (Post)Socialism and Its Other*, ed. Dijana Jelača, Maša Kolanović & Danijela Lugarić (London: Palgrave MacMillan), 345–50.

CIN. 2018. *The Land of Toxins*.

Duraković, Ferida. December 2018. Personal Correspondence.
Husanović, Jasmina. 2015. 'Governance of Life and Femininity in Bosnia and Herzegovina: Reflections on Affective Politics and Cultural Production' in *Genre and the (Post-)Communist Woman: Analysing Transformations of the Central and East European Female Ideal*, ed. F. C. Andreescu & M. J. Shapiro (New York: Routledge), 117–132.
Lewontin, Richard & Richard Levins. 2007. *Biology Under the Influence: Dialectical Essays on Ecology, Agriculture, and Health* (New York: Monthly Review Press).
Lorey, Isabel. 2015. *State of Insecurity: Government of the Precarious* (London: Verso).
Nixon, Rob. 2011. *Slow Violence and The Environmentalism of The Poor* (Cambridge, MA: Harvard University Press).
Pupavac, Vanesa. 2005. 'The Demoralized Subject of Global Civil Society' in *The Global Civil Society: Contested Futures*, ed. Gideon Baker & David Chandler (London: Routledge), 52–68.
Sassen, Saskia. 2014. *Expulsions: Brutality and Complexity in the Global Economy* (Cambridge, MA: Belknap Press).
Soss, Joe, Richard C. Fording, & Sanford F. Schram. 2011. *Disciplining The Poor* (Chicago: Chicago University Press).
Šehabović, Šejla. September 2017. Personal Correspondence.
Šehabović, Šejla. December 2018. Personal Correspondence.
Zupančič, Alenka. 2018. 'Apocalypse Is (Still) Disappointing', *S: Journal of the Circle for Lacanian Ideology Critique*, 11: 16–30.

CHAPTER 11

'A Marvellous Leeway': Walter Benjamin's Idea of Europe

Vivian Liska

On 7 April 1919 the then 27-year-old Walter Benjamin writes to his friend Ernst Schoen:

> After taking my exams, I want to learn languages, as you know – to have the European sphere behind me [...] I am expecting from the future – as soon as it is intrinsically and extrinsically feasible for me – to leave Europe. Both are inextricably intertwined and it sometimes weighs heavily on me: because I can't carry this out as an act of violence; but I see leaving Europe as a necessity I will have to face.[1]

Den europäischen Kreis im Rücken haben: 'To have the European sphere behind me'.[2] The ambiguity of the expression, in which Europe appears as a support and a resource, but also as a threat and a burden, as well as a place one turns one's back on and leaves behind, contains in essence the paradigmatic and simultaneously singular ambivalences of this German-Jewish thinker, who for many is the epitome of a European intellectual of the inter-war period. According to Hannah Arendt, Benjamin feared, if he were to immigrate to America, 'being dragged up and down the country to be exhibited as the "last European"' (Arendt 1970, 17–18). Neither this departure *in extremis* nor the emigration to Palestine took place. After more than two decades of hesitation about leaving Europe, Benjamin committed suicide in 1940 while fleeing from the Nazis. His suicide at the French-Spanish border became the symbol of a failed departure from a Europe to which so many Jewish intellectuals fell victim because they were unable, or able only too late, to make a break with the old continent.

---

1 Thus in the correspondence (Benjamin 1994, hereinafter referred to in the text as CWB), 140. This and other quotations have been slightly emended. The German edition, *Gesammelte Briefe* (Benjamin 1966 ff.), is referred to in-text as GB.
2 This text is a slightly modified and shortened version of a chapter in *Escape to Life. German Intellectuals in New York: A Compendium on Exile after 1933*. Eckart Goebel, Sigrid Weigel (eds.), Berlin: De Gruyter, 2012.

Between Benjamin's initial reflections on leaving Europe and his death, he produced works – he spoke of a 'telescope' – with which he re-examined the peaks of European cultural achievement – from Kant and Goethe, Shakespeare and Hölderlin to Baudelaire and Proust, Kraus and Brecht – and at the same time viewed the foundations of the social and historical developments that prepared the ground for the European catastrophe about to take place. This work was accompanied by Benjamin's long farewell to Europe, vividly documented in his letters. From his earliest plans to leave the old continent in the context of an initial interest in Zionism in 1912 to his final, desperate attempts to escape the Nazi terror, Benjamin considered the possibility of emigrating from Europe in letters written in almost every phase of his life. The fact that he remained until it was too late has repeatedly been described – most forcefully by Hannah Arendt – as failure, as fate, as misfortune and clumsiness of an unworldly intellectual. Indeed, although the situation had long been dangerous, it was only in the final months that Benjamin seriously tried to procure means and possibilities – money, affidavits, visas – to enable him to leave. Benjamin was quite aware of the risk involved in this postponement. In July 1940 he writes to Gretel Adorno: 'I continue to live in the spirit appropriate to one who is exposed to risks he should have foreseen and that he ran in (almost) full consciousness of the dangers involved.' That remaining in Europe, however, was something more, and different from a delayed and finally unsuccessful attempt to escape, is evident from his numerous reflections about his leaving.

Benjamin understood both options, emigration and remaining in Europe, in terms of almost metaphysical categories. To him the claim of both possibilities is absolute, its mood the subjunctive, its fundamental figure of thought the aporia: 'My mission,' Benjamin writes to Florens Christian Rang in 1923, 'could not be fulfilled here [in Europe], even if it were here. It is from this perspective that I view the problem of emigration. God willing, a solution can be found.' (CWB p 216) If Benjamin sees in the rejection of Europe and his turn towards Palestine and Jewishness 'ein Gebot, das philosophisch durchdacht sein wollte' [a commandment that needs to be thought through philosophically], then equally he describes his work oriented towards Europe – above all his magnum opus, the *Arcades Project*, which because of the sources required also binds him physically to the old continent – as his essential calling. Benjamin never solves the conflict, but its insolubility, demonstrated in frequently varied formulations is linked to one of the core aspects of his thought. This dilemma has a parallel in his conception of Europe to which Benjamin remains faithful to the last. It is revealed in Benjamin's correspondence with friends and acquaintances conducted over almost three decades.

In the continuities of style of those passages from his letters in which Benjamin envisages departure – through all the changes in his private life and in political conditions – there can be seen a commitment to an idea of Europe that he defended to the last and for which his whole work stands. Europe is to him neither a geographical nor a political and ideological realm. In a letter to Rang he talks dismissively of the earlier preferences of their common friend Erich Gutkind, who 'carelessly dedicated himself to what was European. He did this in a way that would necessarily one day reveal itself, and had to reveal itself, as a mistake to anyone with eyes to see. For me, on the contrary, circumscribed nations were always central: German or French.' (CWB 214) Europe is not important to Benjamin as a democratic, cosmopolitan association of states, but as an indispensable workshop or, as he put it, as 'writing factory' (*Schreibfabrik*) and 'production enterprise' (*Produktionsanstalt*) as well as a mode of thinking and an attitude toward life. In the sediments of the decaying heterogeneous intellectual tradition of Europe he finds at once the material, the tools, and the procedure to investigate the state of this tradition - its possibilities and dark depths, its reach and relevance - and recasts it for a new purpose. Benjamin's idea of Europe takes shape not only in terms of contents, but in forms of speaking and thinking, leading to a critical distance and a saving critique of the existing and the given. Consequently, in what follows, my concern will be less with a biographical reconstruction of Benjamin's failure to leave than with an analysis of the textual figures and figures of thought through which for more than two decades he expresses his need to leave Europe and, even more, his resistance to such a departure.

1 Necessity and Act of Violence

First of all, the fundamental questions: Why go – and why stay? The variety of changing necessities, that is, the compelling motives *for* an emigration from Europe which Benjamin cites over the years can broadly be reconstructed from Benjamin's letters: initial encounters with Zionism which, as he already writes to a school friend in 1912, confronts him 'als Möglichkeit und damit vielleicht einmal als Verpflichtung, 'as a possibility and hence perhaps one day as a duty' (CWB 17); the recognition of the potential significance of Hebrew, which ultimately can be learned only in Palestine, for his own thinking, particularly in the context of his studies on the German Tragedy; the emigration of acquaintances and friends, Gershom Scholem, above all, to Palestine; failed love affairs and an increasing feeling of loneliness and isolation; disappointment at the failure of his university career - latent anti-Semitism and academic conservatism led to the rejection of his habilitation thesis; the financial difficulties related to this rejection, became acute in later years; hopes of professional possibilities outside Europe; anti-Semitic violence in European cities and the foreboding that there is no place for Jews, and not only for them, in Europe; more generally the increasingly dark social and political situation, as a result of which 'Europe has become uninhabitable' and lacks 'air to breathe' (B VI 244), and, already from the 1920's, an awareness of the irreparable decay of Europe which was confirmed by Hitler's seizure of power. Finally, there is the urgency, following Benjamin's internment in the Clos St. Joseph camp near Nevers, with which the necessity of a flight from Europe became a question of survival.

These various necessities conflict with those attachments to Europe that would make leaving it an act of violence inflicted upon himself. The reasons for staying or for postponing emigration appear just as diverse as those for leaving, only they are more complex. There are too many, and their formulation too often sounds like an excuse, to take each one of them at face value. Benjamin's existential and intellectual bond with Europe, so it seems, lies beyond all concrete justifications. In the early years the reasons to stay usually come from Benjamin himself. First, there is a rejection of political, territorial Zionism in favour of a 'Zionism of the spirit' which can only be realized in Europe: 'The best Jews,' Benjamin writes to Ludwig Strauss in 1912, 'are today bound to a valuable process in West European society.'[3] Then there is the question of Hebrew: the possibility of also learning it in Berlin or Paris in conjunction with the complaint, influenced by Scholem, of the 'hideous' revival of Hebrew as practiced in Palestine (to Gretel Karplus, 25/5/1935, GB V 93). Finally, and increasingly, there is the impossibility of being able to devote the necessary time and attention to Hebrew, as this would distract him from other, 'more European' work.

Soon after first considering the possibility of a later Zionist 'duty' Benjamin emphasizes his ties to Europe. In a further letter to Ludwig Strauss he writes: 'To me it is pointless to ask whether Jewish Palestine-work or Jewish-European work is more urgent. I am bound here.' (GB I 71) The placing of the two hyphens speaks volumes. In the first case it stands between Palestine and work, while 'Jewish' remains separate, in the second it is placed between Jewish and European. Benjamin is tied to the 'here' of Europe, an idea of Europe, that has entered into a union with Jewishness. Consequently, the place of Jewishness is Europe. It is betrayed by the 'Palestine Zionists'. 'I did not find,' writes Benjamin in the same letter to Strauss, 'that the Zionists had a Jewish life, that they had more than vague ideas of the Jewish spirit [...] They propagate Palestine and booze German. They are half people. Have they ever thought through school, literature, the inner life, the state in Jewish terms?' It is hard to say, from all this,

---

3 Quoted from Benjamin 1966, 1: 64. The letters to Ludwig Strauss are not included in the English edition of Benjamin's letters.

whether Benjamin remains in Europe because Palestine doesn't appeal to him or whether he wants to cast Palestine in an unflattering light in order to stay in Europe.

Professionally, and even more so with respect to his spiritual and intellectual development, Benjamin doubts whether there are possibilities for him outside Europe. There may 'also be no place in Europe' for him, yet 'is there more room for me [in Palestine] – for what I know and what I can do – there than in Europe? If there is not more, then there is less' (CWB 417). Even as an outcast his place is in Europe, even if there is no place for him there. Benjamin responds to the emigration of friends with hope about the special meaning of 'distant friendships', which can only develop their true potential in the intensity of an exchange of letters. After a failure to meet Scholem he writes to the latter: 'it may well be fitting to have a small ocean between us when the moment comes to fall into each other's arms "spiritualiter".' (CWB 623) And more importantly, it is precisely the emigration of a large number of Benjamin's intellectual Jewish acquaintances that requires him to stay. 'It would also be bad for Europe, if the cultural energies of the Jews were to leave it.' (to Ludwig Strauss 10/10/1912, GB I 71) Later, the letters only hint at one of the principal reasons for his rejection of emigration to Palestine, his relationship with the Russian Communist Asja Lacis, who influences him not only emotionally but also ideologically against plans for emigration at a time when he was closest to realizing them.

Concrete remarks on the political situation and on the anti-Semitic threat in Europe are noticeably rare in Benjamin's correspondence. Where he mentions them, he talks of the 'anti-Semitic ideology' in the same breath as Zionism. Benjamin's awareness of the political state of affairs in Europe, which would cause him to emigrate, is balanced by doubts about conditions in Palestine. These apply both to the internal Jewish situation and to relations with the Arabs. On the tension between the eastern Jewish immigrants, the majority of whom are strictly observant, and the 'enlightened' Western Jewish immigrants, he asks his interlocutor: 'How does one propose to resolve the pressing religious issue between Western and Eastern European Jews? Does one not fear religious wars? Is not the union of two cultures such as the west and east European Jewish ones something like a leap... into chaos?' (GB I 62) In 1929 he notes the breakdown of relations with the Arabs. Even in 1936 the situation in Palestine appears to him to be at least as threatening as that in Europe. (GB III 317). To him this threat is less to the physical presence of the Jews in Palestine than to the spirit of Jewishness. He fears, that 'the material actions of the Arabs' could hardly be more harmful than the 'psychological reactions of the Jews'. He sees no prospect of an improvement in the situation. (GB III 316) To him the rescue of the spirit of Judaism is by no means guaranteed in Palestine, quite the contrary: 'What becomes of the hopes that Palestine raises, beyond allowing ten thousand Jews, even one hundred thousand Jews, to eke out a meagre existence. A circumstance that, as absolutely essential as it is, may well not run its course without proving to be a new and catastrophic danger among all the dangers threatening Judaism' (CWB 526) The few passages in which Palestine appears in a positive light are ambivalent. For example, in his reaction – no doubt intended to be humorous – to Scholem's enthusiastic description of his stay in the cabbalist town of Safed. Benjamin concludes with relief, 'that, even in much of Palestine, things proceed in a more human and less Jewish fashion than someone who is ignorant of Palestine might imagine' (CWB 243). Benjamin is hardly interested in becoming less ignorant. Only rarely and half-heartedly does he ask about the country. 'I will enjoy looking through a travel guide to Palestine,' he announces in June 1924, but then again only 'as soon as I have the opportunity' (CWB 243). The intention is not mentioned again.

In part, Benjamin cites outward circumstances that prevent him from leaving. These change depending on his situation: first, there is work that still has to be completed before a departure – the doctorate, the habilitation, various commissioned pieces as well as trips already planned within Europe, concern about his dying mother, visitors expected from abroad. In his final years the real obstacles to leaving Europe increase: no passport, no money, no visa, physical and mental exhaustion, and finally a border guard who blocks his escape. Yet even in the last two years of his life as the situation in Europe becomes ever more pressing and departure more difficult, it is not only external circumstances that hold him back from emigration. The work on the Arcades Project is increasingly at the centre of his life. For that he must stay in Paris, in Europe, 'for me, nothing in the world could replace the Bibliothèque Nationale' (CWB 621). The actual title of the project is 'Paris, Capital of the XIX. Century', its actual aim a stock-taking of the European condition and its foundations. As early as 1930 Benjamin is calling this work 'the theatre of all my conflicts and all my ideas.' (CWB 359) It increasingly demands all his attention and the subordination of all other 'dispositions', finally also those that could have saved his life. Even in the desperate attempts at flight of his last months there is still evidence of the need to save an idea of Europe that, he believes, can be seen only in the lives of those it is preparing to expel. In his letter to Adrienne Monnier of 21 November 1939 Benjamin describes what is at issue in his project, which he continues working on until the last moment: 'Espérons que les témoins et témoignages de la civilisation européenne [...] survivent à la fureur sanglante d'Hitler' (GB VI, 334) 'Let us hope that the witnesses to European civilisation [...] will survive the murderous rage of Hitler, along with their accounts of it'.

(CWB 613) The witness does not survive, his testimony remains. It also includes Benjamin's letters: He explicitly assigns the epistolary genre to 'the sphere of "testimony"' (CWB 149). This is true in a very special way of Benjamin's letters about the possibility of emigrating from Europe. If letters, for Benjamin, belong 'to the history of the continuing life of a human being', then these epistolary reflections contribute to the survival of European civilisation that is in the process of being destroyed.

2 Deferral and Aporia

Leaving Europe would be an act of violence, but is, at the same time, 'a necessity I will have to face.' In 1919 Benjamin describes the question of emigration, which will occupy him for two decades, with uncanny clarity as an aporia. The simultaneity of the 'necessity' of departure and the inability to execute it proves to be not only an existential challenge or an ideological choice but a continuing philosophical problem. Benjamin describes what 'philosophical problem' means in a letter to Rang: 'You may be pleased to see that I, for my part emphasise that nothing in your deliberations is derived from what we could call philosophical principles precisely because they are not deduced from theorems and concepts, but born from an interplay of ideas' (CWB 218). Benjamin's reflections on emigration and so on his dilemma – he talks of 'difficult decision', 'weeks of struggle', of 'tremendous conflict' and 'horrid competition' between Europe and Palestine, the European and the Jewish – are not to be derived from principles, from existing ideas, but are generated by such an 'interplay of ideas'. In this case the idea of Europe and the idea of Judaism. To Benjamin they come together in the 'jüdischer Literat,' 'the Jewish man of letters' (GB I 83), in the 'idea of the man of letters' (GB I 63), who bears 'the new social consciousness' (GB I 64), which freed of well-worn patterns of thought and ways of behaving, and in the simultaneity of close observation and critical distance, reveals an alternative to 'das Gegebene', to what exists. This alternative consists in an 'interplay' of antitheses, which Benjamin describes in relation to Kafka's writing, as an 'ellipsis between Jewish tradition and modern big city dweller'. This Kafka-style ellipsis also determines Benjamin's own deliberations on the question of emigration.

Arendt writes, that Benjamin 'did not need to read Kafka to think like Kafka' (1970, 17). This is particularly true of those passages in Benjamin's letters in which he considers his departure from Europe. They are couched in a strikingly odd style, which leads Arendt to talk of Benjamin's 'curious endless consideration [...] of emigration to Palestine' (1970, 35). These passages are consistently marked by his aporetic way of writing – the staging of an insoluble situation – which displays a conspicuous similarity to Kafka's *stehender Sturmlauf*, the repeated about-turns characterizing Kafka's writing method. The curiousness and even more, the endlessness of Benjamin's consideration of emigrating from Europe are of the same stamp.

The core of these considerations is delay. On 1.8. 1928 Benjamin writes to Scholem: 'Meine Reise nach Palästina [...] [ist] beschlossne Sache [...] Zunächst der Termin meiner Ankunft. Dieser wird sich vielleicht [...] verschieben. Das hängt [...] davon ab, ob ich mir vorsetzen kann, die Passagenarbeit noch bevor ich Europa verlasse abzuschließen' (GB III, 403 f.). The rest of the letter describes the importance 'not to hurry with the end of the work' Two weeks later Benjamin explains to Alfred Cohn, 'why he remains in Berlin for a thousand and one reasons' (GB III, 409). Something of a fairy tale shines through in this formulation. On 22.5. 1929 one of these reasons is that he began the essay on Proust 'from a thousand and one perspectives' (GB III, 462). In countless variations he sounds like in this letter to Gretel Karplus (Paris, 30. 12. 1933): 'The decision, for which I still would have to find the strength, would be to go away from here. I still have to delay this.' What Benjamin has to await changes with the years and the circumstances; but there are simply too many of them to take the reasons fort he delay at face value. Instead his writing circular arguments, tautologies, contradictions and superfluous justifications, double subjunctives, and reflections in which in every line a 'but', a 'however' or 'nevertheless' interrupt the straight line of the argument and prevent a conclusion. These explanations are marked by constant hesitations, conditions, reservations, hints at vague difficulties and impossibilities.

On 1 February 1923 he writes to Scholem: 'In addition to everything else, it has become impossible to remain in Germany and the prospect of my getting away has not improved in any way' (CWB 205). In a letter of 25 May 1935 Benjamin explains to Werner Kraft: 'The question you raise as to where to live during the war is hard to answer because I can hardly count on external circumstances allowing me to do what seems right to me at such a moment, when whatever action taken probably comes too late in any case, but when one must necessarily act within the space of a few hours' (CWB 487). On 28 February 1933 he talks of being 'absorbed by the problems posed by the next months. I don't know if I will be able to make it through them, whether inside or outside Germany' (CWB 402). In the last years of exile the difficulties are above all of a practical nature. In 1939 Benjamin writes to Scholem: 'The same conditions that threaten my European situation will in all likelihood make emigration to the USA impossible' (CWB 601). There are no doubts facts behind that claim, yet Benjamin's repeated and detailed descriptions of these situations remind one of his remarks about Kafka: 'There is nothing more memorable than the fervour with which Kafka emphasised his failure' (CWB 566). Benjamin's descriptions of the failure of his decision to leave Europe are memorable above all where he both reflects on and fervently enacts them.

Often there is, in Benjamin's hesitation, a self-ironic undertone: 'Begin April', he writes to Scholem on 5. 3.1924, 'I want to get away from here at all costs. How I will finance this I don't know yet. I'm ready to some sacrifices from my library. For now I compensate for the pain this thought causes me by daringly buying books' (GB II, 433). Benjamin is ready to sacrifice part of his library to raise money for his departure. In the following lines he draws a list of expensive books he just acquired.

Benjamin himself talks of his own 'pathological hesitancy', but the path by which he reaches this self-knowledge casts a light on its function: 'I am unfortunately in no position at all to counter your reproaches' [about the postponement of his departure for Palestine and the learning of Hebrew linked to that] he writes to Scholem on 6 June 1926,

> they are absolutely justified and I am up against a truly pathological inclination to procrastinate in this matter. I have unfortunately occasionally experienced this inclination with regard to other matters. To be sure, it does seem that you misinterpreted the brevity of my last letter. It resulted from my haste to let you know that this business – [his departure for Palestine] - had *finally* got started. And this, of course, is all the more significant, the more complicated my inhibitions were. (By the way, you have only an incomplete picture of their nature and scope and, insofar as they are of a purely personal nature, I must wait to fill you in on the rest until I can do so in person.) ... My coming in the fall depends strictly on my material circumstances. On nothing else, given good health. On the contrary, you may rest assured that now I have begun, I will absolutely go on with Hebrew, here or over there, quite independently of when I leave for Palestine. (CWB 350)

These lines are a typical example of Benjamin's Kafkaesque writing: He admits his hesitation and habit of procrastination, and then takes back his confession with opaque justifications, which could only be clarified in the event of a decision – that is, on arrival in Palestine. He talks of complicated inhibitions and a few lines later advances *solely* financial reasons for the postponement. He describes his inability to decide as a character trait and immediately after that announces his decision to come with a great show of resolution. He takes back the certainty of his coming with a single condition – independent of any inner state –, seals this one uncertainty and quickly adds a second, only to go off in the opposite direction with the very first word of the subsequent sentence. Now he splits the 'matter' – the emigration and the learning of Hebrew – lets the journey to Palestine slip off into vagueness and ends with the assurance that he 'will absolutely go on'. In the midst of all this vacillation there comes the explanation, that it is precisely the continuing inhibitions – the hesitancy, the postponement – which determine the weight of the decision. In these lines the dynamic of Benjamin's 'curious endless consideration(s)' becomes evident: They are insoluble and yet decisive precisely in their insolubility.

Benjamin repeatedly emphasises the insolubility of his situation. On 25 April 1930 he writes to Scholem:

> And I must once again put off giving a definitive answer to the question [of coming to Palestine]. Not, to be sure, for much longer. And not without telling you that in one respect [...] it is insoluble in its alternative form. [...] But whatever this decision may depend on, it will be made soon – however much, on the one hand, it is embedded in circumstances that seem to be totally alien to it and, on the other hand, in that procrastination that has been stretched to the limit and that is second nature to me when it comes to the most important situations in my life. Having begun to loosen the extremely tangled knot of my existence in one place [...] this 'Gordian knot' [...] will also have to be unravelled.' (CWB 364/5)

Now, as is well known, Gordian knots cannot be unravelled but only cut by a blow from a sword. Even more significant is the fact that here Benjamin locates his wavering not between Palestine and Europe but between 'alien circumstances' on the one hand and procrastination itself on the other. Hence that 'procrastination... stretched to the limit' becomes a possibility, an attitude in itself, opposed to the 'alien circumstances'. It can, however, only be attained performatively and not conceptually, since hesitancy, expressed conceptually, would cancel itself.

Benjamin's deliberations on emigrating from Europe pile up to such an extent that they become an end in themselves and the apparent goal – a possible decision – disappears from view. As with Kafka, hesitancy, *Zögern*, becomes the way itself: it makes it possible to ward off a decision. Yet this hesitancy is not merely a passive inability to decide. What matters is the process of hesitation itself. Benjamin, whose hesitation is so like that of Kafka, calls this process in Kafka his 'gesture'. Of Kafka's gestures Benjamin says that there are none which are not affected by the 'ambivalence in the face of decision' (*die Zweideutigkeit vor der Entscheidung*) . This ambivalence is, Benjamin continues, itself 'decisive', because it reveals 'the middle of events' (GS II 2, 419). As in Kafka, this gesture – as Werner Hamacher has pointed out – 'hesitates before every meaning and every doctrine and is nothing but such hesitation; stalling, postponement' is itself 'a decision, but not one that decides *on* or *for* something, not one that passes judgment, sets up a law or makes an example – then it would belong in the realm of predicative language [...] and would presume what can only be disclosed in it' (Hamacher 316). What on the other hand is disclosed in Benjamin's gesture of hesitation is a space, which is free of the dictates of 'foreign circumstances' and requirements and in which something else than the given is conceivable.

Arendt comes close to the meaning of this space when she writes:

> What in these letters seems like indecision is in reality the consequence of the bitter insight that no solution is adequate for reality, that a solution would lead him into a lie of solving problems [...] He would thereby lose the possibility of an awareness of his situation [...] even at the risk of becoming inacceptable for his contemporaries. (Arendt 1970, 221)

What is unbearable for Benjamin's contemporaries – she may be thinking of Scholem here – is Benjamin's hesitation, because they are expecting an ideological stand, because the situation is urgent, and makes a decision necessary. They don't tolerate the philosophical and political value of considering the future as something unknown, that can not be deduced from the given. The 'Ambivalence before the decision' is however, not only, as in Arendt's comment, a way out or a space of insight, and it is not only to be understood *ex negativo* – as a space corresponding to the negative reality. It is also a space beyond necessity and impossibility, where the possibility of salvation lights up.

3   Europe as Leeway

In his great Kafka letter to Scholem of 1938 Benjamin calls this space *ein herrlicher Spielraum*, a 'marvellous leeway'. It is 'the space,' he specifies, which the (coming) catastrophe will not know' (CWB 564). The catastrophe will not know this space of thinking, free of preconditions, because it knows only the already given and thought. In it there will be no opening to something else and no way out. Not to know this space – its necessity and possibility – that *is* the catastrophe. Benjamin's hesitation creates, like Kafka's gesture, the space which stands against this catastrophe. It takes place not in a decision between two possibilities – here Europe, there Palestine or the Jews – but 'in the middle of events', in hesitancy itself. This discloses neither a concession nor a compromise, nor resolution in a third way. Instead it emerges from the interplay of opposites which simultaneously stand undiminished in opposition to each other, in all their radicalism. 'I don't concede any compromise,' Benjamin already writes in 1926. Only in the paradoxical transformation of one into the other, only where both the idea of Europe and the idea of Judaism each proceed 'radically in their own sense' is such a hope given (GB III 158–159). Benjamin's 'pathological hesitation' and the profound despair that accompanies it appear like the fear we find in Kafka, of which Benjamin writes: '[It] makes a mess of the process', delays action, but is 'nevertheless the only hopeful thing in him' (GS II, 2, 431). Benjamin's hesitation prevents him from being saved, and yet it is precisely that which he believed has to be saved.

'For Benjamin,' writes Gerhard Richter,

> the moment of undecidability is [...] not something negative that needs to be transcended. Rather, the perpetual navigation of the relentless difficulties that can never be understood once and for all is the very condition of possibility for any political hope. Benjamin gives the promise lodged in this hope the name 'Europe'. (Richter 2002, 59)

As accurately as this formulation in some respects captures Benjamin's hope, it is lopsided in giving it the name 'Europe'. For Benjamin the 'marvellous leeway,' *der herrliche Spielraum* before a decision arises as an ellipsis between the European and the Jewish. In a text of 1923 to which he initially gave the title 'Thoughts towards an analysis of the condition of *Mitteleuropa*' Benjamin speaks of the 'leeway lent by freedom'. There he describes this space as 'that more or less evident irony with which the life of the individual demands to run its course as distinct from the existence of any community in which he finds himself' (GS IV, 919). In 1923 Benjamin calls this space the 'most European of all goods', yet in the present 'it has disappeared as far as the inhabitants of *Mitteleuropa* are concerned' (GS IV, 3, 919). In 1938 Benjamin localizes the origin of this space in the Jewish mystical tradition. It is that which makes Kafka's work the 'precise complement of its epoch' and allows him to be, as an *individual*, 'devoid of all collective principles and conditions.' It is this space, emerging from the conjuncture of the Jewish tradition and European ideas of freedom, which determined Benjamin's deliberations on emigration. And it is this possibility, this possible space, which Benjamin wishes to rescue as a complementary world to the lurking catastrophe. Precisely by not being brought to a conclusion, his deliberations, like Kafka's gesture, point to a way out of the given order and thereby to an opening to something to come, which is still unnamed and unknown. This saving, complementary alternative world arises for Benjamin from a leeway of freedom, which recognizes the catastrophe, a leeway which will disappear with the catastrophe of the destruction of a Europe interwoven with Jewishness.

Benjamin illustrates Kafka's 'marvellous leeway' by way of a well-known passage in *The Nature of the Physical World* by A.S. Eddington, which presents a humorous view of modes of behaviour in modernity:

> I am standing on the threshold about to enter a room. It is a complicated business. In the first place I must shove against an atmosphere pressing with a force of fourteen pounds on every square inch of my body. I am sure of landing on a plank travelling at twenty miles a second round the sun – a fraction of a second too early or too late, the plank would be miles away. I must do this whilst hanging from a round planet head outward into space, and with a wind of ether blowing at no one knows how many miles a second through every interstice of my body. The plank has no solidity of substance. To step on it is like stepping on a swarm of flies. Shall I not slip through? No, if I make the venture one of the flies hits me and gives a boost up again; I fall again and am knocked upwards by another fly; and so on. I may hope that the net result will be that I remain about steady; but if unfortunately I should slip through the floor or be boosted too violently up to the ceiling, the occurrence would be, not a violation of the laws of Nature, but a rare coincidence. [...] Verily, it is easier for a camel to pass through the eye of a needle than for a scientific man to pass through a door. (GB VI, 110)

Eddington describes in the form of parody the impossible enterprise, in full awareness of the known physical facts – the gravity of the atmosphere, speed of the earth's rotation, spherical shape of the planet – of walking through a door. It is questionable whether Benjamin knew that here he was also describing himself. 'In all literature,' writes Benjamin, 'I know no passage which corresponds to the same extent to the Kafka(esque) gestus'. One could, he writes, 'without any effort match almost every passage of this physical aporia with sentences from Kafka's prose pieces.' And, one might add, with Benjamin's considerations on leaving Europe. It is indeed easier for a camel to pass through the eye of a needle and for a physicist to pass through a door, than for Benjamin to leave Europe. And yet he does leave it – real, existing Europe – in his mind, he leaves it at the point in his thinking where he enters the ellipsis of the interaction of his idea of Europe and his idea of Judaism. He leaves a Europe that has become uninhabitable; he leaves it in his passages on the necessity and the act of violence of leaving it, he leaves it in his hesitation, which opens up the 'marvellous leeway,' his escape route and the only hope that remains. That is what Benjamin is talking about when he quotes Kafka, that there is an 'infinite amount of hope – [but] not for us' (Benjamin 1970, 116). There is an infinite amount of hope in Benjamin's farewell to Europe, only not for him. Yet in the texts he has left behind and in the letters which arrived in Jerusalem and are preserved there, Benjamin leaves Europe in the same manner as the Chinese painter, whose story Benjamin frequently repeats. 'When the former showed his friends his most recent picture, there was a park in it and a path leading to a small door. But when the friends turned round to the painter he was gone and in the picture. There he was walking on the narrow path towards the door, he paused in front of it, turned round, smiled and disappeared through it' (GS II, 3, 1261). On 20 June 1931 Benjamin writes from Berlin to Scholem in Jerusalem: 'Ich habe meine bisherigen Verhältnisse nun in solchem Grade bereinigt, dass der Entschluss nach Palästina zu übersiedeln mir nicht schwerer fiele als vor die Tür zu gehen' (GB IV, 46). 'I have now settled my affairs to such a degree that a decision to immigrate to Palestine would be no more difficult for me than to walk out the door' (CWB, 381).

Works Cited

Arendt, Hannah. 1970. 'Introduction: Walter Benjamin 1892-1940', in: Walter Benjamin, *Illuminations*, ed. Hannah Arendt (London: Cape).
Benjamin, Walter. 1966 ff. *Gesammelte Briefe*, ed. G. Scholem & Th.W. Adorno (6 vols., Frankfurt /Main: Suhrkamp).
Benjamin, Walter. 1970. 'Franz Kafka: On the Tenth Anniversary of his Death'. In Id., *Illuminations*, ed. H. Arendt (London: Cape).
Benjamin, Walter. 1994. *Correspondence, 1910-1940*, ed. G. Scholem & Th.W. Adorno (trl. M.R. Jacobson & E.M. Jacobson; Chicago: Chicago University Press).
Richter, Gerhard. 2002. 'Sites of Indeterminacy and the Spectres of Eurocentrism', *Culture, Theory and Critique* 43.1.

Index

Abraham, Nicolas 160
Adorno, Gretel 187
Agamben, Giorgio 42, 163–165, 177
Agbabi, Patience 109
Alexander, Jeff 54
Alfonso vi, King of Castile and León 154–155
Andreas-Salomé, Lou 144
Andrukhovych, Yuri 164n19, 165
Arendt, Hannah 54, 186–187, 192, 196
Arsenijević, Damir vii, 11, 170–184
Assmann, Aleida 87–88
Auden, W.H. 105–106
Azeglio, Massimo d' 114–115

Bachmann, Veit 80
Balibar, Etienne 6, 72, 74
Barraclough, Geoffrey 122
Barreto, Danny M. 161
Barthes, Roland 158
Bassin, Mark 71
Baudet, Thierry 94
Bauman, Zygmunt 2, 47, 54, 68–70, 74
Beck, Ulrich 159–160
Beeren, W.A.L. 130–131
Bejhanović, Aldin 178–179
Benedict, Ruth 123
Benjamin, Walter 12–13, 62, 158, 186–199
Benoist, Alain de 93–94
Bergman, Ingmar 97
Bergson, Henri 19n6
Bhabha, Homi 40
Bialasiewicz, Luiza vii, 6, 66–80
Bignall, Simone 164
Biti, Vladimir vii, 1–13, 36–49, 99
Boldrini, Lucia vii, 8, 99–118
Borges, Jorge Luis 68–69
Brandt, Willy 54
Brown, Wendy 180
Buden, Boris 176
Bush, George W. 97
Butler, Judith 42

Cacciari, Massimo 66
Casanova, Sofía 152
Cassin, René 93
Chaadaev, Peter 10

Chaadaev, Pyotr Yakovlevich 139–140
Chakrabarty, Dipesh 37
Cliteur, Paul 94n10
Cohn, Alfred 193
Conrad, Joseph 7
Coudenhove-Kalergi 93
Crépon, Marc 19n5
Curtius, Ernst Robert 108–109
Custine, Astolphe, marquis de 140

Decaux, Emmanuel 76
Delanty, Gerard vii, 3, 53–64
Derrida, Jacques 6, 29, 46–48, 60, 66–67, 72–76, 78, 158
Detienne, Marcel 11, 151, 153
Diderot, Denis 137
Domínguez, César viii, 151–166
Dostoevsky, Fyodor 142–143
Downey, Anthony 164
Drakulić, Slavenka 100–102, 106–108, 118
Drakulić, Slavenka. 101–103
Duchêne, François 70–71
Duggan, Christopher 114
Duraković, Ferida 172
Dziub, Nikol viii, 151–166

Eddington, A.S. 198
Elalamy, Youssouf Amine 104–105
Enzensberger, Hans Magnus 110, 116n36
Erdoğan, Recep Tayyip 96
Ernst. Cassirer 118
Esposito, Roberto 42, 78n9
Etkind, Alexander 144, 161

Fanon, Frantz 92–93
Farage, Nigel 94
Fassbinder, Rainer Werner 97
Fellini, Federico 97
Fioramonti, Lorenzo 71
Foster, E.M. 92
Foucault, Michel 159, 161–163, 165
Francis, Pope 78–79
Frazer, Nancy 163
Freud, Sigmund 45–46, 144
Friedell, Egon 143–145
Friedman, Susan Stanford 151

Gadamer, Hans-Georg 60
García ii, King of Galicia and Portugal 154–155
Gasché, Rodolphe VIII, 2–3, 17–34, 46–47, 99n1, 109n18
Geertz, Clifford 123
Gellhorn, Martha 110
Giesen, Bernd 54
Golemo, Karolina 152, 153n6
Grande, Edgar 159–160
Greene, Graham 85, 96–97
Groys, Boris 144–146
Gutkind, Erich 188

Habermas, Jürgen 6, 48, 63–64, 66–67, 72–74
Hamacher, Werner 196
Hansen-Löve, Aage VIII, 9–10, 136–146
Hatoum, Mona 107–108
Hazard, Paul 91
Heidegger, Martin 31–33, 69
Heller, Margaret 109
Herder, Johann Gottfried 1, 46, 91
Hofmannsthal, Hugo von 44–46, 145
Hooper, Barbara 71
Husserl, Edmund 18, 20–21, 26–27, 30, 46

Inaga, Shigemi IX, 8, 121–134
Irving, Washington 90

James, Henry 97
Jaspers, Karl 60
Jelloun, Tahar Ben 102–103, 105
Johnson, Boris 96
Juncker, Jean-Claude 79

Kabakov, Ilja 145
Kafka, Franz 13, 192–199
Kant, Immanuel 31, 33, 43–44, 138
Karplus, Gretel 189, 193
Keats, John 96–97
Kieslowski, Krzysztof 97
Korek, Janusz 164
Kraft, Werner 193
Kramsch, Olivier 71–72
Kristeva, Julia 47
Kudō, Tetsumi 9, 129–133

Lacis, Asja 190
Lakhous, Amara 115–116

Le Pen, Marine 94
Leerssen, Joep IX, 1–13, 85–97
Leibniz, Gottfried Wilhelm, Freiherr von 137–138
Lessing, Gotthold Ephraim 90
Letta, Enrico 78
Levi, Primo 108, 118
Lévi-Strauss, Claude 124
Levy, Daniel 54
Lewis, Martin 109
Liska, Vivan IX, 1–13, 186–199
Lowell, Percival 123–124
Lucarelli, Sonia 71
Lutosławski, Wincenty 152

Makavejev, Dušan 97
Mann, Thomas 92
May, Theresa 117n38
Meier, Christian 54
Melas, Natalie 151, 164
Michel, Foucault 49
Mogherini, Federica 79
Monnet, Jean 93
Monnier, Adrienne 191
Montalbán, Manuel Vázquez 111–115, 117–118
Montesquieu 114
Montesquieu, Charles de Secondat, baron de 90, 114
Mori, Ōgai 9, 124–127, 133
Mozart, Wolfgang Amadeus 90
Mufti, Aamir R. 151, 164
Musil, Robert 45–46

Nancy, Jean-Luc 30n15
Nietzsche, Friedrich 40, 44, 143
Nora, Pierre 58

Obama, Barack 78–79
Orbán, Viktor 94, 96

Pasolini, Pier Paolo 97
Patočka, Jan 17–27, 28n12, 29, 31, 60
Popper, Karl 87n3
Povinelli, Elisabeth 41
Povinelli, Elizabeth A. 163
Prodi, Romano 72

Ramnoux, Clemence 22
Rang, Florens Christian 187–188, 192
Rei, Mariña Pérez 153n6

Renan, Ernest 43
Rhodes, Cecil 55
Ricci, Matteo 91
Richter, Gerhard 197
Rigney, Ann 88n5
Rivas, Manuel 11, 153–155, 159–163, 166
Rodrigues, João 123
Rossi, Ernesto 99–100, 118
Rothberg, Michael 58
Rougemont, Denis de 93
Rousseau, Jean-Jacques 91
Rumsfeld, Donald 73

Said, Edward W. 92–93, 164
Sakai, Naoki 121
Sancho ii, King of Castile and León 154–155
Sansom, George 122
Sarkozy, Nicholas 93
Sassen, Saskia 172
Saura, Carlos 97
Scholem, Gershom 188–191, 193–196, 199
Schultz, Martin 79
Schumann, Robert 93
Scott, Walter 90
Šehabović, Šejla 172–173, 183–184
Sidaway, James 80
Spengler, Oswald 143
Spinelli, Altiero 99–100, 118
Staël, Madame de (Anne-Louise-Germaine) 92, 114
Stasiuk, Andrzej 11, 153, 157–163, 165–166
Strath, Bo 61
Strauss, Ludwig 189–190

Svirsky, Marcelo 164
Sznaider, Natan 54

Takeyama, Michio 9, 126–129, 133
Tarkovskii, Andrei Arsen'evich 97
Tassinari, Fabrizio 72
Taylor, Charles 163
Tocqueville, Alexis de 117
Todorov, Tzvetan 6, 72, 74–75
Tomić, Milica 175
Torok, Maria 160
Trebacz, Gosia 152
Trump, Donald J. 96–97

Vázquez, Isabel Castro 165–166
Vernant, Jean-Pierre 22
Villar, María do Cebreiro Rábade 161
Voltaire 90, 137

Warner, Michael 163
Weale, Albert 118n39
Weber, Max 92
Welles, Orson 85
Wenders, Wim 97
Wierzejska, Jagoda 165
Wigen, Kären 109
Wolff, Larry 152n1

Yeats, W.B. 85, 89
Young, James 58

Zambrano, Maria 66
Zurita, Jerónimo de 156